THE ART OF CASE ANALYSIS

or

*How To Improve Your College Performance
By Developing Better Classroom Discussion Skills,
Better Writing Skills, Better "Blue Book" Testing Skills,
Better Team Skills, Better Numbers Skills, And Better Presentation Skills*

Third Edition

ROBERT RONSTADT
*Professor Of Entrepreneurship
Pepperdine University*

Lord Publishing, Inc.
P.O. Box 242
Wayland MA 01778

(800) 525-5673 voice
(508) 358-1666 fax

Library of Congress Catalog Card No. 7645719
ISBN - 0-930204-01-8

*The title of the first and second editions was <u>The Art Of Case Analysis: A Guide To The Diagnosis Of Business Situations.</u>

ACKNOWLEDGEMENTS & DEDICATION

I am grateful for the help of many superior teachers who have made helpful comments about <u>The Art Of Case Analysis</u> over the years. These include Rudy Winston, David C.D. Rogers, Robert Pitts, Jack Stamm, Harry Seward, Nazir Bhagat, John Dory, Richard Moxon, Kathryn Harrigan, Jeff Shuman, Jack Hornaday, Jack Duncan, Bob Pavan, Ted Gautschi, James Lee, and many others.

A number of years ago, Nancy Tieken made many good suggestions when I began thinking about a third edition. More recently, I am indebted to Ms. Cindy Lundquist, Associate Librarian par excellence at Pepperdine University for her contributions regarding electronic databases. Also, numerous students have provided valuable feedback for which I am extremely grateful.

Though I am alone responsible for errors or deficiencies, I have no doubt that the original work and this third edition would be far weaker without the able editing and publishing talents of Rebecca Lord.

■ ■ ■ ■ ■ ■

I dedicate this book
to my son, Jason
and my daughter, Kate
for the love and happiness they've given us
over the years.

CONTENTS

PART ONE
THE REVOLUTION IN LEARNING AND THE CASE METHOD

PART FOUR
CLASSROOM STRATEGIES & TACTICS

PART FIVE
WRITING, PRESENTATIONS, AND EXAMS

PART SIX
KEY ANALYTIC TOOLS FOR BUSINESS ANALYSIS

CONTENTS (cont.)

CONTENTS (cont.)

PART NINE
CASE & TEAM MATERIALS
(Tear out and copy these items to insure sufficient quantity for all your classes)

OTHER INFORMATION OF INTEREST

PART ONE
THE REVOLUTION IN LEARNING
AND THE CASE METHOD

■ ■ ■ ■ ■ ■

Preface
Reflections After 20 Years Of Case Study...
Or Why We Must Move Beyond The Case Method

Last year I had the good fortune to teach at a business school that was also known for its outstanding professors of liberal arts. Very few of these professors, however, "professed" in the traditional sense. What I mean is that none were strictly lecturers. Instead, all utilized a variety of teaching methods. And all required student participation in one form or another.

Having visited a number of schools over the last few years, I believe this particular school was not an exception. Most universities with quality undergraduate programs have adopted these teaching innovations. Very few, if any, provide liberal arts programs where lecturing is still the exclusive pedagogy. For many, lecturing is not even the dominant pedagogy.

But just thirty years ago, my own classroom experience as a student was dominated by the lecture method, and I believe it was the norm. Students were, for the most part, "lectured at." There was little room for real interaction, other than the perfunctory Q&A period that rarely followed a lecture.

This change in teaching methods is quite profound, even revolutionary by academic standards. Looking back, I believe the programmed addition of student involvement in the learning process represents the single most significant change in college classroom life and the college learning experience over the last three decades. From a long term perspective, this single shift in classroom teaching will continue to have an enormous and positive impact on learning in the decades ahead. It is an academic revolution.

Of course, such interaction is still evolving at many institutions. But what I wrote about the case method exclusively for graduate business students just 17 years ago, is clearly applicable to many students, including undergraduate liberal arts students. In one form or another, the basic approach of the case method has spread across the academic landscape.

Many revolutionary changes are occurring in our world today. The globalization of society, multicultural diversity, new economic systems, the information revolution, genetic engineering, the struggle for female equality and freedom... are just a few. All are significant. But no less significant is the way people learn, how they are educated, and how they use their educations to improve the human condition.

The case method represents progress in the history of pedagogy, i.e., the art of teaching. While this book is about the case method, I want to suggest at the onset that (as students and teachers) we need to move beyond the case method, while retaining its best features. I will discuss in a moment specifically what we need to move toward. But first we need to understand the case method, or what we should move beyond.

The case method is an offshoot or variation of the "socratic approach" which is another name for proactive interaction between teachers and students. This proactive interaction takes the form of a process of questions and answers. Good teachers don't provide answers <u>per se.</u> They provide questions...not just any question, but probing questions, questions that cause students to learn by discovering the answers for themselves. A fundamental assumption of the socratic approach is that such self-discovery leads more frequently to real learning... learning that involves not just the intellectual awareness of knowledge but the ability to apply this knowledge to new situations.

One of my most basic beliefs is that this assumption about self-discovery and learning is true for many students. I also believe that the socratic approach to learning is particularly useful when stock answers won't suffice. Physical science enjoys a level of constancy that is nonexistent in the social sciences or any activity associated with the affairs of human beings. In the physical sciences, problems can be replicated, often under laboratory conditions. A right answer exists, and it is always the same.

But in business, and other human activities, variables shift and unique conditions continually surface. There is no permanent "right" answer. But there are often better answers. To find them, questions must be asked so that the better answers can to discovered. The intent is "to learn" a better course of action, to find a better decision, to discover a better way.

At least, that is an objectivist's interpretation. Those involved in this process professionally know the distinction between "teacher" and "student" isn't always so clear. A popular refrain among teachers is "we learn from our students." For those addicted to learning, this fuzzy relationship is actually quite lovely, though hardly constant. For eventually, students must also learn to ask penetrating questions.

Unfortunately, for the student, that is the "real" student, this relationship initially appears messy and confusing. And it is. But, as my son is fond of saying, "not to worry." One of the positive paradoxes of the case method is that this messiness is like life itself. And unlike a nicely packaged lecture, life seldom reaches our doorstep in finely wrapped containers.

FROM THE SOCRATIC METHOD...TO THE CASE METHOD

To reduce this messiness somewhat, we move from the pure socratic approach to the case method. The case method provides a measure of order by providing a documented situation... a written case...as a basis for discussion. Sometimes this written document is augmented with a film of the protagonists, or even their actual appearance in class. But whatever the precise format, "a case" is provided whereby we can step into someone else's situation. A case, when well conceived and executed, is a wonderful mechanism that allows students and teachers to experience vicariously the worldly lives of practitioners... at least up to a point.

For cases are not "histories" per se, but a selection facts and inferences that present a "situation." This situation may be a problem someone faces, or an opportunity. The key is that this situation requires action. Our action may differ from the action taken by the actual practitioners because we bring a different set of skills and values to the situation. That's to be expected. What's critical is learning how to deal with unique situations that, like unique human beings, still resemble one another.

And it works. The process of putting yourself in some's shoes gives you the opportunity to engage your knowledge, to assess facts, organize them, analyze them, think creatively about them, and then to communicate what you would do. Vicarious experience. That's what the case method is all about.

Why? Because we all agree: experience is the best teacher. Unfortunately, real-world experience is terribly expensive, not to mention time-consuming. The compromise of "vicarious" experience... the opportunity to learn from situations experienced by others...is better than the alternative: being told by professors what you should do.

FROM THE CASE METHOD...TO THE PRACTITIONER METHOD

The case method represents educational progress. Like the socratic method, the case method moves beyond rote learning and spoon-fed lecturing. Yet the "structure" or presence of a case helps to insure that the feet of both professors and students remained somewhat immersed in the mud of reality.

But the case method is not enough. The classroom experience that uses the case method does not prove students actually can formulate and implement decisions "in the real world." It doesn't prove that they can produce. It doesn't prove that they will become an excellent employee, manager, owner, or leader. In too many instances, it is not even a reliable indicator.

One response to this deficiency is "hands-on" experience, not just vicarious experience via business cases. Today, many academic programs offer field courses, internships, consulting assignments, residencies, and other course projects that actually involve real business assignments. Still others are combining real world experience with the case method and "hands-on experience" by getting students out of the classroom and involved in practitioner activities or situations. For instance, a case on a business situation involving a bankruptcy auction would be coupled with an assignment to visit an actual auction of a business. Another involving a legal dispute would see students attending small claims court. Getting students to "pound the pavement" to produce strategic plans, marketing plans, production plans, and traditional business plans is an increasingly common assignment in courses where students traditionally never strayed from the classroom.

I encourage you, as students, to take practitioner-based courses whenever possible. I encourage professors to offer them. These courses, and the experiences they provide, represent a move beyond the case method of learning. It is a welcome move. It is a move of relevance... one that is consistent with the practitioner heritage of the case method. It is a move that is consistent with a larger societal trend toward the decentralization of all human activity. It is a move away from the pseudo-science of business that has found a welcome home in far too many business programs.

I want to stress that I am not recommending the abandonment of the case method, just as I would never jettison lecturing. There is right time and place for lecturing, and for learning by the case method. But we need to improve. The current state of business learning, particularly the traditional MBA, is testimony to that need. New subject matter is not the only solution. New pedagogical approaches are also needed. What I'm dubbing as a "practitioner's approach" is just one possible improvement.

To compete in today's global village, we must get students out of the classroom for some portion of their learning experiences while still finding ways to insure academic value. International programs that simply trade domestic classrooms for foreign ones are not the answer. A practitioner's approach means finding creative ways to share and learn from real world experiences that contain "on line" decision making.

Of course there is a price for relevance. With the greater relevance of a practitioner's approach comes uncertainty. For students and teachers, the jump to academic enterprises that involve "hands-on" experience is yet another leap into uncertainty. "Practitioner learning" means discomfort for those teachers and students who enjoy the comfortable certainty of lectures. But practitioner learning also means discomfort for those teachers and students who have become acclimatized to the lesser uncertainty of the case method.

Bridging this new pedagogical uncertainty won't be easy. Teachers are the first learners. (Or should I say the first learners should become teachers). And we still need to learn much about providing courses that contain heavy components of "hands-on" learning or practitioner learning.

We must take this risk. To be truly prepared for the 21st century, teachers and students must find creative ways to move beyond the case method.

Chapter One
Developing A Personal System For Case Analysis

"If I only knew how to analyze the case... The class seemed to go far beyond my own analysis, and in directions I never saw. I felt frustrated. I was unable to contribute very much to the discussion. While I feel I am learning from my classmates, I believe I should be contributing and learning more".

This quote by an anonymous student is fairly representative of the feelings experienced by many students when exposed to the case method for the first time. Unfortunately, my experience as a case student and case teacher suggests that for many students, exposure to more cases does not necessarily result in much higher skill levels of case preparation and discussion. All too many students simply become consigned to muddling through their case experiences as best they can.

The principal purpose of this chapter is to help improve the skills of students in case preparation and discussion. A unique feature of our approach is that it looks at case preparation and discussion from the student's point of view. Other works on the case method of teaching have been designed to meet the needs primarily, if not solely, of case teachers and case writers.

But first I must offer a word of caution. This book does not offer "THE" system for case preparation. No such comfortable system exists. It is not even "A" system for case preparation. Rather, it contains a collection of observations about case preparation and discussion which will stimulate students to develop their own system of case analysis.

The development of a personal system of case analysis is vital and can increase what you contribute to and what you "take away" from a case experience. My belief is that people learn best by doing, by actively participating in the search for knowledge and the development of skills. Cases offer an opportunity for vicarious living and learning which is relevant and productive for individuals faced with the need to make difficult decisions in a logical, analytical and professional manner.

However, the achievement of these goals depends not only on the skills of the case teacher, but also the individual skills that students develop to prepare and discuss cases. Hopefully, this book will contribute to your development of these skills and thereby heighten what you take away from what is usually a fascinating and productive learning experience.

Before you begin reading these pages, I would like you to consider carefully two suggestions.

First, if you have no (or little) prior case exposure, I recommend you review this book after gaining some case experience. Some of the messages about case preparation and discussion will assume substantive meaning only after you have struggled through some challenging cases.

Second, carefully evaluate after some period of time what you have done to develop a personal system for case preparation and discussion. How have you modified, improved, and extended the ideas presented in this book?

Why should you go to all this trouble? The main reason is that the development of any system of case preparation and discussion must be tailored and re-tailored to fit your particular evolving skills and capabilities. Most importantly, once you begin developing a personal system of case analysis, you will find it helpful long after you leave school. A personal system will help you to develop skills in analyzing new and changing situations and to communicate your analysis effectively and efficiently in either oral or written form. Consequently, the skills you develop that comprise your personal system of analysis and communication can be utilized throughout your professional career. More than just facts or information, these skills can be among the most important benefits you derive in your educational program.

Unfortunately, my experience is that insufficient thought is devoted by most students to developing a personal system for case preparation and discussion. I believe this statement is true even when we are discussing students in an MBA program that is totally committed to case teaching, much less undergraduate business programs or executive management programs where students confront a limited number of cases without having much prior case exposure.

For instance, the average Harvard MBA has the opportunity to read and prepare between 500 to 700 business cases before graduating. Some Harvard MBAs become extremely adept at case preparation and discussion, especially in the second year of their program. These students generally make significant contributions both inside and outside of class (and their grades usually reflect it).

One reason for their success is that often they have developed a personal system for not only the preparation of individual cases, but a system for handling a heavy case load over an entire semester.

Yet, not all MBAs become proficient with case analysis and discussion. In fact, my impression from attending many second-year classes is that sizeable numbers of MBAs never become very good at case preparation and discussion, despite their exposure to a large number of cases. And others never realize their full potential in class. Many of these students are as talented as their more successful counterparts. They have worked as hard (perhaps harder) than the more successful students. I believe the difference is that the less successful MBAs have not developed a personal system of case preparation but merely have picked up some of the "tricks of the trade" as they move through their MBA experience.

If MBAs in case-intensive programs have difficulty developing a personal system of case preparation, what about other students who experience far less than 500 to 700 cases? My experience is that these people travel through their MBA, undergraduate, or executive management programs with little or no idea of the need for developing a personal system of case preparation and discussion. For instance, students may prepare 50 to 100 cases before they begin to discover some systematic procedures for case analysis and discussion. This slow rate of discovery is simply a wasteful and needless hindrance to the learning process.

Consequently, the basic purpose of this publication is to help you increase your level of analysis, discussion, and self-learning at a faster rate than if you must, so to speak, "rediscover the wheels" of case preparation and discussion.

Some of my colleagues no doubt feel such slow, tedious rediscovery is necessary for you. Ideally, I agree with them. But the fact of the matter is that a sizeable number of you will never make the rediscovery because you won't encounter a requisite number of cases. I believe most of us agree that each student should travel a road of self-learning and development. But I also believe that, as teachers, we can assist you along this difficult road. I have no doubt that you will discover considerably more about the process of case preparation and discussion beyond what is covered in this book. Hopefully, this book will simply motivate you to get started sooner than otherwise.

Chapter Two
The Two Basic Conditions For Classroom Success

How can you best insure success when entering the classroom of a case course?

First you must learn "the basics" of case preparation and discussion. The chapters of Part One cover the fundamentals of case activity, and I believe they will help you to improve your performance.

But despite your comprehension of these chapters, despite even the amount of work you actually put into a case, I feel there are two overriding conditions for classroom success in a case course:

    1.   You must always be at least adequately prepared; and

    2.   You must listen and generally respond to what is being said by your instructor and fellow students.

I believe the principal reason good listening is so important is that the effectiveness of case discussions is determined not only by individual efforts but by the performance of the class as a whole. Case classes vary in their collective ability to analyze a case during class discussion. Also, case groups learn to improve their collective performance over time by improving individually but also by improving as a class. Essentially, the class learns how to police itself, thereby limiting the digressions made by individual members.

Digressions are very frequent with classes that are new to the case method. Why? Many people simply have not been placed in an environment that forces them to listen and respond to what is being said by other members of the class. For instance, you may find it advantageous at times to shift the conversation in another direction. And you may attempt it. But remember, blatant digression from the flow of dialogue will weaken, if not negate, anything you say.

No doubt you will observe some students too busy thinking about what they are going to say, rather than listening to what is being said and responding to questions or statements made by other students or the instructor. Being a good talker will not automatically make you a good case student. You must participate in a discussion with others, not create a dialogue with yourself. First and foremost, this means you must listen to what others, especially other students, are saying.

Good listening skills are necessary by they are not enough. You must also be prepared to contribute to the discussion. Why? There are several reasons.

First, you have the responsibility of sharing your ideas with your classmates in order that your classmates might learn from you, just as you have learned from them. Beware of the tendency to rationalize your silence by telling yourself, "But I have nothing worthwhile to say." I have rarely found this position to be true.

Second, you have a responsibility to subject your ideas to open debate and criticism. You will never be able to improve your ideas (and the process that produced them) if you do not disclose them. Of course, the implicit fear is that we will fail in front of our peers... that we will perhaps suffer an emotional and intellectual bloody nose. Yet, how many times have you heard someone say, "I've never learned more than when I've failed."

Can you possibly maximize your learning without taking some risk, without perhaps even some suffering? I believe the key is to know you are really risking very little. Neither your life, your fortune, your job, nor your business are at stake. Yet, someday they will be on the line and your success will be influenced by your decision-making ability. Is it not better to learn your trade while you have very little to lose?

Third, the development of effective communication skills will be fundamental to your future success in professional life. Both strong verbal skills are acknowledged by successful professionals as critical ingredients to their achievements, and interestingly the one (along with written communication) they find most lacking in recently graduated seniors and MBAS. Consistent participation in class will enable you to develop the precious verbal skills you will need later in life.

The fulfillment of these responsibilities for classroom participation requires good preparation. Yet, the perception of what constitutes good preparation and good classroom performance varies widely among students. In terms of class discussion, most case instructors consider the quality of your contribution more valuable than the quantity of your contribution. Nevertheless, the discussion of cases has a distinct bias in favor of the aggressive, articulate student. When all is said and done, you are better off having over-participated even though you were caught "off-base" once or twice, than to have not participated sufficiently because you refused to take the risk.

Some students will reject this environment as totally inequitable to them. However, you best remember that much of your professional life will revolve around your ability to persuade others of the value of your ideas and the analysis which supports your ideas.

Other students will simply reject the whole notion of role playing or living vicariously through some business situation. They are, unfortunately, failing to take advantage of a tremendous opportunity. . . the opportunity to improve themselves by learning from the actual experiences of others, as well as the opportunity to learn how and when to apply various techniques. Both opportunities cannot be dismissed lightly since strong philosophical and pragmatic arguments can be made that knowledge and techniques are simply not learned unless they can be applied.

Chapter Three
Learning's Secret Weapon: Team Learning

"The thing I regret most about my study group experience is that I chose to join the same group with a close, personal friend. We had known each other socially for some time and we'd had many good times together. But we had never worked together and it didn't work out. Unfortunately, this bad experience has also affected our friendship."

This disclosure by an undergraduate student was one of several observations made by 115 students who participated in a confidential survey about their semester-long experiences in study groups for Business Policy at Babson College. Their responses were part of a study to determine what elements helped make some study groups more effective than others. Many of their most common observations indicated some very clear advice for students wishing to establish effective study groups. Let's examine this advice as it falls into two broad categories: 1) advice about group formation; and 2) advice about the operation of the study groups during the semester.

Forming Study Teams

How a study group was formed appeared to be a major factor determining their success. Some key descriptors of successful group formation were: earliness, balanced size, commitment, diversity, compatibility and dependability.

"Earliness" referred to when successful study groups were formed. Student responses indicated that the most effective groups were formed very early compared to the formation of all study groups. In fact, the study groups which reported the least problems throughout the semester were formed "before the semester ever began." Of course, many other reasons could also be responsible
for the lack of difficulty experienced by these groups but the rationale explaining why early formation was a success factor seems reasonable. For instance, the group that forms before the first class:

1. has a wider choice of available members and can be more selective;

2. has members that are probably acquainted with one another through previous class work and have an idea of each other's motivation and capabilities;

3. has one less organizing task to perform during the first week of class and can begin substantive course work immediately.

A second predictor of success is the term "balanced size" which refers directly to group size. in our survey, the groups most satisfied with their study groups were neither too large nor too small. The "right" size for our particular situation varied between 4-to-6 members. Study groups smaller or larger than this size experienced different sets of problems related to their size. Study groups with 4-to-6 members seemed best able to "balance" off these different kinds of difficulties. For example, larger groups with seven or more members (some groups reported as many as ten members) encountered problems immediately with coordinating their schedules. Selecting a meeting time and place mutually acceptable to all became increasingly difficult as the number of participants increased and often became the first point of contention and disagreement within a group. Other operating problems also tended to crop up more frequently for the larger groups as the semester evolved. (To be discussed in the next section.) However, some larger groups (7 or 8 members) did have successful experiences under certain conditions. These conditions were:

1.   formation occurred early;

2.   most, if not all, the members knew each other in terms of work/professional performance;

3.   scheduling problems were minor and resolvable;

4.   members No. 6 and No. 7 brought something special to the group in terms of skills or resources (e.g. a great meeting place);

5 .   group members knew that one or two members were sincere, hard-working students but needed extra support or worked well in paired assignments; and/or,

6.   the study group knew that one or more members would be unable to make every meeting for good reasons, but wanted to have at least 4-to-6 members present for each meeting.

This last point underscored the interrelated importance of the term "commitment" in the formation of a successful group of balanced size. Each member had to honestly commit to meeting with the study group for each session when the group was formed. Otherwise a 4-to-5 member group could suddenly become a two or three member group when one or two members subsequently revealed they could not/would not attend each meeting.

But you might ask, what's wrong with a tight, little group of two or three students? Possibly nothing. Certainly you have a better probability of avoiding many of the problems that arise as you add more and more people to a group. Yet you also have a higher chance of not obtaining a sufficient diversity of skills and experiences which may be necessary for superior case analysis. Also, you may overload yourself or at least be unable to reap the rewards of greater division of labor that are possible with a bigger group.

Obviously, the "balancing point" regarding group size may be different for your particular course. The results here suggest that a smaller two-to-three member group may work well if the course is not particularly difficult, comprehensive and especially where study groups are not utilized to any great extent. Conversely, you probably should have at least a four-member group for tougher courses where study groups are the common practice but be very cautious about adding more than six members.

Two other factors, "compatibility" and "dependability" were mentioned one way or another as important considerations for students when forming a study group. For example, good communication was perceived as a difficult goal to attain within a study group if participants were not comfortable or compatible with one another. As one student expressed it, "the 'best and the brightest' are not always the best people for your study group. if you feel intimidated, you won't open up."

Unfortunately, the legitimate need for a relaxed, open atmosphere apparently leads some students to select personal friends since they know they will be comfortable and can communicate well with these people. Here the dependability factor comes into play. Some friends simply turn out to be undependable in a group situation. Why isn't clear. But these sad experiences do not mean you should unilaterally reject having friends in your study group. As another student explained, "I'm glad I was in a group where I really knew two people well. Besides being friends for a long time, I knew I could work well with them." The key point is his last sentence. You must have a feeling for their dependability and how well you will work together. Overall, the ideal situation seems to be to have "acquaintances" as opposed to "friends" that you know are serious students with whom you will be comfortable and productive. Form your study groups sufficiently early to insure you have compatible members with a diversity of skills. Finally, assess the course and the skills and resources of prospective group members to determine the appropriate size of your study group.

Effective Team Operations

Numerous things should and should not be done in order to develop and maintain an effective study group. My experience plus the feedback from our student survey suggest several "do's" and "don'ts."

First, do verbalize explicitly what will be the ground rules for your meetings. Perhaps it's no surprise to you, but many groups do not formalize what they expect from study sessions or from each other besides showing up and being reasonably punctual. These requirements are not sufficient. You should communicate beforehand precisely what will be expected of each student at the group meetings. The following are some suggested guidelines:

1. Each person must have read the case thoroughly and performed an appropriate amount of analysis "before" a group meeting.

2. Each person will be expected to attend all group meetings and give these meetings scheduling priority. Naturally, exceptions are made for legitimate excuses (health, emergencies, unavoidable business trips for part-time students, etc.).

3. Each person will be given the opportunity to speak at the meeting and no one will be allowed to monopolize a meeting. Everyone must try to contribute something.

4. Useful contributions made by individual students will be respected and rewarded. These people will be given first option to present their contributions in class.

5. Group goof-offs or parasites will not be tolerated. These individuals will not receive the benefit of the group's work if they do not attend meetings and are not prepared to contribute. in serious instances of irresponsibility, they will be expelled from the group.

This latter point may seem harsh but I want to emphasize that such action should be taken only in severe, blatant instances. Although they are usually a small minority, some people will be irresponsible. A few others have developed the ability to manipulate people to a high art form. Study group members generally regret not taking action against these students. Although they admit the decision to take action is difficult, they also report they were glad after the semester was over that they did take group disciplinary action.

On the other hand, students often report they regret taking action to break up a group, leave it themselves, or expel someone when antagonisms developed because of personality conflicts, power/leadership struggles, or various procedural issues. Students who choose to "weather the storm" are usually happy they decided to work out these difficulties after the semester was completed.

Students devise a number of creative rules and mechanisms to help them overcome or avoid dysfunctional group situations. Study groups that do not develop similar procedures either explicitly or implicitly tend to experience more internal conflict and less group cooperation. The central problem which appears to cause internal disruption is productivity - or more properly, the lack of it. While survey data do not prove this point conclusively, discussions with group members suggest that personality clashes, power struggles, loss of group cohesiveness, etc. become critical disruptive factors when group output is insufficient or marginal given the time invested.

What then are the rules or procedures that will help productivity?

First and foremost, you must find and agree on a place that is conducive to productive meetings. A good place means no distractions. It means no ringing telephones, blaring TV's or disruptions from non-group members if you must meet in dorm lounges or student rooms. In short, a good place means no interruptions. It also means, according to student surveys, having a large table to sit around where you can write comfortably and, optimally, a blackboard.

Second, besides a specific meeting place, you should also set a specific time to meet and establish a set routine. A set time will save members from wasting the time needed to coordinate schedules and communicate a changing or "flexible" meeting time. It will also save you from possibly missing a meeting because you didn't hear about the new meeting hour.

Even more important, establishing a specific meeting time means more than setting a starting time. Productive study groups also set a *finishing time*. Given student responses, I suggest a maximum meeting time of two hours per case and stick to it. Why? You will find that you will avoid other distractions and discussions. As one student aptly explained: "We all knew we only had two hours for our meetings. Everyone showed up on time and we got right down to work. Socializing, joking and digressing were kept to a minimum. We couldn't afford it."

What's more, the alternative of long, open-ended meetings can be disastrous. Another student notes, "The meetings went on and on, some lasting three to five hours. Looking back on it, we wasted too much time. People would show up late and later lose interest. We spent too much time on small details and didn't move along. Then people would get tired and irritated."

Third, students found they saved time and were much more productive when they agreed to be open and frank with one another. "We had an unwritten rule that helped greatly. We all agreed that if anyone was digressing or off the point, we'd let each other know it and not get upset about it. The same held for class. If I were off base continually in class, my group members were to let me know."

Fourth, you should determine explicitly how your group will handle the leadership function. Some groups agreed on a leader to chair meetings and coordinate activities and individual assignments. Other groups decided to rotate the group leader position in order to give everyone an opportunity to develop leadership skills. Other groups did nothing and regretted it. Bids for power occurred and met with success and quiet resentment or destructive clashes of wills and personalities.

Fifth, determine how and when you will implement an appropriate division of labor for *each* case. A fixed assignment for all cases (e.g. Jones will always do the financials) is probably better than no division of labor. But management cases often differ considerably and productivity will be higher at group meetings if you can tailor assignments for each case (e.g. most of the financials are given in XYZ case so Jones should do something else).

But who should decide specifically who does what? Several successful groups gave this authority to the group leader who had the responsibility to read ahead and determine and make assignments before other group members read the case. Specifically, group leaders decided who should specialize, the areas of specialization, if members should all work independently and in different areas, if paired assignments should be made for difficult areas, or if one or more students should work on the same area but independent of one another. Duplicating assignments worked well when the group leader felt:

1. an assignment was particularly difficult;

2. a need for a check on critical areas or a need to have at least two people knowledgeable about the area;

3. a need to help students who were weak in a particular area;

4. some members simply worked better in pairs or small teams rather than alone.

Sixth, whether or not you rotate the leadership position, you should decide on a schedule to rotate assigned roles to give people the chance to improve their weaknesses. First, discuss your strengths and weaknesses up front. Strengths usually coincide with your principal interests, e.g. your undergraduate major, graduate areas of concentration, or related employment experiences. Obviously, you generally should lead from strength initially and for particularly important case assignments. Accounting or finance majors usually are prepared best to "push numbers" while marketing people should do the marketing initially and so on.

But you can overdo a good thing and eventually the group will be no stronger than its weakest link. However, the group's total performance will improve, especially in critical situations, as individual weaknesses are improved. An effective group leader will schedule assignments to give non-number pushers an opportunity to "run the numbers" while the accounting/finance experts work on sensitive human behavior issues. When roles are shifted, paired assignments may be prudent initially for individuals weak in some specific area. Some members may resist working in unfamiliar areas. However, a major trap is for each member to specialize continually in their strongest suite. Remember, if nothing else you will learn to ask better questions about your weaker areas while also understanding better the analysis of the group experts when you do some work in their areas.

These six general procedures should foster group productivity. However, you may still find your study group is unable to attain close-knit cohesiveness and sufficient productivity. For instance, you may discover your group is too small or too weak to produce top level work. Whatever the reason, a permanent or temporary merger with another group may be the answer. A temporary merger means consolidating the study groups for particularly difficult assignments. Also, a trial merger for one or two sessions is often a prudent way to discover if the combined groups are indeed better than the original teams.

Larger study groups may experience just the opposite. No matter what they do, some group members may not work well together. Sub-groups may be more productive for some assignments when groups are too large and unwieldy. Shorter "general sessions" can be used to bring the sub-groups together.

Toward Spirited Cooperation...Rapidly

Various theories or models of group development exist which describe the behavioral stages groups experience as they become productive working units. Like individuals, some groups mature and become productive at a rapid rate. Other groups, in a sense, never grow up. Even for "developing" groups, some mature all too slowly and painfully while others develop quickly with seemingly little effort.

Yet the effort is usually there. Members of successful groups often must make sacrifices to maintain and promote the development of their group. They listen. They arbitrate. They encourage. They tolerate, interpret, and support. Members must be prepared to both lead and follow at different times. Most of all, they find discover a basis for trust.

The members of successful groups make these efforts in order to move through various stages of group life. This process of group maturity often involves five steps:

1. getting acquainted;
2. defining reasonable goals and work tasks;
3. competition for power and influence;
4. workable cooperation; and
5. spirited cooperation.

How rapidly a study group gets through the first three stages and attains at least "workable cooperation" determines its ultimate success. The goal, of course, is "spirited cooperation." Then some fantastic things are possible and learning itself soars. A key message of this chapter is that spirited cooperation will have a greater chance of occurring if a study group is formed properly and institutes some simple operating rules and procedures.

Chapter Four
Ethics, Cases, And The Classroom:
A Microcosm Of Life

This chapter can be the **most** important one of the book for you. I've discovered over the years that students often get into trouble because they encounter ethical problems that are not recognized as ethical dilemmas because they occur in new contexts and environments. Nevertheless, specific ethical problems exist that are related to the use of cases by teachers and students.

The principal kinds of case-related ethical problems are:

1.　　passing on case notes or old case reports to students who have not yet taken the course, thereby giving them an unfair advantage;

2.　　discussing the case with someone who has not yet had the case in class but expects to have it at a later time;

3.　　spending considerable effort attempting to find out "what happened in the case" in order to look good (as if what the company did was the correct answer, or that someone else's " right" answer is right for you);

4.　　contacting a case **company** without permission to gather more information about the case situation;

5.　　blowing the cover of a disguised case;

6.　　taking advantage of other group members by letting them do the bulk of the work - the group parasite syndrome.

A professional code of ethics must be recognized and followed by students regarding their treatment of cases. I believe two principal elements of this code are:

1.　　you should not provide information on a specific case to people who have not yet had the case in class;

2.　　one does not seek or provide information about the case situation other than what is provided in the case, unless *explicitly* permitted by your instructor.

Cases represent a considerable investment in time and money. Generally, it takes about 30 to 40 days to research, write, and get a case approved for classroom use. Including expenses, I estimate the average cost of a case is approximately $2500. Yet, many cases are written that are not used more than once or twice in class. For various pedagogical reasons, four or five cases may be written that do not work well in class. If the costs of the less effective cases are included in the total cost, the approximate cost of developing a quality case is around $10,000.

While these figures are only rough estimates, they serve to illustrate the value of a good case. My impression is that most students do not realize the damage they can do by passing on notes, etc. No doubt your instructor will realize what has happened before too long. Unfortunately, the need to withdraw or shelve many good cases will have a direct impact on the quality of your course since the inventory of good cases is limited.

What should you do if your roommate approaches you and says, "You had the XYZ Company yesterday, didn't you? How did your class handle it?" However, you respond, I advise you not to act terribly offended. The situation is usually one where the person making the inquiry may not realize the nature of the inquiry and the position he/she places you. Unfortunately, the routine of obtaining packaged information from lectures has conditioned and confused some students into thinking they can always obtain prepackaged, spoon-fed answers. How they obtain the answer doesn't matter. After all, if you can buy course notes of Professor X's lectures on the open market, what's wrong with asking a friend for information on a case?

Indeed, you can obtain "answers" about a case situation. Yet, this information gathering is not learning. Perhaps the most important step you can make in your educational career is the realization that you will *learn* only through your own efforts. A second step is the realization that you have a responsibility to help others to learn. Providing notes or extensive verbal information about a case is not helping an individual to learn.

Certainly professors can and should vary their case offerings and thereby reduce the temptation to obtain "inside" information on particular cases. But in the end, the case system can flourish only if students respect an ethical code. All too frequent scandals in business and government suggest w,e require not only more classroom discussion of ethical conduct in professional life, but also more practice while in school. One place to start is by observing and maintaining an ethical code for case study.

PART TWO
WHAT TO DO BEFORE GETTING TO CLASS
■ ■ ■ ■ ■ ■
Chapter Five
Reading a Case Efficiently

The first task of case reading is to determine what kind of case you are reading. Several basic kinds of cases exist. Each requires a different type of analysis and, consequently, a different kind of reading. Four types of cases are identified below, along with some general reading instructions.

1.   Highly Structured Cases

This type of case is generally short with little or no excess information. The facts of a problem are reasonably well-ordered and stated. A "best" solution often exists and you are expected to apply some known tools or model to derive the solution. An example is a short case demonstrating the use of breakeven formulas.   Read the case to determine the appropriate analytic tools or formula to use.

If you already know what formulas or models to apply, review them before reading the case to identify the specific facts or data you need to "set up the problem." Then read the case and identify the necessary data for solution.

2.   Short Vignettes

This type of case is generally used to introduce key concepts. However, you may encounter them in other courses as first-day or in-class cases when your instructor needs a short teaching vehicle for some reason. Again little excess information is presented. The case may vary in length from one-to-ten pages with one or two exhibits. A "best" solution usually does not exist in the sense of a right answer that is derived from a formula. However, your instructor probably hopes you will be able to identify and apply one or more management concepts in discussing the case. The application of these concepts will allow you to present a "better" solution or recommendation, than if you analyzed the case without them. Consequently, read the case vignette, searching for possible ways to apply concepts you have learned recently in your class or concepts you are clearly expected to know from earlier courses.

3.   Long Unstructured Cases

These unstructured cases may vary in length from ten-to-fifty pages with several exhibits. The case writer has attempted to reflect the reality of a situation by supplying all or nearly all the information associated with the situation. Irrelevant, excess information exists while enough relevant information may not be available. The existence of qualitative factors does not usually permit a "best" solution. The underlying problems and/or opportunities are unclear.

Despite these obstacles, the case situation covers a terrain where knowledge exists in the form of preferred practices or even theory. A body of concepts and defined teaching objectives exist. For instance, many upper-class, MBA, and executive management classes will encounter the long, unstructured case and the reading recommendations subsequently presented in this chapter are intended expressly for this type of case.

4. Ground-Breaking Cases

Advanced MBA, doctoral, and some executive management classes may encounter cases where both the students and the instructor are engaged in an exploratory mission covering new ground. The terrain is new because the business situations are totally new and little, if any, knowledge exists which is based on systematic research.

Relevant concepts, teaching objectives, even approaches to the business problems or opportunities posed by the new situation, have not been identified. As you read these cases, you must be prepared and capable of extending (not just applying) existing, tangentially related theory or practices in order to build upon existing knowledge. Simultaneously, you must be ready to structure and organize the case data in completely new ways which may bear little or no resemblance to existing concepts.

Reading Objectives and Scheduling

Your main objective is not only to read the case, but to comprehend its contents as efficiently as possible. Considerable emphasis is on "efficiency" because time is generally a constraint. Other cases must be prepared, other papers written, other assignments completed. Consequently, an advantage accrues to the student who can read and comprehend a case in a minimum amount of time.

However, a "minimum amount of time" does not mean reading the case once quickly the night before your scheduled class meeting. Few people can absorb, comprehend, and analyze a case with so little effort. Most cases must be read at least twice. Even more than two readings may be required to realize a top-notch job on a case. For instance, few students realize that their instructor may have read the case several times and have virtually committed the case to memory.

Obviously, you do not have to go to these extremes. However, you must get a simple procedure embedded in your mind. With rare exception, you must plan to read a case more than once.

With this rule in mind, you should consider scheduling specific periods of time (each two to four hours in length) which will be devoted exclusively to case reading if you must prepare several cases per week. During this time, you will read anywhere from three to six cases, depending on the length of the cases.

Many students find it helpful to read all or most of their cases for the week on the preceding Friday, Saturday or Sunday. This early reading gives them plenty of time to ponder the case, discuss it with study group members, and generally feel less pressured. Whatever else happens during the week, at least they've read the case and had some chance to think and talk about it before class. Remember, a good deal of learning occurs "in background mode" for human beings. But you must read the case before you can think about it...even subconsciously.

A Reading Procedure

Most cases are divided into two basic parts: 1) the text; and 2) the exhibits.
One reading procedure is to divide your initial case reading in terms of these two usual divisions.

Understanding The Text: First, familiarize yourself with the text by carefully reading the first page or so (which usually describes the *situational context* and/or the key problems and opportunities faced by the principal protagonists in the case). Look for the situational context and reread it until you understand it thoroughly and can restate it in your own words. If the situational context is not stated in the first few pages of the text, you should immediately begin to look through the case for it. Often, you will find a description of the case situation on the last page of the text when it is not introduced on the first page.

Once the case situation is understood, the next step is to quickly skim the rest of the text of the case, noting the main headings and perhaps reading the initial sentences of lead-off paragraphs.

<u>Understanding The Exhibits:</u> After gaining quick familiarization with the text, you should quickly leaf through the exhibits, noting their basic type. Does the case have a Balance Sheet and Profit and Loss Statement? Is there an organizational diagram? Is there a biography of principal case characters? Is there an exhibit which has already worked out certain key financial ratios?

You can often save much valuable time if you know what kinds of exhibits already exist in the case. It is surprising the number of students who begin reading and analyzing a case on Page One and begin collecting facts and performing analyses which are available to them later in the case.

Your quick review of the case exhibits will prove more effective if you keep in mind that there are essentially two kinds of exhibits:

1.   exhibits common to most cases - financial statements, an organizational diagram, etc.;

2.   exhibits unique or specific to the particular case.

At this point, I recommend taking a careful glance at the common" exhibits simply to see if there is anything strange or "uncommon" about them. For example, if you find an uncommon treatment of inventory, or you discover some "reserve" account you've never seen before, note it down as a potential area for careful scrutiny. Often, a preoccupation for understanding anomalies in the exhibits pays off. If you crack these strange exhibits or entries, you will almost always have something worthwhile to say in class simply because many of your fellow students will not have exercised the intellectual muscle to decipher or understand these anomalies.

Once you have familiarized yourself with the rough contents of the case, begin to read the text from the beginning at a comfortable pace. Rarely underline. It takes too much time. Limit yourself to jotting brief notes in the margin - notes which never repeat what is said in the case, but reflect your observations about a topic or issue, including the identification of concepts you feel may be relevant to a particular paragraph for future analysis. At this point, be certain you refer to exhibits as they are mentioned in the case so you understand the context of their reference.

Be careful you understand complex descriptions of a technical or organizational nature. Separate fact from opinion. Distinguish between what a person or persons are "saying" versus what they are actually "doing." Are they the same? Try to note what "isn't being said," and ask yourself "why?"

After finishing with the text, examine each exhibit carefully, making sure you understand the purpose of the exhibit and its principal component parts.

The day or evening before the case is due, you should read the case again. I suggest a slightly different procedure for reading the case the second time. First, review the first page or situational context, wherever it is located in the case. Then, instead of reading the text, begin with the last exhibit and work backwards through the exhibits, making sure you understand each exhibit and continually keeping an eye open for the "non-kosher" exhibit or entry. This procedure is recommended because many students become tired during the first reading or tend to hurry to finish the case. Consequently, their comprehension of the last few pages and exhibits is probably weaker than the first parts. Especially during periods of time crunch, it may prove prudent to begin your second reading where you have done the weakest job the first time around.

CASE PREPARATION SHEET

■ Name of case, class, and date . . . .

■ What is the situational context of the case? . . . Mr Palmer is an *upscale* mens suits manufacturer
who is losing market share to imports and low-cost manufacturers.
He's not sure what direction to take.

■ Who are the principal players? . . . Palmer clothing, the govt., his domestic &
foreign competition.

■ What are the pertinent facts provided in the text? <u>INDUSTRY</u>: recent recession hurt demand
as imports moved in. Dollar vs other countries has risen. Much underutilization.
Many majors took long run positions of demanding manufacturers sell
below cost to put independents out of business. Manufacturers were supposed
to make up losses with volume, further tying them to majors. Mr Palmer
had trouble getting people to work as welfare provided almost as much
means. Soft wear clothing is a new trend that other manufacturers have
begun producing. No amt of modernizing could make domestic apparel cheaper.

■ What are the pertinent facts provided in the exhibits? Men's apparel has grown at a much
slower rate over 20 yrs then any other type of apparel. & Imports of
cotton, wool & man-made fiber has increased dramatically. The tremendous
fall of the apparel/textile trade balance is lead by the drop in apparel
trade balance. The hourly wage of apparel & related industry workers
has increased at a much slower rate than those of other manufacturing
industries. Employment in these industries has fallen as compared to
the almost 10 yr employment growth for other manuf. industries.
More casual clothes are being produced by the men's apparel industry.

■ What concepts apply?
- essential industry argument
- tariffs vs subsidies & other direct price influences
- Quotas / Quantity Controls

■ What is hard to understand? Why? . . . .

Chapter Six
Analyzing and Preparing a Case for Discussion

You will need two distinct but related skills to generate effective case analysis for classroom discussion.

The first skill is obvious: you must generate a meaningful analysis of the case assigned for discussion. One general approach to analysis is offered over the next few pages. Subsequently, specific types of analysis are presented for the preparation of cases.

The second skill is less apparent but just as vital: you must translate or package your analysis into some form that will allow you to present it in class. You may have a great case analysis "on paper," but unless you can tell the class about it, your actual classroom performance will not reflect the quality of your analysis. The final section of this chapter offers some suggestions for translating your analysis for class presentation.

The Analysis

The kind and level of analysis you perform for any given case should depend on your classroom discussion role and your strategy for the course (covered in Chapter Six). For instance, students with heavy case loads (i.e., three cases or more per day) may find it impossible to do a comprehensive analysis on every case.

The purpose of this section is to outline a simple but effective approach to case analysis regardless of specific strategies. This approach is summarized into four steps

1.   Determine the key case issues and case positioning (i.e., why the case is assigned now!);

2.   Determine if there are any principal "unassigned" questions that relate to key case issues;

3.   Determine the general analytic approach you should take to analyze the case;

4.   Determine how to focus your analysis (i.e., select the appropriate tools and facts needed to support some recommendation);

5.   Determine the specific level or type of analysis you will perform for class.

Most students begin their analysis by working through the questions assigned by the instructor. While this may be an appropriate way to start case analysis, it is not always the most effective way to analyze a case. Following the assigned questions may provide an adequate analysis, one you can live with, but my experience is that it rarely yields a comprehensive analysis.

After your initial skim reading or before your second reading, I suggest asking a few fundamental questions.

What do you think are the key issues of this case?

Why was the case assigned now?

Are there any bidden issues?

The answers may not be readily apparent. if you cannot answer these fundamental questions, you may want to ask other students in your class. Keep these questions in mind and continually try to answer them even, if necessary, while class discussion is in progress. A sudden breakthrough about the underlying purpose of the case may allow you to apply some analysis and observations you have made already about the case.

After class, you may wish to ask other students or the instructor what the key issues were, and why the case was assigned if class discussion did not make this clear to you.

Unassigned Questions

If you wish to obtain a good grasp of the case, you should attempt to determine the principal "unassigned" questions pertaining to the case. The identification of these questions may require nothing more than a little common sense, taking into account the nature of the course and topic of the case.

Another way to determine the unassigned questions is to ask yourself what kinds of questions you would ask your classmates if you were teaching the class. Many case instructors do not follow the assigned questions, but tend to flow with the discussion as it unfolds, seeking to ask those questions which will help you to make worthwhile classroom contribution. What kinds of questions do you think will be raised by class discussion of the case?
If you can spot just one or two of these questions, you can be ready for them. The probability is also high that you will be the one selected to respond to these questions. Few other hands will be raised when these questions are asked by the class or your instructor.

Analytic Approaches

There are many approaches to case analysis. Which approach you select will be based partly on the kind of case you are reading. For instance, marketing cases will require the application of marketing concepts and marketing conceptual frameworks. Likewise, a body of financial knowledge exists that is relevant for the analysis of finance cases. But whichever approach you chose, you should keep in mind that the identification and evaluation of alternative courses of action is a common approach for most cases. You should also attempt to form opinions about these alternatives.

However, never forget that effective case analysis means providing support for your position or opinion. You may or may not be expected to analyze all the alternatives. Such analysis, in fact, may be impossible, given your time constraints. However, whatever opinion you form or recommendation you present, it must be supported with facts drawn from the case, other acceptable data, or even perhaps with your own experience.

Analytic Focus

The determination of some focus for your analysis is a critical step. Most cases, especially good cases, reflect the real world by providing an overabundance of information and detail about a particular business situation. A tremendous amount of inefficient time will be spent by the student who tries to analyze every fact and push every number in a case. Good case analysts are always asking what are the pertinent facts for analysis? What are the relevant numbers that should be pushed?

Superior case analysts go one step beyond identifying the relevant facts and numbers which are given in a case. Rather they ask: given my analytic approach, what are the facts and numbers I need to analyze a particular issue or alternative regardless of what I think is given in a case? The superior analyst is also prepared to say: If these numbers or facts are not provided in the case, what can I assume they are? In short, a superior case analyst is ready and willing to make creative assumptions.

Many students, especially those without prior management experience, feel such "assuming" is unrealistic and not representative of "the real world of business." As any experienced manager will tell you, such creative "assuming" frequently occurs because managers rarely have all the information required to make a decision, nor the
time and money to acquire the missing information. A fundamental problem of life is that decisions must be made almost always with incomplete and often imprecise data.

Finally, whatever you recommend, your classroom performance will be enhanced immeasurably if you produce some quantitative analysis to support your position. Many students will stop short of "running numbers" when supporting a position. Some students may even reject, consciously or unconsciously, the idea of pushing numbers. Yet, the creative use of simple quantitative analysis in support of a qualitative position is one of the most valuable skills a student can learn through continual exposure to the case method. It is a skill which, once it becomes a reflex action, will arm you with a distinctive advantage over most managers. Part Six of this book presents a number of valuable, frequently-used techniques, which you should master.

The Specific Level and Types of Analysis

There are probably almost as many specific levels/types of case analyses as there are cases. Five kinds of case analyses are presented as follows. Can you think of others?

1.   The Comprehensive Analysis

Provides in-depth treatment of the key issues of a case, including pinpointing principal recommendations for action and quantitative and qualitative support for them.

2.   The Specialized Analysis

Focuses on a particular question or issue in a case and provides an in-depth analysis . . . one much more detailed than most of your classmates will provide.

3.   The Lead-off Analysis

Focuses on analyzing what you believe will be the initial question asked by your instructor. A lead-off analysis is similar to a specialized analysis; however, some important differences may exist. Depending on the lead-off question and the instructor, you may not "necessarily" be expected to go into great detail about a particular issue but rather identify the major issues/alternatives for discussion.

4.   The Hit-and-Run Analysis

Provides a surface or generalized treatment of assigned questions and explicit issues. Hit-and-Run is part of a "holding" or "survival" strategy, designed to keep you out of trouble, i.e., being unprepared.

5.   The Integrating Analysis

Takes many forms, but basically incorporates information from sources other than the assigned case. These sources may be industry notes, technical notes, annual reports, personal experience, etc. The purpose of this analysis is to utilize information from these non-case sources to enrich an analysis of a particular issue.

Translating Your Analysis for Discussion

When you think you are through with your analysis, you are probably not quite finished. You have one more important step to perform: translating your analysis into a form which will enable you to present it in class.

A great many students will often do a good job of analysis, but end up becoming frustrated in the classroom when they find they are not able to present their analysis to the group. Packaging your analysis for presentation is a skill all of its own, one you will continue to use after leaving school.

Several techniques exist which can help you to present your material. One I find useful is to envision how the case teacher can write or diagram what you have to say on the blackboard. For instance, can you develop a simple matrix or decision diagram showing the key alternatives, or make a simple list of the pros and cons of each alternative? Instead of a diagram, can you refer key aspects of the analysis to a particular exhibit in the case? For some complex relationship mentioned in the case, can you start off by posing a problem that leads your instructor to write a simple list on the blackboard?
For example:

> "Well. . . . I have to admit I had a lot of problems understanding the different kinds of lease arrangements that were described on pages seven and eight of the case. Consequently, I tried to determine what were the unique distinctions of each lease possibility. Lease number one had these distinctive elements . . . Lease number two had . . . etc."

A second useful device for presentation is to relate your analysis to some common experience shared with the class during a previous case. Is your analysis similar to one presented in an earlier case?

Perhaps the most effective way to present complex or extensive analysis is through the use of transparencies for an overhead projector. Unfortunately, you may be able to use transparencies only if your instructor regularly uses an overhead projector. However, if one is available, you can use transparencies to communicate considerable information which otherwise may be impossible to convey to the class. *

*Also, I should note to my teaching colleagues that the level of class discussion is often raised several notches if students are encouraged and able to use transparencies.

Two ways exist for you to make transparencies. You can buy blank transparencies and a special pen (regular pen and pencil won't work) for printing directly on each transparency. Or you can print or type your message on regular paper, xerox it, and then pass the xeroxed copy through a special machine which your library, audiovisual or student secretarial services usually have for making transparencies.

A few extra tips about making and presenting transparencies can make the difference between a good and poor presentation:

1.   Don't write. Print using large bold letters.

2.   Use blue or green ink if producing transparencies directly (black, red, yellow, etc. don't work well).

3.   Limit the information on any one transparency as much as possible. Break down complicated exhibits into two-to-three transparencies. Try to use no more than fifteen-to-twenty words per transparency.

4.   Use capital letters or largest type when presenting typed visuals.

5.   Determine beforehand if you should show the transparencies yourself or merely hand them over to your instructor for display to the class, e.g. you may want to handle the presentation if you have several transparencies, to avoid confusion.

6.   If you show the transparencies yourself, face the class -not the screen. You can use a pen or pencil to point to key words or calculations directly on the overhead projector and the image will be reflected on the screen for the class to follow.

7.   Present each transparency only when you cover the point it conveys. Remove it as soon as you or the class moves on to a new point to avoid distraction.

8.   If you've produced some extensive analysis or transparencies, tell your instructor before class the general nature or content of your transparencies so he or she will weave you into the discussion process, if the proper occasion should arise.

One final message. However you decide to communicate your analytical work to the class, be certain you crystallize or reduce your analysis to a few simple points. Don't overwhelm your mind trying to memorize every detail of a set presentation. Even when such memorizing is possible, it's too easy to get knocked off a narrow trend of thought by a student or your teacher who asks a simple question of clarification that you did not consider. Flexibility is critical. You must be able to respond to the give-and-take of an on-going discussion which may or may not include some constructive cross-examination.

Chapter Seven
Discussing a Case in Class

What's the ultimate position you can attain in a case course? Once you've demonstrated your superior ability to your teacher, the best thing you can do is give others a chance and support their attempts to improve their skills. A friend who teaches using the case method summed up this role for me one day when he was discussing an unusually outstanding student (let's call him David)

> "David never said a word the entire class. But he was there. If the class had stumbled or stalled, I know he would have entered the discussion and bailed them out."

Many ways exist to participate in the discussion process. Yet, few of us will obtain the ultimate position of David -- participating even though we say nothing at all. Indeed, rather than refrain from talking about a case, the objective for most of us is to find ways to break the ice and enter the discussion process.

I have three recommendations for increasing your participation in class:

First, you must develop an understanding for the process of discussion in your class. Some rudimentary knowledge of the discussion process itself will make it easier for you to participate. Second, determine beforehand the discussion role or roles you will play in your class. At least develop an awareness of various discussion roles which you may employ if the opportunity arises. Third, be aggressive. I am not recommending "talking for the sake of talking," but rather a strong spirit of participation or a mental attitude where you are anxious to take the offensive in discussing a case.

The Discussion Process

The discussion process for most case classes will include:

1. identification and analysis of the case situation;
2. the analysis of key alternatives; and,
3. recommendations for specific action.

However, you should be aware that this process is often altered depending upon the nature of the case and the approach taken by your instructor. For instance, a case discussion may start off with the teacher calling for specific recommendations for action, then getting into the situational context of the case, and then seeing how these recommendations hold up. The point, however, is to know what is happening when it is happening and anticipate where the discussion is going.

Let's assume, for the moment, that the class discussion follows the specific process outlined above. For example, the lead-off question involves the definition and analysis of the situational context of the case. This lead-off question may be broadly stated, (e.g. "Well, Mr. Jones, what's the situation? -- What's going on here?"). Or the lead-off question may be stated specifically, (e.g., for a production class, "What are the particular process choices open to Mr. Jones, and what is the capacity for each alternative?").

I believe this latter question points up the need for analysis in defining the particular situation of the case. When first exposed to the case method, many students will simply describe the situation as it is explained in the case without determining if this explicit situational context jives with the facts given in the case. For instance, a finance or business policy case may find the principal managers planning for the long-term capital needs of the organization when an examination of the financial statement shows that a cash crisis exists.

In fact, whenever financial statements are given, you should ask what is the financial health of this organization. Is it mildly ill? Or does it have some severe problems which require a rapid and perhaps drastic operation? Or is it lean and healthy? Knowing the financial position of an organization alone provides you with a foundation for further analysis. But whether the case is finance, marketing, control, or policy oriented, the careful definition of the situational context of the case will provide a basis for identifying realistic alternatives.

The second part of the discussion process usually involves an analysis of these key alternatives. Part of this analysis may involve discussion of the appropriate tools to use for analysis. In any event, you should have already asked yourself what are the appropriate tools for analysis, and, given these tools, what kind of information or data you require for analysis of the alternatives.

The process of discussion in many instances will involve the application of tools which yield a quantitative analysis of the alternatives. Given some quantitative ranking of the alternatives, the discussion will often involve or lead to a qualitative assessment of the alternatives. For instance, even though alternative number one has a better ROI (Return on Investment) or net present value, than alternative number two, do some qualitative reasons exist why you would still recommend alternative number two over the "more profitable" alternative?

At this point, the process of discussion often shifts into an analysis of what should be done when and how. More emphasis will be placed on this part of the discussion process in programs and courses that are attempting to foster a sense of administrative action on the part of its students.

Throughout the discussion process, I can't emphasize enough the importance of listening carefully to the person chosen to lead the discussion. Careful listening is especially critical during the lead-off period when you may still be shuffling your own papers or trying to get your own thoughts in order, instead of listening to what is happening. Do you agree or disagree with what the lead-off speaker is saying? Why do you agree or disagree? Understanding your position relative to the discussants will enable you to move quickly into the discussion process.

Discussion Formats

Beyond these simple observations about the discussion process, I believe the role and attitude you assume and the discussion formats adopted by your instructor will be the major determinants of the kind of discussion that takes place in class. Let's look first at some discussion formats you may encounter in a case course.

Knowing what is happening during class discussions means knowing partly what your teacher is doing. Your instructor may use at least six different discussion formats. All six approaches are related to the socratic form of teaching. In using the socratic method, your instructor will not answer questions or spoon-feed you information but will answer questions with other questions in the hopes that you will be guided to discover and articulate your own answers.

1. Teacher-to-Student: Cross-Examination Format

The flow of discussion will be mainly between your instructor and you. An observation, position, or recommendation you make will be scrutinized through a series of questions whereby the logic of your statements is exposed. The tone may be adversarial but stay cool and do not mistake the active questioning for personal badgering.

2. Teacher-to-Student: Devil's Advocate Format

Again the discussion is usually between your teacher and you but may be open to other class members. Instead of active questioning of your position, your instructor may assume a role or position (often an extreme, and seemingly untenable one) and ask you and possibly others, to refute the advocated position. The critical point in this kind of exercise is to determine at some point if your teacher's position is indeed untenable. You must think and reason actively on your feet, marshalling and weaving case data, conceptual or theoretical information, your own relevant experiences, and common sense.

3. Teacher-to-Student: Hypothetical Format

This discussion format is similar to the preceding ones but differs in one key respect; instead of questioning your position or assuming a devil's advocate position, your teacher will pose a hypothetical situation which is an extreme variant or outcome of your position or recommendation. You will be asked to assess the hypothetical situation in terms of your recommendation. Such an exercise often forces the logic underlying your recommendation to the surface where it can be examined. You must be alert and open during this discussion process to the possible need to modify and reshape your position.

4. Student-to-Student: Confrontation and/or Cooperation Format

Valuable contributions and insights often occur when the discussion flow is completely between students. For instance, a fellow student may challenge your position on grounds of logic or by providing new information you did not consider in your analysis. You or another student may try to rebut the challenge with still different insights and analysis. The power of group discussion and collective analysis often becomes apparent in these situations. Through a spirit of positive confrontation and cooperation, the opportunity to learn is heightened far beyond what can be learned through individual effort.

5. Student-to-Student: Role Playing Format

Your teacher may ask you to assume a role and interact with other classmates who are assigned roles. I find most students enjoy putting on someone else's cap" and interpreting how to act in a given situation. Sensitivities for how others may react are heightened and you begin to inquire regularly (rather than ignore) how others might act given your decision to pursue some course of action.

Some students, unfortunately, reject role playing as contrived and artificial. But this argument is true of all professional (and most purely academic) education. Because something is contrived, does not mean it is valueless. Case learning is itself a vicarious experience, one that most closely approximates the real world. You may not be in love with role playing but it can be beneficial, if not for you, at least for others.

6. Teacher-to-Class: The Silent Format

Your instructor may raise a question which is directed at an individual initially but gets extended to the entire class because no one is able to answer the question. Three discussion paths are possible at this juncture: 1) your instructor will provide clues in the form of additional questions or information; 2) under certain circumstances, your instructor may provide the answer (as Socrates rolls over in his grave); 3) your instructor may do nothing but assume a very silent position until someone works out the problem.

Option 1 has been discussed and Option 2 presents no problem. The issue is how to contend with a silent impasse. Two approaches exist. First, if you feel you know the proper direction, go back to the proverbial drawing board and do some quick analysis. Perhaps a couple of fast financial ratios is all you need. Second, if the problem and required analysis appear more complex, you may be better off thinking how you can go about solving the problem rather than trying to determine an answer. For instance, you may say: "I'm not sure what the answer is to your question, but I would try to solve the answer in the following way. I think a "pro forma" cash flow will tell us if we have the time and resources to follow the business direction recommended earlier. In order to have a meaningful cash flow, we must determine the relevant period over which to track cash inflows and cash outflows. If you think this kind of analysis is appropriate, perhaps we can try to make a rough estimate now."

Discussion Roles

The kind of classroom role you assume will probably relate to the kind of analysis you have done for a particular case. Eight discussion roles are outlined below which relate to the kinds of analysis discussed in Chapter Three. I have no doubt that many other kinds of roles for discussion exist, ones that you may find comfortable and effective to use in the classroom setting.

1. The Expert Witness Role

Relates to someone who has done either a comprehensive or specialized analysis, that is to say, has in-depth knowledge about one or more case issues.

2. The "Bail'em-Out"Role

Relates to someone who has done sufficient analysis which allows them to wait until the class gets stuck (which generally occurs during the quantitative analysis of the alternatives).

3. The "Assume-a-Personality" Role

Relates to someone who has done sufficient analysis of a particular person (and/or their position in an organization). Assuming an identity can be very effective for not only entering class discussion but for continual re-entry. For instance, if you identify yourself as Mr. Jones, the V.P. of Manufacturing, the likelihood is that the class and your instructor will continually refer to you during the discussion for your particular "manufacturing" opinion.

4. The "Get the Facts Out" Role

Relates to someone who has done essentially a hit and run analysis. Because of the surface or holding nature of your analysis, you must enter the discussion process as quickly as possible when your topic arises. The reason is that whatever you have to say will be quickly covered by a great many other students who have probably done as much or more analysis than you have.

5. The "Industry Expert" Role

Relates to someone who has analyzed the impact of industry trends on the particular case situation.

6. The "I've Got Experience" Role

Relates to someone who integrates relevant past experience into the case situation.

7. The "Questioning"Role

Relates to someone who generally asks key questions that are directed at other students about their analysis, its purpose, and where it is taking the discussion. The "questioning" role can be very effective if the questions are phrased to help fellow students expand and improve an analysis.

8. The "Wrap it Up" Role

Relates to someone who integrates different analyses presented in class and relates them to the major issues of the case. The student assuming this role must pay close attention, note the key messages of class discussion, and try to link them together. Essentially, you are preparing an answer to a question that is often used by case instructors at the end of class. No matter how phrased, this question boils down to something like: "Well, what have we learned from our discussion today?" In attempting to answer this question, I should note a word of caution. Employing the "wrap it up approach" involves more than mere repeating of what has been said. The key is integrating class findings in such a way that your summary, indeed, exceeds the sum of the parts.

On Taking the Offensive

Like life itself, class discussions can be great fun, boring, incredibly insightful, terribly confusing, infuriating, creative, and inspiring. But whatever happens on a given day, what you take away from a case course depends mainly on you. Why? Because over the length of a course, case discussions are ruthlessly just. The old maxim holds: "What you put into it is precisely what you get out of it." And your classroom efforts also apply to your written reports. For instance, professors often "blind grade" exams and reports in case courses. We follow this procedure where I teach, yet I find a high positive correlation between strong, active classroom participants and good written work.

I believe a spirit of active participation will probably be one of **the** most critical determinants of your ability to enter the discussion process and be a strong participant. The old football saying, "The best defense is a good offense," seems to hold especially true for case discussions ... at least as long as the offense is in fact a good offense.

Conversely, the worst situation is to hang back, say nothing day after day, and wait nervously for the moment when your teacher brings the discussion to you. Under these conditions, you are obviously not choosing your time and place for battle.

The next worst situation is to enter the discussion process only when you can do so without risk. The opportunities you will have to discuss an issue with 100% confidence are few. Yet, the number of discussion opportunities multiplies considerably if, for example, you are willing to enter the discussion process with only 70% to 80% confidence. A spirit of active participation will enable you to take the risk you must take to do an effective job.

Finally, I should note that if you are an active participant, you cannot realistically expect to be right all the time. After all, good learning comes partly from making mistakes. And you can expect to make errors of analysis or reasoning. If your classmates or your professor reveal an error, do not defend it to the death. Defending a defenseless position is foolhardy and the mark of a poor manager who cannot recognize plain facts because of an emotional need to always be right. Remember, people do not do poorly in case courses for being honestly wrong. They do poorly for not doing.

Chapter Eight
Recording Case Findings

Failure to summarize the key points learned from class discussion is often a fatal habit many students develop. I still find it amazing that some students will sit in class for 60 to 90 minutes listening to the collective analysis of the class, and then fail to record the principal discoveries made by the group.

Frailty of memory requires that observing, participating, and recording be treated as a unified undertaking. You simply are not finished with a case until you record your observations.

Although the pressure of class schedules makes recording difficult, an incremental investment of five minutes can pay big dividends after you have put in several hours on a case. If you are still unconvinced as to the importance of recording your findings, remember that eventually exam time will roll around. Nothing is more depressing than seeing a pile of cases with only your pre-class analysis. No doubt you will recall that a number of good points were made in class, but unfortunately you can't remember what transpired in each of 25-to-30 classes.

A Note-Taking Procedure

Be precise and selective in your note-taking. Some students feel that they have to write down every word people say in class or everything the teacher writes on the blackboard. These are bad habits. During most of the class period, you should be listening and watching -- not writing, in addition to trying to listen and watch. If a major revelation occurs to you, make a quick note. Your notes should be brief, something to jog your memory when you summarize at the end of the class or later the same day.

The "FIG" List

Some students find it useful to take and summarize their case notes in the form of a "FIG" list. Using this system, notes are grouped and listed as either "facts, ideas, or generalizations." For example, a class in Starting New Ventures resulted in the FIG list shown below.

THE "FIG" LIST
May 10th Class - Session No. I

Fact 1:   Retail businesses tend to have higher failure rates that most other kinds of new businesses.

Fact 2:   The average life span of a business is said to be six years, but averages are very misleading.

Fact 3:   It is not possible to buy time when running a business operation, and there is no such thing as a sure deal.

Fact 4:   There are 2,210,000 gas station businesses in the United States.

Fact 5:   There are 2,350,000 grocery stores in the United States.

Idea 1:   The concept of "interstice theory" - turns on the overlap area of large corporations that are too small for large companies to get involved with but great for small business ventures. An example would be producing wooden spools for large cable and wire manufacturers.

Gen 1: To start a business you need several resources, among these resources are: people, capital, and an idea.

Gen 2: A business that is considered marginal will return a lower profit than that realized if one had decided to work for someone else.

Gen 3: The entrepreneur's basic goal is to maintain a level of survival.

Other students may simply wish to summarize the key messages of classroom discussion. These key messages can be methodological, e.g., "The case discussion revealed how an analytic tool (contribution analysis) was applied and made sense of the case data." Or perhaps the key message is conceptual and relates to the subject matter: "The case provided an excellent example of a company that had not spelled out an explicit strategic direction."

But whatever note-taking system you use, don't put summarizing off past that day. You've invested too much, and with another round of cases coming up, you will tend to forget what happened in a particular class. Also, you will not have an up-to-date summary which may help you to analyze the next round of cases.

Special Tips Regarding Classroom Films & Videos

Don't revert to a couch potato if your instructor shows a film or video. Too often when I've shown a video clip, I see some students slouch down into their seats, get real comfortable, and prepare to "zone out." Video cases and various other kinds of course films are becoming increasingly available. They represent a huge investment, not just to make, but to rent.

So when your instructor dims the lights, don't go to sleep. Now is the time to stay alert. Ask yourself, "why is this film being shown at this point in the class?" Also, don't assume too much if you've seen a particular film before. You probably weren't watching the film in terms of the context and subject matter of the course.

Finally, as the film progresses, you generally can't take extensive notes, given the lack of lighting and the pace of the film. But you can jot down a word or two to remind you later about the film's key facts (including who the protagonists are), critical events or decisions, as well as any major ideas or generalizations that come to mind.

PART FOUR
CLASSROOM STRATEGIES & TACTICS
■ ■ ■ ■ ■
Chapter Nine
Classroom Strategies

The purpose of this chapter is to provide a longer term view or strategic perspective of the case preparation and discussion process over the duration of a course - whether it is a semester course for MBAs or undergraduates, or shorter, more intensive programs.

This kind of course or program overview is vital, especially for the one-shot executive programs where there will be no next semester.

Most people experiencing cases for the first time do not develop a strategy that is relevant to their particular situation. Most likely, you will be in this group. If so, you will probably approach the course by muddling through each case as an independent exercise with little consideration of classroom dynamics or your own competitive position. Most likely, you have not thought out the best way to make a meaningful classroom contribution, maximize your learning experience, while receiving the best possible grade you can achieve.

In order to maximize your classroom performance, you should develop a strategy for the entire duration of your semester course or executive program.

Developing a viable strategy for an entire course requires developing an appreciation for the principal variables affecting classroom activity under the conditions of case discussion. I believe the following story will illustrate these variables.

One of the first case courses I had in business school was a little number called Control. Since I didn't have much business school background, I wasn't quite sure what the term Control meant, or what would be expected of me in class. Like most of my fellow students, I was a little nervous the first day of class.

There were about 80 students in the room, and the teacher called on someone sitting right next to me. I breathed a sigh of relief thanking my stars he hadn't called on me. I'd read the case carefully and tried to analyze it as best I could. But quite frankly, I was a little more than lost.

I didn't know the fellow sitting next to me, but he seemed eager to start and quickly explained the course of action he would recommend. After five minutes, he was still going strong, sounded terribly convincing, and had most of us listening intently with open mouths. 'Boy,' I thought to myself. 'This guy really knows his stuff.'

After ten minutes, the student (let's call him Mr. Jones) offered to show a few viewgraphs of his supporting analysis, and he spent the next 15 minutes walking us through his analysis. I was flabbergasted.

Finally, he ended his presentation. Without any surprise or fanfare, our teacher thanked Mr. Jones and quickly turned to another student. 'Now, Mr. Davis, what do you think about Mr. Jones' analysis?' 'Damn,' I thought to myself, 'Is this what the teacher expects?'

Needless to say, everyone came to class for the rest of the term extremely well prepared. However, after a week or so, we began to miss Mr. Jones, who hadn't showed up for class since the first day. What had happened?

The case teacher had used a "shill" on us. It was a setup, with the instructor bringing in a former student to provide an example of an outstanding analysis and presentation. 'Dirty pool,' we cried. But the point was made. The case teacher had clearly conveyed to us what he felt was a good case analysis and presentation. None of us ever equaled Mr. Jones' performance. But we had something in mind to strive for, and the instructor never had to push us to strive to do better and better, pursuing some illusive unknown level of performance.

I believe this little story says three things that have strategic implications for you.

First, the information the narrator provides about himself should make it clear that he could never have been Mr. Jones on the first day of class, given the narrator's skills and resources relative to the subject matter.

Second, Mr. Jones was capable of being a "classroom authority" from Day One. That is, he had the necessary skills and resources in the subject matter to do a comprehensive case analysis and presentation.

Third, the case teacher revealed his expectations for case analysis and discussion very clearly. He also revealed something about his classroom style. For instance, he didn't ask for volunteers. He called on specific individuals, thereby making the decision about who would do the talking.

No doubt, many variables can affect strategy for a case course. But for the most part, I believe a good strategy can be formulated by assessing these three key variables.

1. Your skills and capabilities relative to the course subject;
2. The skills and capabilities of your fellow students -- what they bring to the subject matter, compared to what you bring to the class;
3. The case teacher's approach and style in case teaching.

What do you know about these three variables for any particular course? You probably know a lot more about the first variable (your „kills and resources), compared to the second and third variables. in fact, you may know little or nothing about the capabilities of your fellow students and the particular kind of case method employed by your prospective case teacher.

Consequently, the first few sessions of your course should be viewed partly as intelligence gathering sessions. You may have enough information to formulate a tentative strategy before ever entering the first class. However, a prudent course of action dictates holding off a session or two before committing to a particular strategy or, more properly, a particular set of strategies. The exception, of course, is if you are a Mr. Jones, i.e., a potential classroom authority on the subject matter, having perhaps taken the course as an undergraduate, worked professionally in the particular subject area, etc.

First, ask yourself what you know about the course. Are you confident in your understanding of the main concepts and tools that will be used in this course? Do you know what they are? Do you know where this course is going or are you uncertain about its direction? Do you perhaps have some knowledge or skills which relate to part of the course but not the rest of it? Is the course oriented toward quantitative analysis? Are you comfortable pushing numbers?

Second, you should use the first few sessions to assess the capabilities of your classmates and their skills relative to you. Who's doing the talking? Are they answering the questions or are they straying from the subject? Who's hanging back, saying very little or nothing? Why? Do you know if they otherwise are good students? How would you rank yourself compared to the students in this class? Are you in the top or bottom 20% of this particular class? In a class of 40 people, can you find eight of your classmates doing a better job than you? ... Or likely to do a better job?

Third, you should use the first few sessions to gather information on your instructor's style and approach to case teaching. How active a role is he/she playing in the discussion process? Does most of the dialogue occur between students or between individual students and the instructor? Is the instructor leading or channeling the discussion in some specific direction? Or is the instructor content to go where the class discussion leads? Does the instructor like to sprinkle the case discussion with lecturettes about particular tools or concepts? Does the instructor end class with a summary of the case or topics covered during the class discussion? Will the instructor perhaps make this summary at a later date? Or does the instructor refrain from any lecturing, while generally ending class without comment (on the grounds perhaps that this serves as an incentive for students to do their own thinking). Will your instructor help the class over analytic bottlenecks when no one in the class has the appropriate analysis?*

*Be cautious about generalizing about an instructor's style across courses. For example, the same instructor will probably use completely different teaching styles with a class that is new to the case method versus a more experienced class.

Obviously, you may not be able to answer all these questions about your classmates and your instructor over the first few sessions. Yet, I advise assessing the information you collect during this early period and use it to begin developing a course strategy. Once you have developed a strategy),, however, you should continue to assess the capabilities of your classmates and be alert for any changes in teaching approach by your instructor. Because the future is rarely certain, you must remain open to the need to rapidly change your strategy as the course evolves.

Formulating a Course Strategy

One way to formulate your strategy for an entire course or program is to think in terms of sets or combinations of classroom roles and case analyses. The reason for a flexible set of case analyses and discussion roles is the dynamic nature of the classroom experience over the duration of the case course. For instance, your skills and resources will be changing, hopefully improving, as you learn more about the subject matter and about your instructor and classmates. Also, the skills and resources of your classmates will be improving. Finally, you may have other courses or assignments to consider.

Exhibit 1 shows an example of three different strategies for a case course, assuming you have either weak, average, or strong skills/resources relative to your classmates. I call the three strategies:
1.   The Classroom Authority;
2.   The Contender; and,
3.   "Here Comes Swaps."

For ease of presentation, I've divided the course (covering 12 weeks) into three equal segments. The task is to develop and implement a strategy that is relevant to your capabilities for each major segment of the course.

For example, assume you have very strong skills for a particular course. You feel you can do a comprehensive case analysis early in the program and assume a classroom role as an "expert witness."

Fine, but what do you do for an encore? You cannot possibly do a comprehensive case analysis in every case course. Even if you are capable of such a feat, your instructor and classmates will not permit it. No one likes to hear the same person all the time, no matter how right he/she is. As a colleague once quipped, "That's called lecturing."

Exhibit 1 shows two possible courses of action. During the middle part of your course, limit your efforts to in-depth specialized analyses at points where you believe the class will bog down. The instructor and the class will be grateful.

During the last part of the course, let "the contenders" take over this "bail'um out role." Do your best to help weaker students and concentrate your efforts on other courses or subjects, while coming to class prepared to do at least an adequate job.

For non-horse racing fans, Swaps was a successful racehorse famous for come-from-behind, homestretch drives. During most races, Swaps would generally hold down last place and appear to be out of the running until Fuming into the homestretch. Then, the announcers would suddenly exclaim, "And here comes Swaps!"

Of course, other strategies exist beside the three I have outlined in this chapter. in fact, quite possibly the three strategies mentioned here do not fit your situation or your needs. If this is the case, develop one that makes sense for you. The easiest thing to do is forget about it, and that will not help your contribution nor your performance in class.

Exhibit 1
STRATEGIES FOR CASE COURSES

	"The Classroom Authority"	"The Contender"	"Here Comes Swaps"
Beginning of Course First 4 Weeks of Course	Strong skills and resources relative to class	Average skills and resources relative to class	Weak skills and resources relative to class
	Comprehensive analysis/big splash	Specialized analysis	General/surface analysis
	Establish yourself as classroom expert	Go in-depth on a particular question, issue or role. Also questioning role	Lay low, if possible, questioning role — hit and run role — low risk/low gain
Middle of Course Weeks 5-8	Lay low. Do specialized analyses oriented at where you believe class will get stuck. "Bail 'em out role."	Expand specialized analyses. Attempt leadoff analysis. Try to become an "expert" if none exists.	Specialized analysis of explicit issues or questions assigned as your skills improve.
End of Course Last 4 Weeks	If necessary, reassert your position as class expert. Most likely, General/Surface Analysis Hit and Run Role. Help weaker students out of class. Concentrate on other courses/subjects where you are weak.	Comprehensive analysis at least once. Specialized analysis of stumbling points. Be ready to carry the ball if weaker students fumble.	Expand specialized analyses. Attempt leadoff analysis. Provide evidence of big improvement down the home stretch.

Chapter Ten
Classroom Tactics

Besides strategic considerations, you will make a number of tactical decisions, perhaps unconsciously. These tactics should be carefully considered. Also, you should develop a repertoire of useful tactics for handling tough classroom situations. Knowing how to handle these difficult situations or taking advantage of unforeseen opportunities will foster a sense of ease that is conducive to making meaningful contributions in the classroom.

A healthy knowledge of classroom tactics can help you to gain control of almost any situation arising out of the case preparation and discussion process.

A number of problems and opportunities related to case preparation and discussion arise inside and outside the classroom. You can better contend with these problems and take advantage of the opportunities by developing tactics to deal with these situations. The tactics discussed in the ensuing pages are but a few of a long and changing list. You must continually ask yourself how could I have handled that situation? What should I do if it should happen again?

On Selecting a Seat

Perhaps your very first tactical decision in a case course is where you decide to sit in the classroom. Most students will not give a great deal of thought to this particular decision, especially if they are new to the case method. After all, this decision may not be particularly important for a lecture course, unless one has a hearing or sight deficiency. However, the decision where you sit in a case course can be extremely significant, especially if your instructor decides to "freeze" the seating arrangement for the duration of your program or course. (This is a frequent procedure taken by many case teachers because of the need to learn student names rapidly.)

Your seat selection is important because, depending on the layout of the room, some seats will be more visible than others to your instructor. In fact, this visibility factor provides a useful way to categorize seats:

1. Conspicuous, High Visibility seats;
2. Moderate Visibility seats;
3. Low Visibility seats; 4. Hideouts.

Where these scats are located depends on the layout of the classroom. For example, Exhibit 2 provides a diagram of what is thought to be an ideal classroom seating arrangement for case teaching. The diagram shows a multi-tier, semi-circular classroom where students can easily converse with one another, as well as with the teacher. Rows 2 and 3 are approximately at the eye level of the professor standing in the "pit."

Seats designated "C" are conspicuous, high-visibility seats. These seats are in sharp contrast to those denoted "H" or Hideout seats, which are outside the easy vision of the instructor. Assuming the classroom will be filled, these are the seats where you may get lost in the crowd until you are ready to surface. Also, you may be interested in a "hideout" if you know you have a tendency to talk too much in class.

Exhibit 2
SEAT VISIBILITY IN A CASE CLASSROOM

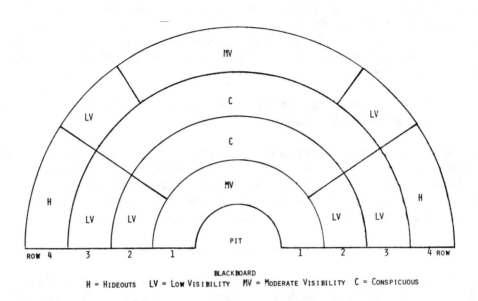

H = Hideouts   LV = Low Visibility   MV = Moderate Visibility   C = Conspicuous

But perhaps you don't want to get lost in the crowd. If you are soft-spoken, a little shy, or desire not to play an active role in the early part of the course, I recommend sitting in seats that are low or moderate in visibility vis-a-vis the instructor. The moderate visibility seats near the front of the room are particularly suitable in the case of shyness. These seats will allow you to look only at the professor and forget about most of your classmates behind you. Some students sitting in the back rows become distracted or freeze up when asked a question and the entire class turns and looks at them.

What these comments suggest is that the kind of seat you select should depend upon a) the kind of strategy you are adopting for the course and the skills and resources you bring to this particular course; and b) a personal evaluation about how you perform in group discussion situations of varying class size.

As indicated earlier, analysis of your skills and resources involves assessing your knowledge of the course content. However, knowledge about the course content is not the only factor you must assess. You must also consider your experience and capabilities for verbal communication in front of potentially large groups of people. For instance, do you have a problem speaking in front of other people, particularly large groups? Are you apprehensive or tentative about joining in classroom discussions? Do you generally find yourself doing the lion's share of talking at group meetings? Do you sometimes find yourself not listening to what other people are saying? Do you have a strong booming voice, or do people sometimes have a problem hearing you, especially in a large room? Do you think well on your feet? Or are you prone to freezing up in the presence of other individuals when hit with an unexpected question?

On Being Conspicuous

The number of times you are likely to be called on during the semester is a function not only of where you sit, but to some extent, how you stand out compared to your classmates. Early in the course, your personal evaluation should include some consideration for how conspicuous you are relative to your classmates. If you are the only woman in a class of 80 men, if you are the only black person in the class, if you are considerably older than the other students, if you are a foreigner with a strong accent, you may expect to stand out amongst the crowd.

For better or worse, your conspicuousness will result most likely in your being called on more frequently, not only by the teacher, but also by your fellow students, to give "your particular point of view." The fact that you are conspicuous may be upsetting, especially if you are not prepared for the situation. However, with a little thought, you can probably think of a number of ways to turn your conspicuousness to your advantage.

On Handling Questions

You should consider carefully how to handle three kinds of questions.

1. The leadoff question asked by the case instructor.

2. Other questions asked by either the case instructor or your fellow students.

3. Questions you ask which are directed either to the case instructor or your fellow students.

First, the most critical rule about handling the leadoff question is that you must provide some kind of answer which will hopefully stimulate further discussion - even if you have not prepared the case adequately. The only possible exemption from this rule is if you tell the case teacher before class that you are not ready to participate in class discussion for some legitimate reason. (I don't advise doing this more than once per term.) If you have not made such a declaration to your instructor before class, you have given up the right to respond, "I'm not prepared to answer." or "I pass." (which is at least better than saying "I'm not prepared."

Declining to participate is a gross tactical error, one which will embarrass you and the teacher. The incident will also tend to stick in the teacher's mind and no doubt influence the opinion he/she forms of you as a student. From that point on, you will be on the defensive and be constantly under pressure to prove yourself to your instructor.

Once this "non-sidestepping" rule is adopted, you will find that you will tend never to come to class unprepared to answer at least the leadoff question. If you feel ill-prepared, you must deal with the situation as best you can. Try to answer the question, while looking for an opportunity to redirect the conversation into an area where you feel you have something to say. In the worst possible case where you have nothing to say about the leadoff question, you can often still do well by taking an aggressive posture and stating outright, "I didn't understand this, but I did look at the following..."

Remember: some case teachers feel that the leadoff question and who answers it is one of the most important decisions the instructor makes. Consequently, you should try to decide if any pattern exists in the way the instructor is determining who will deal with the leadoff question. For instance, the instructor may be selecting people who have had prior experience within the industry associated with the case. Perhaps your instructor is selecting people who have not yet participated in class. If a pattern exists, and you identify it, you may be able to predict when the probability is high that you will be asked to start class discussion.

When fielding a question from your instructor or another student, never fall back on the crutch by saying, in effect, "There just isn't enough information to answer this question." Usually a case provides more than enough information to answer most questions, and even where the information isn't readily available, your instructor is likely to ask you, "Well, what kind of information would you need, and how would you use it?" Consequently, the key question to ask about any question is, "What kind of information do I need to answer this inquiry?" Having gone through this thought process, the sophisticated case student may use the "not enough information response" as a gambit, knowing full well that he or she will be pushed to analyze their own question further.

Finally, my impression is that students should consider more carefully the kinds of questions they pose during a case discussion. There is a right and a wrong time to ask a question, and often a student will pose a question which is nothing more than a digression from the mainstream of the conversation. And even when the question is pertinent to the discussion, the student who asks the question must be prepared to attempt some kind of answer. A favorite ploy of most case teachers is to turn a question back to a student to see if you can figure out the answer.

On Controlling Digressions

Anyone is capable of digressing from a conversation at times. Consequently, I think it is useful to differentiate between frequent offenders versus someone who makes an occasional slip-up.

If a classmate unintentionally digresses from the conversation, attempt to politely and casually redirect the conversation back to the earlier streams of discussion, e.g., "That's interesting, Mr. Davis, but I'd like to address the point made earlier . . .," or "That's true, perhaps, but I don't feel that we have fully discussed or solved the problem we were discussing regarding. . . "

Stronger measures will undoubtedly have to be taken with frequent offenders, e.g., "Well, unfortunately, I don't think this is relevant to our discussion. What is relevant is . . ."

At this point, you might ask why doesn't the instructor step in and control frequent digressions. No doubt, your teacher will control digressions to some extent. However, your instructor may also allow them to occur. After all, digressions by group members will be a part of your future business life and it is important for you to learn how to police or control group discussions.

On Group Activities

One of your most important outside class activities in a case course is to find and develop good study group members. My impression is that skill levels and experience are less important than people who are willing to work conscientiously and diligently. You may find it helpful to have a mix of talent in a study group, but I believe the critical factor is selecting people you feel will get together regularly and make- a concerted effort.

Of course, you can make it easy or difficult to get together. I suggest looking for group members where the circumstances make it as easy as possible to get together and establish a routine early in the course.

If you or your group are extremely weak in an area, say the bottom 5% of your finance class, try to enlist the aid of a class expert, if possible. And don't feel badly about it. You may not be able to pay him or her back directly, but perhaps someone else is helping him or her in another course, or you are helping someone else in another course. if you are a class expert, remember this kind of cooperation is vital in a case course and the more you try to teach others in your study group, the more you will learn yourself.

On Relating Outside Experience

One of the key strengths of the case method is the opportunity to tap a diversity of experiences. You can often enrich class discussion considerably by relating personal experience to the case situation. Yet beware. It is terribly easy to digress from the class discussion when interjecting outside experience. Finally, don't overdo it. Be careful about relating your experience to every other issue discussed by the class, especially if you are older and indeed more experienced than the rest of the class. After awhile, your forays into personal history encounter the quiet resistance of people mumbling . . . "Damn, here comes Davis again with one of his irrelevant battle stories."

All the tactics in the world won't help you if you don't "stick to the point."

PART FIVE
WRITING, PRESENTATIONS, AND EXAMS
■ ■ ■ ■ ■ ■
Chapter Eleven
Writing Great Reports

Over the duration of a course or program, writing case reports and other kinds of papers are often important activities for you in terms of your grade and as valuable learning experiences. Some observations about these activities will hopefully improve your productivity, while reducing the uncertainty faced by you when writing a "WAC" (Written Analysis of a Case).

Most WACs are relatively short reports from five to ten typed pages of text, plus a number of exhibits. Some WACs are assigned as completely individual efforts. Others may be partial group efforts, permitting students to discuss the case and analyze it and perhaps even prepare common exhibits while still requiring an individual effort in writing the text.

Generally, a case assigned for write up is more complex and difficult than the cases that students must prepare solely for class discussion, especially where the case teacher is permitting partial group effort. WACs are generally tougher, longer, more complex cases than classroom cases because the instructor expects you and members of your study group to spend more time reading and analyzing the report case.

Scheduling Time and Tasks

However, you must budget your time cautiously when writing a report case. It is equally easy to spend too little or too much time on a written case analysis. And it is not altogether clear from either a learning or grade viewpoint which extreme is worse. Plan to spend anywhere from 12 to 15 hours over a two-to-three day period. You may spend as much as 20 to 25 hours, assuming the case represents a significant challenge to you. The main danger of spending more than 25 hours is that you will probably begin to lose perspective as fatigue becomes a factor.

I think many students and study groups make a related mistake by failing to define the different tasks they must perform well to produce a good report. If these tasks are not carefully defined, you may budget too little or too much time to them. Regardless of the "total" time you spend on your report, you must allocate an appropriate amount of time to several different sub-tasks. I have divided these tasks into six steps which I believe are necessary to produce a good report. The suggested times in parentheses are rough estimates for a difficult 30 to 40 page case and a written report of 6 to 8 pages (about 2000 words) with a maximum of eight exhibits.

1.   Initial readings of case and individual analysis (4 - 5 hours).

2.   Initial group meeting.
         Analysis of facts and existing situation.
         Problem identification with group work assignments (2 - 3 hours maximum).

3.   Re-read case and perform analysis (4 - 5 hours).

4.   Second group meeting (2 - 3 hours maximum).

5.   Organize paper (5 - 7 hours).
                  Determine key messages
                  Produce first draft

6.   Rewrite paper (2 - 3 hours).
                  Final proofreading of typed version

All six tasks can be grouped into two activities: analysis and writing. Over the last five years, I have read over 3000 WACs and if I can make any generalization, it is that most students regardless of grade do not spend sufficient time on the writing portion. My impression is that too much time is spent with the analysis portion and particularly with group analysis. Remember, every extra hour of analysis may mean one less hour for writing and yet you have produced an extra hour's worth of information you must sift and translate into written form. This snowball effect may render you powerless to utilize, absorb or accurately describe and integrate all your analysis into a cogent, meaningful document that makes persuasive sense to someone reading it for the first time. The end-result is often a writer's nightmare as the following conversation demonstrates.

Student: "I put in so **much** time, I never expected this grade, but I've re-read my report and see the problems. I didn't realize it was so weak when I wrote it."

Teacher: "Why not? Tell me precisely when you wrote the paper and under what conditions."

Student: "Well, our study group met over the weekend. We put in a lot of hours but we didn't have our final meeting until late Monday afternoon. I started organizing and writing Monday evening, but it took longer than I expected and I didn't finish typing it until 4:00 in the morning. Then I got a few hours sleep and handed the paper in at our Tuesday morning class."

Someone once said, "There is no such thing as good writing --only good re-writing." However, our imaginary (but not atypical) student has left effectively no time for re-writing and insufficient time for absorbing, organizing and writing up group and individual analysis.

I want to stress the need to schedule properly your time for a case write-up, particularly the writing/rewriting functions. The written analysis of a case can be an extremely rewarding learning experience. It represents probably one of the few opportunities in your academic career where you **can** test and improve written communication skills within your chosen professional field. Consequently, the dividends for immersing oneself in this exercise can be substantial. But plan your attack wisely.

Most individuals are weak in translating their case analysis into a piece of written communication that accurately reflects their findings. Such translation is not easy, especially when the WAC's word limitation prevents the case analyst from writing more than a half dozen or so pages.

Putting Your Report Into Perspective

This word limitation is the source of the guiding principal for writing a good case report. "Keep it Simple."

What does this advice mean? It means - don't be literary, don't be fancy, don't try to weave together too many intricate thoughts in a complex scenario of your perceptions of the case. Such attempts are high risk. Unfortunately, after hours of note-taking and analysis, you will find it difficult to be straightforward. But remember, given no more than seven or eight pages of text, you don't have the word space to do more than present and defend one or two principal messages which are the main products of your anal@,sis.

Another pragmatic reason for adopting a very straightforward, one, two, three approach is that your instructor or reader will probably not spend more than 15 or 20 minutes on your paper. Remember, if a teacher or grader has at least fifty papers, at 20 minutes per paper, they have nearly 17 hours of non-stop work ahead of them.

Basically, what I am saying is that you will be lucky if you get 20 minutes. You will also probably get a reader who will not want to dig out your thoughts. Chances are your boss in the business world will have similar time constraints. The point is your main ideas and supporting analysis must be easy to spot and follow in your report.

The question is how do you produce such a document. First, you must do a good job of reading and analyzing the case. In terms of reading, you must do the kind of reading job you would expect to do if you were attempting a comprehensive case analysis for class discussion. You must know the facts of the case cold. Plan to read the case twice, preferably three times, before meeting with your study group. You must not be hazy about fact versus opinion, about what is said, versus what is done, about complex human relationships or technical descriptions.

Before beginning your analysis, I believe it is prudent to ask two questions about the case assigned for write up.

First, do you think the WAC is basically a review case? What conceptual similarities or differences does the WAC have compared to other cases you have discussed in class. In other words, has the WAC been assigned by the case teacher to determine if you have learned the principal lessons and/or techniques discussed in cases prior to the WAC assignment.

Second, is the WAC possibly of the new ground breaking variety? That is, does it require that you extend or project what you already know into new areas not yet covered by the course?

I do not mean to suggest that all WACs can fit neatly into this dichotomy. in fact, many WACs will have both review and forward looking elements in them. The point is that if you can provide specific answers to these questions, you may be able to apply techniques used in other situations to new and unique business situations.

Often, a key aspect of a written case analysis is to assess the future effects of your recommendation or proposal. Again, you Must actively search for quantitative as well as qualitative support for your recommendations. Breakeven calculations, return on investment calculations, cash flow projections, and pro forma financial statements are extremely powerful evidence in support of your proposals.

Organizing Your Report

Once you have completed your analysis, *do not start writing.* Spend a fair amount of time on thinking about how to present your findings in an efficient and clear way.

Up to this point, you probably have spent a considerable amount of time, including some agonizing moments reading and analyzing the case. A common temptation is to write the report following the step-by-step path you experienced in doing your analysis. Try to remember that your instructor or reader has no desire to share such agony. Often it is far wiser to begin your paper *not* at the beginning of your analysis, but at the end. Can you sum up in one sentence what is the principal output of your analysis? This message should be the principal thesis of your paper and clearly stated in the first few paragraphs. The rest of your paper should be devoted to a) noting why you chose this key message; b) the other alternatives you did not choose and why; and c) the evidence supporting your observation or alternatives.

I believe a prudent approach for writing the rest of your paper is to develop a key message outline for each paragraph. Remember, ease of reading is critical. Limit your paragraphs to one key message and you are liable not to develop problems of transition and logic. A paragraph that is a page and a half long will probably contain a number of different ideas which may be difficult for the reader to identify and in any case will make him or her suspicious.

Presenting Good Exhibits and Other Suggestions

The proper presentation of data in exhibits can enable you to introduce economically a great deal of supporting evidence. Make sure the exhibits are fully integrated into the text so that the reader can appreciate their impact. Also, make certain that:

> Each exhibit can stand alone;

> The title explains the purpose of the exhibit; and,

> The reader will be able to understand the nature and source of the exhibit without referring back to the text.

Before a final draft of the paper is typed, ask someone to read your written analysis. At the very minimum, read the paper out loud to yourself. Often hearing what you have said in addition to seeing what you have written will enable you to identify the rough areas in your write-up.

Also, be certain you to do the following.

1. Number all pages.
   Reason: Courtesy. Allows the reader to refer to your page number when making comments.

2. Number all exhibits, numbered them sequentially in the text, and given each a clear title.
   Reason: Clarity and ease of reading.

3. State the key message(s) of each exhibit in the text and at the bottom of each exhibit if appropriate.
   Reason: Clarity. The reader may want to know what you think is critical about the exhibit.

4. Highlight references to exhibits made in the text by underlining them or putting them in parentheses.
   Reason: Courtesy. The reader may wish to refer to them after reading the paper.

5. Do not repeat information that already exists in the case, e.g., recounting evolution of company.
   Reason: Wasteful. The reader is familiar with such information.

6.   Avoid wordy constructions and the passive voice . . . e.g., overuse of "there are, there is, it is".
      Reason: Conciseness and brevity.

7.   State the principal message of long sentences first and avoided long introductory clauses.
      Reason: Clarity and ease of reading.

8.   Qualify all unqualified pronouns, e.g., "It seems to be true"... or "This was..."   Instead of using the pronoun "it" or "this," say what you really mean. State what "it" or "this" refers to.
      Reason: Clarity and conciseness. Also the use of unqualified pronouns is often an unintentional way of producing logical inconsistencies.

If you have writing difficulties (who doesn't?), I suggest you:

1.   Buy a copy of an ageless, succinct (78 pages) classic, *The Elements of Style,* by William Strunk and E. B. White, 2nd edition, MacMillan Publishing Co., New York, 1972.

2.   Budget additional time for writing and re-writing.

3.   Re-read your paper completely after it has been graded and make notes of writing problems you will try to avoid the next time around.

4.   Read the paper of a group member who appears to have done a good writing job.

After the paper is typed, proofread it carefully for typos, omitted words and sentence, inappropriate or misleading words, etc. Pencil in changes where necessary. You haven't produced the *Magna Carta* so don't be concerned about neatly disfiguring your cleaned, typed version.

One final point: Before writing your first report in any course, one of the first things you should do is ask your instructor if he or she will put an example of what they consider a good written report on library reserve. Some case teachers may not wish to comply with this request for good reasons. The supply of good cases for written analysis is not always abundant, and your professor may not wish "to kill a good case" by placing it on library reserve. Also, good written reports for one case may mislead students into applying similar kinds of analysis and organization of their papers which are inappropriate for their report case. However, an example of a good report can help give you a better idea of your instructor's expectations and, if possible, he or she will probably be happy to make one available.

Chapter Twelve
The Secrets Behind Great Presentations

The first secret you need to know is that there are two basic kinds of presentations. Choose the wrong one for your audience and you are guaranteed a disappointing performance. The first type is informational. Think of it as the classic military briefing given to the general staff. Content is the key. The recipients want information, clearly delivered in the least amount of time. Theatrics be dammed.

The second type of presentation will contain information, but it's main objective is to motivate, uplift, or enthuse. Motivational presentations require style. Theatrics be praised.

A presentation filled with information to an unmotivated sales staff won't do the job. Conversely, a rousing talk that fails to provide a plan of attack may also come up short. Some talks clearly require a mix of information and motivation. Your job is to determine the right mix.

The next secret is to have and state a thesis right at the beginning of your talk. Take a position and defend it. This thesis or position is the same as the thesis you'd develop for a short report... with one major difference. For a talk, you are constrained by time. Clarity and conciseness are even more important. The best advice I've heard here is from one author who says you need to be able to state your key message or thesis is 10 seconds or less. If you can't, you haven't thought your talk through.

Another version of this advice is the three step approach: 1) tell them what you are going to tell them; 2) tell them; 3) then tell them what you told them. It sounds simplistic. But it works.

A fourth secret is to remember to get their attention and keep it by avoiding common distractions while creating empathy with the audience. Don't be afraid to take plenty of time before starting your talk. Embrace the silence. Let all eyes and ears focus on you. Remember, your first words should be real attention getters. Your first few sentences should contain your thesis or position. If you start too quickly, some people will miss these most important points. If you have team members with you, make sure they are sitting down and unobtrusive. Use eye contact with several different members of the audience to create empathy.

The very best speakers can keep a audience spellbound without using props, slides, overhead transparencies, film clips, etc.. The rest of us should make ample use of them. But make sure they work. Transparencies that can't be read by anyone are worst than no transparencies at all. The secret is to use props to "bring your talk to life." To give it some zip or pizzazz. Props can provide information. But they should do more. They should help you to get and keep an audience's attention.

The following "presentation worksheet" is meant to guide you toward making better presentations as well as give you some idea what instructors consider about presenters.
A more detailed version is provided in Part Nine.

Exhibit 3
PRESENTATION WORKSHEET

CLASS, TOPIC & DATE: . . . .
. . . .
. . . .
. . . .
. . . .

THESIS: . . . .
. . . .
. . . .
. . . .
. . . .

OPENING: A Real Attention Grabber: . . . .
. . . .
. . . .
. . . .
. . . .
. . . .

HOW MOTIVATE AUDIENCE TO BELIEVE IN MY THESES: . . . .
. . . .
. . . .
. . . .
. . . .
. . . .
. . . .
. . . .

PRESENTATION AIDS: WHEN, WHERE, HOW MOST EFFECTIVE: . . . .
. . . .
. . . .
. . . .

HOW CLOSE WITH IMPACT: . . . .
. . . .
. . . .
. . . .
. . . .
. . . .
. . . .
. . . .
. . . .

Chapter Thirteen
Taking Exams Successfully

There are two main types of case exams:

1. the take-home case exam; and
2. the in-class "sit-down" case exam.

The latter exam is also a variation of the tradition "blue book" exam. Consequently, I've chosen to conclude this chapter with six steps or guidelines for successfully taking blue book exams.

Take-Home Case Exams

The take-home exam enables you to read and analyze the case at your leisure. Some instructors may also ask you to write your exam at home and simply submit it at some appointed time and place. Or you may have to come to class to write your exam. In this instance, you will probably be unaware of the particular questions your teacher will ask you about the case.

In either case, take-home cases are usually long, complex cases which often involve the use of rather sophisticated analytic techniques, much like written report cases. In short, you will probably receive a case that is extremely complicated - one you may not be expected to complete during a shorter exam period.

Under these test conditions, a history of strong efforts at case analysis throughout the course pays rich dividends. For example, the practice about asking what are the potential unassigned questions can now be seen. in order to focus one's pretest analysis, you must first think of the right questions to ask yourself.

If the case is distributed before the exam, read and analyze it as you would read or analyze a case for a write-up or for a comprehensive presentation in class. You probably can analyze the case using many of the same questions that have been assigned for other cases during the term. Ask yourself, which ones apply to this case?

In-Class Case Exams

"Sit-down case exams" are generally three-to-four hour exercises where you are given the case for the first time and asked to read, analyze and write up your analysis. One important thing you should know about this kind of final exam which distinguishes it from the take home variety is that the sit-down exam allows your teacher to provide a "you see it or you don't" type of final. This kind of exam case is often too easy for regular class use or certainly as a report case or take-home exam. But under the pressure of a four-hour time limit, it often provides a vehicle for your instructor to determine if you have digested completely the major concepts of the course.

Of course, you may encounter other kinds of final exams. Some are integrative in that they try to summarize various aspects of the course. Others may be specialized finals that focus on only a particular part of the material covered in the course. In any event, you should try to assess the kind of final exam you are analyzing soon after receiving it.

Before taking a sit-down exam, you have to prepare for it. However, unlike the take-home final or the final exams for most lecture courses, preparation for a case final is relatively light. You have already done most of the work, hopefully. Before tackling the exam case, I suggest reviewing the cases you have had and the key findings you have recorded about these cases. I also suggest preparing a list of the main skills you have learned from the course that the teacher may expect you to apply on the final exam. Can these skills be incorporated into a simple conceptual framework for analysis of the course subject matter?

Beyond these small preparations, perhaps the best preparation is an alert, rested mind. Staying up late, "cramming" for tomorrow's exam may work for a take-home case exam or other types of final exams. But sitting down already mentally fatigued for a "sit-down " case exam qualifies you for observation for suicidal tendencies.

Another word of caution: most case instructors will allow you to bring materials, class notes, etc. to class. If you feel more secure bringing these kinds of materials along, by all means, do so. But be careful not to become overly dependent upon them. Also, make sure the materials are relatively well organized and easy to handle in class. All too often, students waste valuable time searching for something through a mountain of notes. I've even seen some students panic at not being able to find some reference notes.

And panic is perhaps your greatest enemy. Taking a case exam is a challenging activity. You must read, comprehend, analyze, organize and write about a business situation you have never seen before. Reading and analyzing an exam case may alone take as much as three hours. While watching the time slipping away, you may begin to get nervous and tighten up. Yet there is no cause for alarm. Your write-up can only be as good as your analysis which in turn depends upon the quality of your comprehension of the case. Generally, the written portion of the exam does not have to be long. Also, you are better off writing a few pages that are right on target, rather than pages of comment and analysis that just do not hang together.

Since time is a factor, the development of good case analysis skills during the term is a critical prerequisite for success in a four hour sit-down exam. If you've developed a lot of bad habits, e.g., excessive underlining, unfocused analysis, etc., you will probably find yourself hard pressed to finish the exam.

To save time, I believe you should try to perform your analysis in a neat and organized manner on scratch paper, keeping in mind that you may be able to easily convert some of this preliminary analysis into exhibits to be included in your write up.

Be certain that your analysis answers the exam questions. This sounds obvious, but often your reading of the case provides observations and opportunities-for analysis that are not necessarily related to the question asked by your instructor. Temptations for sidetracking continually surface.

Spend ten or fifteen minutes on deciding how to present your written analysis. One way to organize an exam is to list your principal findings or observations and then note your main supporting evidence for each finding. in some exam situations, you may simply be able to transfer these lists. For instance, you might say, "I recommend the following action for these reasons: 1), 2), 3), etc." This kind of exam presentation is often easy for the reader to identify what you are saying. Also, it lists the key points without burdening you with the task of writing a complex essay with all the transitional problems inherent in such an exercise. However, do not mistakenly think that an outline or list approach exempts you from explaining how you derived your recommendations. Good supporting analysis or explanation is required. Where appropriate, the generation of quantitative support for your key recommendation or proposal will separate you almost always from many of your colleagues.

But whatever stylistic approach you take in writing up the exam, you must strive, even sweat, for quality of content yet simplicity of presentation. And here you should remember that a good write-up of a case exam often contains no more than a few key messages that are well defended and supported by your analysis. In fact, no more than one or two critical observations may be required for the "you see it or you don't" type of final.

Blue Book Exams: How To Take Them

I hate to think about the number of blue book exams I've taken as a student. I never did very well with them and one reason I experienced greater success in graduate school was that I was able to take less blue book exams and write more term papers and other kinds of reports. In fact, I never fully realized why I underperformed with blue book exams until I was grading them as a young assistant professor. Then a number of things became clear.

Ever wonder why the following happens? John and Bill both know the subject equally well. They've studied the same amount and spent the same time preparing for the exam. But John finishes the blue book exam 20 minutes ahead of Bill and gets a better grade. The reason for the different grade is simple. John knows how to take blue book exams and Bill doesn't.

What does John know? He knows that presentation, simplicity, and clarity count. Most of all, he knows that, despite the fact that these blue book exams are also called essay exams, most of his professors aren't looking for an "essay" per se. What they want to know is whether John grasps certain information or concepts and can interpret, synthesize, or possible apply this information in some way. And like it or not, John also realizes that his professor won't be able to spend more than 15-to-20 minutes on his particular blue book exam. [Remember, 40 blue books multiplied by 20 minutes is 800 minutes or roughly 13 hours of work. Counting time for sanity breaks, grade recording, and feedback, we are talking at least two days of work]. The key message is you must make your points fast and make them easy to identify.

Now let's see how John operationalizes what I've just said.

> First, John reads the question very carefully. He becomes dedicated to answering this question and not some other question he feels is more relevant or one about which he has more (extraneous) information.

> Second, he outlines his answer on scratch paper or in the blue book itself. His first step in outlining his answer is simply to list the key points or observations related to the question's topics. His second step is to order these points. His third step is to identify a major argument, position, or thesis that ties these points together. This thesis or argument will be his first sentence or opening paragraph. He will also re-state it in a different way to conclude his argument (essay).

> Third, John decides to print his answer because his penmanship is lousy. He also decides to print every other line and every other page in order to make his answer easy to read. If he is really tight on time, he will just list his key points. Assuming he has ample time, he will explain each point or follow the question's instructions to compare, contrast, amplify, etc. this point with additional information.

> Fourth, John will re-read his answer, checking for mis-spellings, omitted words, or unclear expressions. He won't hesitate to write corrections in the margin or use a footnote approach to add information he should have included.

Fifth, John will highlight the most important points of his answer. How will he do this? Well, John also comes to class with a yellow highlighter and/or a minimum of two pens with different colors. He's now using the pen with red ink to underline key points. By the way, John never uses a pencil. It's too hard for the professor to read. He'd rather cross out words than use a messy eraser. But he doesn't have to cross out many because he's outlined his answer, he's keeping it simple, and he's sticking to the point.

Sixth, when the graded blue books are returned, John will always do two things that Bill never does. He will re-read his own blue book, no matter how painful that may be. He will look to see how his answers can be improved. After all, he may see a variation of the same question on the final exam. Finally, he will read someone else's blue book who did better on the exam that he did. That's easier said than done. John goes out of his way to find someone cooperative. If necessary, he will even go to his professor and ask to see an "A" exam.

Follow these six steps and you will improve your performance. Success breeds success, and nothing is more discouraging than studying hard for a test, only to perform poorly because no one ever told you how to take a blue book exam. If you feel you should be writing better blue book exams, stop beating your head against a wall. Resurrect one of your recent blue book exams and analyze it or retake it following these six steps.

PART SIX
Key Analytic Tools for Business Analysis
■ ■ ■ ■ ■
Overview

A problem with most management textbooks is that they provide much more information than you need to do an outstanding analysis of a business situation. Also, the most relevant tools for case analysis are often spread across several different textbooks oriented toward specific disciplines or functional areas. The tools presented in this section have been selected by me from a variety of sources for your convenience.

The list is not comprehensive, but it represents my best judgment about the analytic tools needed most frequently by students for case analysis. Many of these techniques involve some "number pushing." I have emphasized these tools because my impression is that most students find them more difficult to apply compared to qualitative techniques once they are exposed to the latter.

The brief summaries provided here are meant only:

1.   to identify for you some important tools; and,

2.   to provide a means for quick and convenient review rather than an extensive treatment.

Of course, you should add whatever tools and concepts to this selection that you feel will help you with business analysis.

■ ■ ■ ■ ■

Chapter Fourteen
Some Fundamental Concepts Underlying Business Analysis

This chapter summarizes concepts that cut across functional areas such as marketing, production, finance, etc. and underlie other analytic tools.

The first is the concept of cost structure (i.e. which costs are fixed versus variable costs and how these two kinds of costs are distributed). The second is the concept of "contribution." The third is the concept of "breakeven." The fourth is the concept of "operating leverage."

The Concept Of Cost Structure
(Fixed Versus Variable Costs)

As an organization generates sales of its products or services, some costs remain fixed over some range of volumes while others vary with changes in sales volume. The job of the case analyst is to determine which costs actually vary because of increases or decreases in sales volume versus those that remain fixed over some relevant decision making period. For instance, rent is usually a fixed cost because a constant amount, let's say $2500, must be paid each month, <u>whether anything is sold or not.</u> By contrast, salesmen's commissions are a variable cost because commissions are "vary" directly to sales. No sale, no commission. As sales increase, commission costs rise proportionately.

The Concept Of Contribution

Once total variable costs are identified, they are subtracted from total sales revenue. The remainder is the total dollars "contributed" against fixed costs. This total dollar "contribution" is defined as follows:

TOTAL SALES
-- TOTAL VARIABLE COSTS
_____

TOTAL CONTRIBUTION AVAILABLE
TO COVER TO FIXED COSTS

Where "units" of production are identified, "unit contribution" is found simply by dividing total contribution by total unit output.

Why is it important to know either the total or unit contribution for different products, services, or investment alternatives? The main reason is that it is possible to have high contribution products or services that provide low or no profit. Yet if one looks at profit alone, the temptation may arise to de-emphasize or even drop low or negative profit products. Such action can inhibit a business from covering its total costs since some of these costs are fixed no matter what the organization produces. Because contribution is important, an increasing number of large and small businesses use contribution dollars to evaluate investment alternatives and management performance.

The Concept Of Breakeven

The distinction between fixed and variable costs also allows the calculation of breakeven points for single product businesses or, in more complicated cases, multiple product businesses. Traditional breakeven analysis tells you how many units you must produce so that total revenues (net sales) will equal total costs. Exhibit 4 graphs this relationship.

However, there are at least five different breakeven calculations you should know. Each one solves for a slightly different kind of breakeven. All five calculations have one thing in common: fixed costs are always the numerator. The five breakevens are: 1. volume or unit breakeven; 2. total sales breakeven on a fully loaded accounting basis; 3. total sales breakeven on a cash basis; total sales breakeven for some stated level of profits; and 5) sales price breakeven. Each of these five breakevens is explained below along with their respective formulas and sample calculations. (It will help if you get a calculator now and work through the calculations as you read the following section).

1. Breakeven Volume: In order to calculate the breakeven unit volume (BEV), you must know total fixed costs dollars (FC$) for a particular product plus the contribution per unit (CU$) for the product and/or the unit sales price (SP$) and unit variable costs (VC$) for the product. The formulas for breakeven analysis are:

1) BEV = Total $FC /(UNIT $SP - UNIT $VC)

2) BEV = Total $FC /Unit $CU

Note: the dollar signs in the numerators and denomerators of both formulas will cancel, leaving the product to be expressed in units (cars, TV's, etc,). Also note that both these formulas are exactly the same because just as total sales minus total variable costs equals total contribution, so unit sales price minus unit variable costs also equals unit contribution. In both cases, we are dividing fixed costs by contribution.

Example: we calculate that fixed costs will be $400,000. We will charge $13.33 for the product and unit variable costs are calculated at $9.33. Then:

1) BEV = $400,000 / $4   = 100,000 units

2) BEV = $400,000 / (13.33 - 9.33)   = 100,000 units of product needed
                                               to be sold to breakeven

2. Breakeven Sales On Fully Loaded Accounting Basis. In some situations, you may not know unit variable costs, but only what variable costs are as a percentage of total sales. For instance, suppose you know fixed costs are $400,000 for a given level of total sales, and that variable costs are 70% of total

EXHIBIT 4

BREAKEVEN ANALYSIS

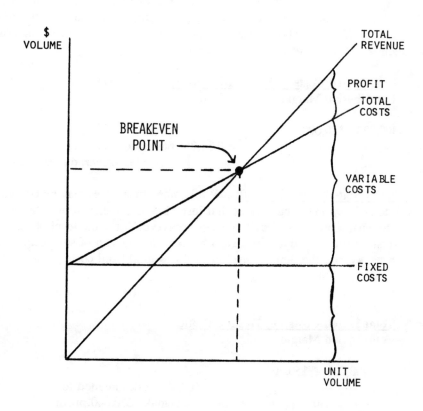

sales. Since "contribution" equals sales minus variable costs, the contribution margin in percentage terms is simply:

Total Sales = 100% - 70%VC = 30% Contribution.

NOTE: The true "contribution margin" is simply the decimal equivalent of this "percentage contribution" of 30%...i.e., the contribution margin (CM) equals .30

You can use this information to solve for the breakeven (BE) sales volume:

$$BES = \frac{Total\ \$Fixed\ Costs}{CM}$$

$$BES = \frac{\$400'000}{1 - .70} = \$1,333,333\ sales\ need\ to\ breakeven\ on\ accounting\ basis$$

3. Breakeven Sales On A Cash Basis. Basically, the previous breakeven calculation says we must realize sales greater than $1,333,333 to begin realizing an accounting profit. Yet some organizations, especially small companies, may be interested in calculating the level of sales needed simply to survive. A difference exists because some accounting costs or expenses don't result in real cash outlays. For instance, depreciation, depletion, amortization, and bad debt expenses are examples of accounting expenses that don't require you to pull out your checkbook and write a check to someone. To calculate a "cash breakeven," you must determine which costs have not resulted in an actual cash outflow (e.g., depreciation). For instance, if depreciation is $20,000, the procedure is to reduce fixed costs ($400,000) by $20,000. Consequently, sales breakeven on a cash basis is:

$$Cash\ BES = \frac{Total\ \$Fixed\ Costs\ --\ Non\ Cash\ Expenses}{Contribution\ Margin}$$

$$Cash\ BES = \frac{\$400,000 - \$20,000}{.30} = \$1,266,666\ sales\ needed\ to\ breakeven\ on\ cash\ basis$$

4. Sales Breakeven For A Stated Level Of Profits. While many businesses may be content to breakeven during tough times, I don't know many businesses that just what to breakeven over the long term. Most business owners want to earn a profit. Calculating sales breakeven for some level of desired profit is easy. It's just the reverse of the procedure for a cash breakeven. Instead of subtracting selected fixed expenses from fixed costs, we add the desired level of profit to total fixed costs. Assume we want to

make $50,000 in profit. Then:

$$Profit\ BES = \frac{Total\ \$Fixed\ Costs\ +\ Desired\ Profit}{Contribution\ Margin}$$

$$Profit\ BES = \frac{\$400,000 + \$50,000}{.30} = \$1,500,000\ sales\ needed\ to\ make\ \$50,000\ profit$$

Once you know the breakeven sales or unit volume, you can compare it with estimates of forecasted dollar or unit sales, total market size, your realistic share of market, and/or your available capacity. Do you have sufficient production capacity to attain breakeven volume? Is breakeven higher or lower than the share of market you can realistically hope to capture? Or, given the total market, what market share must you capture just to breakeven? For instance, is the breakeven level of sales at 40%, 60%, or 90% of forecasted sales? If 90%, how likely is it you will realize breakeven? There certainly isn't much room for error or negative unforeseen events.

5. Breakeven Sales Price. A good way to perform a reality check of your thinking is to calculate a breakeven sales price. Most people have a price for a product in mind when they are preparing their marketing plan. Let's assume the price we had in mind was $9.99. The breakeven sales price calculation will allow you to determine if your assumption about this price is correct, as well as your assumptions about your planned or actual level of fixed costs, variable costs, contribution margins, forecasted sales, and even available plant capacity make sense. For instance, your business may not be able to operate higher than some level of unit capacity nor will it want to operate below some percentage of this capacity in order to avoid laying off people. Let's assume you believe you can sell 100,000 units of your product and you have this level of capacity. The formula for breakeven sales price is:

$$\text{BESP} = \frac{\text{Total \$ Fixed Costs}}{\substack{\text{Units Of Capacity}\\ \text{(or Targeted Volume)}}} + \text{Unit \$ Variable Costs}$$

$$\$13.33 = \frac{\$400,000}{100,000 \text{ units}} + \$9.33$$

What this calculation tells us is that our original thoughts of a $9.99 price just won't fly unless we can somehow reduce the fixed or variable costs involved, produce more than 100,000 units without increasing fixed or variable costs, or increase the price to something above $13.33, assuming we want to do more than breakeven.

The Concept Of Operating Leverage

The concept of operating leverage is a critical notion for business practitioners. Yet my experience is that very few students can explain the concept. Often it is confused with financial leverage.* And some similarities exist. For instance, both concepts are double edged swords because you can have positive and negative leverage. Also, both concepts are relative notions. A company or investment can have high or low leverage only "in relation to" some other company or investment alternative. And both concepts use the idea of levering or increasing resources (debt in, the case of financial leverage and fixed costs for operating leverage) to better accomplish some purpose.

High positive operating leverage simply means total profits increase at a faster rate than increases in sales volume once breakeven volume is achieved, compared to a business with low operating leverage.

---

*Financial leverage is positive when you combine debt with equity to produce a greater return than you can achieve with equity alone after the cost of debt is included. If the net return is lower than the cost of debt, you have negative financial leverage. If the net return is greater, you have positive financial leverage.

Assuming equal breakeven points, a business with relatively high fixed costs will have higher operating leverages compared to a high variable cost business. You can observe this relationship in the breakeven graph shown in <u>Exhibit 5</u>. The gaps (A) between the total revenue and total cost lines for the high fixed cost business have a wider angle of divergence above and below the equivalent breakeven points compared to the gaps (B) for the high variable cost business. Consequently, a 1% increase in volume beyond breakeven for both businesses may result, for example, in a 10% increase in profits for the high fixed cost business and only 2% for the high variable cost business. Another 1% volume increase may mean a 20% increase in profits for the high fixed cost business (double the original increase) versus a jump to 3% for the high variable cost business (or half the rate of increase as the high fixed cost business).

But the same relationship holds for decreases below the breakeven point. Losses will increase at a faster rate for the business with high fixed/low variable costs. Consequently, businesses with high positive leverages can also have high negative ones.

This existence of high operating leverages in high fixed/low variable cost businesses explains why executives in these businesses (e.g., large automobile or chemical producers) place great emphasis on marketing and sales activities. Great profits (and bonuses) or great losses (and the search for a new job) can occur with just small shifts in sales volume above or below the breakeven point for a business with high operating leverage.

However, I should note that once the condition of equal breakeven points is relaxed the relationship can change if the low fixed cost business also has relatively low variable costs. Consequently, you should always determine what is the revenue/cost structure for any organization. The value of this exercise will be worth the effort since you will often discover where to allocate what is usually the scarcest resource in most organizations - management time.

EXHIBIT 5
Operating Leverages of Two Businesses with
Equal Breakeven Points

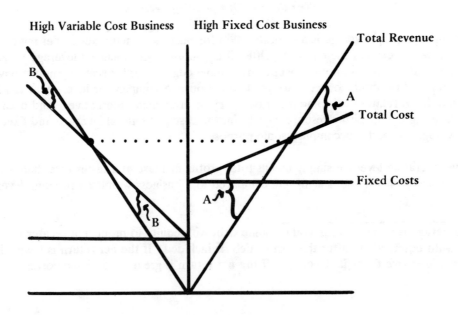

A simple numerical example shows the relationship between management time, profits, costs, and revenues. First, consider the base situation below where two companies have equal sales of $100,000. Both have different cost structures and both are just breaking even and show zero profits.

BASE SITUATION

	High Variable Cost Business	High Fixed Cost Business
Sales	100,000	100,000
Variable Costs	80,000	20,000
Fixed Costs	20,000	80,000
Profits	0	0

Now let's suppose that management spends its tune by making an all-out marketing/sales effort. The effort pays off and results in a 10% growth in sales. However, variable costs also increase as volume expands. For simplicity sake, we will assume variable costs increase proportionately with sales (i.e., also a 10% increase) while fixed costs remain fixed. Currently, sales have increased to $110,000 while variable costs are $80,000 or $20,000 *plus* 10% respectively. The new outcome is shown below.

10% SALES GROWTH

	High Variable Cost Business	High Fixed Cost Business
Sales	110,000	110,000
Variable Costs	88,000 [80,000 + (10% of 80,000)]	22,000 [20,000 + (10% of 20,000)]
Fixed Costs	20,000	80,000
Profit	2,000	8,000

The impact of sales growth for high fixed cost business now becomes evident. Profits have increased to $8,000 for our high fixed cost business or four times the profits realized by the high variable cost business.

However, let's look at one more example before you conclude that high fixed cost businesses always make better profits. Instead of a 10% sales growth, let's suppose our management decides to allocate its scarce time to a program designed to control and reduce raw materials and direct labor (i.e., variable costs). Again, management's efforts are successful and a 10% reduction in variable costs is realized by the new cost reduction program as shown below.

10% DECREASE IN VARIABLE COSTS

	High Variable Cost Business	High Fixed Cost Business
Sales	100,000	100,000
Variable Costs	72,000 [80,000 - (10% of 80,000)]	18,000 [20,000 - (10% of 20,000)]
Fixed Costs	20,000	80,000
Profits	8,000	2,000

Our cost reduction situation shows a much stronger profit performance for the high variable cost business, exactly the reverse of the sales growth situation. Now profits for the high variable cost business are four times the high fixed cost business.

These few examples do not mean that managers should ignore opportunities for sales growth in high variable cost businesses or cost reduction in high fixed cost businesses. They do provide, however, a simple means to determine priorities or relative allocations of time given opportunities for sales growth and cost savings for particular situations.

The Concept Of Integrated Financials

The application of this concept is explained in greater detail in Chapter 17 on Finance Arithmetic. I wish only to define the concept here and explain its importance, since of all the concepts covered in this book, it is the least understood and appreciated... by students and business educators. Yet, the concept of integrated financials is extremely powerful and impacts the very essence of rational decision making.

The concept is defined as follows: Integrated financials are financial projections (at the minimum, a projected P&L, projected Balance Sheet, and projected Cash Flow that are linked together or "integrated" by formulas to constitute a unique financial model that stimulates or reflects a business in all its relevant details. Once this model exists, it allows decision makers to see the financial implications of possible decisions. Integrated financials allow true or valid "what if" analysis.

Experienced practitioners will tell you that any decision, no matter how small, eventually affects all parts of a company. A decision, like a stone thrown into a pond, sends concentric ripples across the water. Everything is affected. When several stones are thrown at once, the affect is pronounced but harder to determine. Waves are rippling across one another as they spread across the pond. Business decisions also come in batches and their net impact is extremely difficult to determine unless you have an integrated financial model. For instance, the opportunities and problems that face business decision makers are rarely single decisions... e.g. sales will increase 10% if I do xyz. In reality, a set of decisions will probably be taken...e.g. sales will increase 10% if I do xyz, and if I invest $50,000 in new equipment, cost of goods will decrease 5%, however I will have to borrow the money at 9%, add 3 new employees, increase inventory purchases, etc. In fact, many sets of decisions or scenarios often are possible.

What impact will each scenario have on profitability, cash flow, owner's equity, breakeven, plus a host of other measures? The computer and the application of the concept of integrated financials allows us to see these impacts. As this concept becomes more widespread and accepted, the decision makers of the 21st century will no doubt look back and wonder how the managers of this century ever operated businesses while being, in effect, half blind regarding the consequences of their decisions.

Chapter Fifteen
Marketing Arithmetic

The following article explains several of the concepts just described from a marketing perspective. It is reprinted with permission from the Harvard Business School.

■ ■ ■ ■ ■ ■

*Note on Marketing Arithmetic and Related Marketing Terms**

This note is about several terms and basic calculations used in the analysis of marketing problems. It is almost always necessary to determine the economic consequences of alternative courses of action, or of alternative sets of assumptions, in the analysis of a marketing problem.

Contribution

The funds available to the seller of an item after subtracting the variable costs associated with it are referred to as *contribution*. A common reference is also made to *unit contribution*—that is, the contribution per each item sold. Assume, for example, that we sell a unit of a product to wholesalers at a price of $100, and that the *variable* manufacturing costs of that unit are $30. In addition, it costs us $3 per unit to ship the product to wholesalers, and we pay a 5% commission to our salespeople ($5 per unit). Under these circumstances, the variable costs associated with each unit of this product are $38 ($30 + $3 + $5). Since we receive $100 revenue for each unit we sell, our unit contribution is $62 ($100 - $38).

This $62 unit contribution is available to cover the fixed manufacturing expenses, overheads, and marketing costs associated with the product, and if all goes well, to provide a profit. *Fixed costs* are costs that remain fixed regardless of the volume of production. Thus, whether we produce 1,000 or 5,000 items, the cost of executive salaries remains fixed, as does rent, insurance, and other so-called overhead expenses. Fixed costs remain unchanged over some reasonable range of the firm's activity. *Variable costs*, on the other hand, are costs that are directly traceable to the volume of activity—the more we sell, the more raw materials we need, usually the more assembly work we need, and the more sales commission we pay.

_____

* Copyright, the President and Fellows of Harvard College, 1981. Harvard Business School. Harvard Case Services #574-082. Reprinted with permission from The Harvard Business School.

Break-Even

Break-even means that our revenue is just enough to pay for both the variable and the fixed costs we have incurred, but only that. We have no profit, we have no losses; we have only broken even.

As a bare minimum, most companies expect a product to break even, that is, not to lose money. Depending on the situation, the appropriate time within which a product should break even may be short (a year, or a season) or long (perhaps as much as five years). For the sake of simplicity, we will assume that the appropriate time period for break-even is one year. It is important to note that under most conditions break-even is not an appropriate goal.

One way to talk of break-even is to say that it occurs when the number of units we sell, multiplied by the unit contribution, is equal to the fixed costs. Thus we calculate break-even as follows: BE = Total fixed costs ÷ unit contribution. If unit contribution is $62, for example, and fixed costs are $100,000, break-even will occur when we produce and sell 1,613 units, (that is $100,000 ÷ $62). If we expect to produce and sell 1,613 units, we expect to break even. But if we produce 2,000 and sell 1,613 we have not broken even. We have incurred losses because our total variable costs are not $38 X 2,000, not $38 X 1,613.

Profit Impact

Few companies are content to operate at break-even. Normally, they require that each product produces a positive impact on company profits. The impact that a particular product will have on company profits is easily calculated, as follows, using the same figures we have been using:

Unit contribution	x	units produced and sold	—	fixed costs	Profit impact
($62	x	2,000)	—$100,000 =		
		$124,000	—$100,000 =		$24,000

Why do we call this $24,000 *impact on profit* (or *profit impact*) and not just plain *profit*? The answer is that there may be a few other costs yet to be charged against the product, such as corporate headquarters overhead, not just product-related overhead.

Suppose we have a certain profit target in mind—a profit impact of $50,000. What will our production and sales have to be to achieve a profit impact of $50,000? The calculation is the same as the above, except that we add the $50,000 profit target to the fixed costs. With fixed costs now at $150,000 instead of $100,000, the resulting calculation gives us 2,419 units. We would then say that if we wish to achieve a profit impact of $50,000, we will have to make and sell 2,419 units.

A similar technique may be used to calculate the effects of a change in our marketing program. Assume that with our present program, we expect to make and sell 2,000 units of a product with a $62 unit contribution. With our fixed costs of $100,000 we saw that this yields a $24,000 profit impact. We now consider raising our advertising expenditure by $50,000, which would increase our fixed costs to $150,000. If we do so, how much volume would the new marketing program have to achieve to generate the same profit impact ($24,000) as our present program? The calculation is as follows:

Present fixed cost	+	Present profit impact	+ additional fixed cost	÷ unit contribution	=	Req. volume

$100,000 + $24,000 + $50,000 ÷ $62 = 2,806

We would have to make and sell 2,806 units for the new program to yield the sam profit impact as the old one which required sales of only 2,000 units. There are other ways to come up with the same answer, of course, but this way at least has the virtue of clarity.

Suppose we improve our product by adding $3 per unit of variable cost. This cuts our unit contribution to $59. If all other costs as well as prices remain unchanged, how much would we have to sell in order to maintain our current profit impact of $24,000? We would then have to sell 2,102 units ([$100,000 + $24,000] ÷ $59).

In calculating the economic effects of a marketing program, one is generally forced to make a number of assumptions. The sales forecast is generally the most critical, but fixed costs, variable costs, and selling prices may also be uncertain. Under these circumstances, it is generally useful to calculate the profit impact of a marketing program under varying sets of assumptions.

Obviously, one can make break-even points or expected profit impact come out any way one wishes by making the appropriate assumptions about sales volumes and costs. For this reason the marketing manager should become adept at appraising the realism of the assumptions on which calculations of these types are based.

Market Share Analysis

One way of assessing the realism of a sales forecast is to calculate its implications for a firm's market share. Assume, for example, that the total market for the product mentioned in the previous examples is 10,000 units, that the market is not expanding, and the we presently sell 2,000 units. We therefore have a market share of 20%. The product manager recommends that we raise our advertising budget by $50,000, which means that we wold have to make and sell 2,806 units to maintain our current profit impact. We shall have to make and sell 806 units above the present level, raising our market share from 20% to 28.06%. How likely is this? Can $50,000 of additional advertising accomplish that? Will our competitors give up 8% of market share without fighting back?

When demand for a product is not static, calculation of probable effect on market share is more difficult. If we increase advertising by $50,000, for example, total demand for the product may increase. If this happens, some of our sales increase may come from increased market share, but some may also come from increased demand. Would the competition then be as likely to retaliate?

Computation of Margin

When a manufacturer produces an item for sale, or when a merchant buys an item for resale, a desired selling price is chosen. This price exceeds the manufacturing cost, or the cost paid by the merchant, by what is called the *margin*. The terms *markup* and *markon* are also often used interchangeably with *margin*, which will be used here. Margin is similar to, though not necessarily the same as, unit contribution (a distinction we shall not clarify here).

Margin, cost, and selling price are related to each other in the following manner:

$$\text{Selling price} = \$1 \left\{ \begin{array}{l} \boxed{\text{Margin} = 40¢} \\ \\ \boxed{\text{Cost} = 60¢} \end{array} \right.$$

Thus, we say that the retailer's selling price of an item consists of the cost of the item (i.e., what was paid for it) and the margin. For many purposes it is useful to express the margin as a percentage. Theoretically, the 40-cent margin might be expressed either as a percentage of the cost or as a percentage of the selling price. If it is expressed as a percentage of the cost, the margin would be 66.67%; that is, the 40-cent margin divided by the 60-cent cost equals 66.67%. When it is expressed as a percentage of the selling price, the margin is 40%—40 cents ÷ $1. The commonly accepted practice is to express percentages—both margins and costs—with net sales as the base. While this is the commonly accepted practice, some industries, companies, and individuals depart from that practice. We will follow the common practice.

If the cost is known and the percentage of margin on selling price is given, it is a simple matter to compute the selling price. Suppose, for example, that a retail merchant buys goods at a cost of $10 and wants a margin of 33⅓ in order to cover expenses and have a chance of making a net profit. What should be the selling price? Since 100% of the selling price is made up of two parts (the cost and the margin), this means that $10 + 33⅓% = 100%. It follows that the $10 cost must be

66⅔% of the selling price. What is 100%—the selling price itself? We have said that:

$$66⅔ \times \text{Selling price} = \$10$$
$$\text{Then:} \quad \text{Selling price} = \$10 \div 66⅔\%$$
$$\text{Selling price} = \$15$$

Similarly, if a wholesaler buys an article for 60 cents and wants a margin of 20%, the selling price is 60 cents ÷ 80% = 75 cents.

Margin percentages are figured on the selling price at each level of business. If it costs a company 75 cents to manufacture an item and it wants a 25% margin, then the selling price must be $1. If the wholesaler to whom the manufacturer sells the item for $1 wants a margin of 16⅔%, the selling price will be $1.20. And if the retailer who buys it from the wholesaler for $1.20 resells it to consumers for $2, that margin will be 40% (.80 ÷ $2.00).

Since some firms and industries use cost rather than selling price as the basis for their percentage calculations, it is useful to know how to convert from one base to the other. On merchandise costing $6 and selling for $10, the margin is $4. This margin, which is 40% of the selling price, would be 66⅔% if computed on the basis of the cost. To make the conversion from either the cost base or the selling-price base to the other, it helps to understand once more that selling price is composed of two parts—the margin and the cost:

$$\text{Cost} + \text{Margin} = \text{Selling Price}$$
$$\downarrow \qquad \downarrow \qquad \downarrow$$
$$\$.60 \qquad \$.40 \qquad \$1.00$$
$$\text{Margin as a percent} = \frac{.40}{\$1.00} = 40\%$$
of selling price

If we want to convert this margin, expressed as a percent of selling price into a margin expressed as a percent of cost, we say:

If 40% is the margin on selling price, then the remaining 60% must be the cost. 40% ÷ 60% = 66⅔% = margin based on cost.

The following formula invariably gets this conversion right:

$$\frac{\text{Percentage margin on price}}{100\% - \text{Percentage margin on price}} = \text{Percentage margin on cost}$$
$$\downarrow \qquad\qquad \downarrow$$
$$\frac{40\%}{100\% - 40\%} \qquad = \frac{40\%}{60\%} = 66⅔\%$$

Suppose we have the opposite question: How to express a margin figured as a percent of cost into one figured as a percent of selling price? We say:

Cost is 100%—that is, the denominator on which the margin was figured.

Since the margin on cost (in the above example) is 66⅔%, then the selling price must be Cost + Margin + Selling Price. (100% + 66⅔% = 166⅔%)

Margin on percent of selling price = 66⅔% ÷ 166⅔% = 40%

The following formula invariably gets this conversion right:

$$\frac{\text{Percentage margin on cost}}{100\% + \text{Percentage margin cost}} = \text{Percentage margin on selling price}$$
$$\downarrow \qquad\qquad \downarrow$$
$$\frac{66⅔\%}{100\% + 66⅔\%} \qquad = \frac{66⅔\%}{166⅔\%} = 40\%$$

Discounts and Chain Discounts

A common practice for the manufacturer is to suggest at what price the product should be sold by a retailer. If the *suggested retail price* is $100 while selling the item to the retailer for $60, the manufacturer is, in effect, proposing a *suggested retail margin* of $40%—that is, ($100 - $60) ÷ $100 =40%. In common usage it will be said that the manufacturer is offering a *trade discount* of 40%. Indeed, the manufacturer may actually quote a price to the retailer as $100 less 40%. If the retailer chooses to sell the item for $90 instead of $100, it will still have to pay $100 less 40%, or $60. The margin will be $30 ÷ $90 - 33⅓%.

Occasionally, discounts from a suggested resale price will be computed in two or more increments. For example, a manufacturer might offer discounts of 40% + 5% on a product priced to be resold at $100. This means that in addition to the original discount (suggested margin of 40% (here $40), the manufacturer has allowed an additional 5%. This does *not* mean 40% plus 5%, or 45%. It means $100 - 40% less 5% of $100 - 40%.

Thus the retailer pays ($100 - $40) - [5% x ($100 - $40)] = $60 - $3 = $57. The 40% + 5% is called a chain discount. The specific percentage link in the chain that is referred to here (5% in the present example) is calculated on the price that is derived after the application of the prior link or links to the suggested retail price. This rather cumbersome practice of stating discounts (or margins) probably arose originally to advise customers of changes in a discount structure. Over the years, the method has become traditional in certain industries.

Terms of Sale

When a manufacturer sells to a wholesaler or distributor, who then sells to a retailer, prices are also generally listed as discounts from a suggested retail price. A product suggested to sell for $100 at retail, with a suggested retail margin of 40% and a suggested wholesale margin of 20%, will be sold by the wholesaler to the retailer at a price of $60 ($100 then 40%), and will be purchased by the wholesaler from the manufacturer for $48 ($60 less 20%). Once again, the margin for a particular institution in the channel of distribution is applied to the price at which the institution sells its goods and services.

Terms of sales are a shorthand method of setting forth the conditions under which a company offers to sell its goods or services. In addition to price, they include a statement of trade discounts, the date by which the amount is to be paid, and shipping responsibilities. For example, terms of sale of $50 per unit, 2/10 e.o.m., 60 days net, f.o.b. seller's plant indicate that (1) the price for which the product is being sold is $50; (2) a 2% trade discount off the price ($1) will be offered if the bill or invoice is paid within a period ending 10 days after the end of the month when the invoice is issued; (3) the total amount of the bill is due within 60 days of the invoice date; and (4) the title and responsibility for the subsequent transportation of the product passes from the seller to the buyer at the former's plant.

Here, the letters *e.o.m.* stand for *end of month*. In their absence, qualifying for the 2% special discount would require paying the bill within 10 days after the date on the invoice. The letters *f.o.b.* stand for *free on board*, a traditional means of expressing the physical location where certain responsibilities for transportation and damage-claim litigation pass from seller to buyer. While these are just two of many different discount and shipping terms, they are perhaps the most commonly used in business today.

Exercises

Horatio Alger has just become product manager for Brand X. Brand X is a consumer product with a retail price of $1.00. Retail margins on the product are 33%, while wholesalers take a 12% margin.

Brand X and its direct competitors sell a total of 20 million units annually; Brand X has 24% of this market.

Variable manufacturing costs for Brand X are $0.09 per unit. Fixed manufacturing costs are $900,000.

The advertising budget for Brand X is $500,000. The Brand X product manager's salary and expenses total $35,000. Salespeople are paid entirely by a 10% commission. Shipping costs, breakage, insurance, and so forth are $0.02 per unit.

1. What is the unit contribution for Brand X?
2. What is Brand X's break-even point?
3. What market share does Brand X need to break even?
4. What is Brand X's profit impact?
5. Industry demand is expected to increase to 23 million units next year. Mr. Alger is considering raising his advertising budget to $1 million.
   a. If the advertising budget is raised, how many units will Brand X have to sell to break even?
   b. How many units will Brand X have to sell in order for it to achieve the same profit impact that it did this year?
   c. What will Brand X's market share have to be next year for its profit impact to be the same as this year?
   d. What will Brand X's market share have to be for it to have a $1 million profit impact?

6. Upon reflection, Mr. Alger decides not to increase Brand X's advertising budget. Instead, he thinks he might give retailers an incentive to promote Brand X by raising their margins from 33% to 40%. The margin increase would be accomplished by lowering the price of the product to retailers. Wholesaler margins would remain at 12%.

   a. If retailer margins are raised to 40% next year, how many units will Brand X have to sell to break even?

   b. How many units will Brand X have to sell to achieve the same profit impact next year as it did this year?

   c. What would Brand X's market share have to be for its profit impact to remain at this year's level?

   d. What would Brand X's market share have to be for it to generate a profit impact of $350,000?

Chapter Sixteen
Accounting Arithmetic

Unlike marketing or finance arithmetic, accounting arithmetic is precise... to the penny. Estimates or future ballpark figures just won't do. Great precision is possible because accounting is concerned almost exclusively with historical data or "actuals" (i.e. actual numbers that were produced in the past or present). Precise data are available.

The job of accounting is "to account" for the transactions of a business in dollars and cents. While accounting numbers are developed and used for management purposes, accounting and accounting arithmetic is driven, in reality, by one primary concern... "financial accounting" or the financial reporting of a business's performance to existing and potential stockholders.

Basic Accounting Statements

In fulfilling its financial reporting obligation, accounting results in the preparation of three different financial statements that provide insight about the status of an enterprise. These financial statements are: the balance sheet, the income statement, and the cash flow statement. Three fundamental formulae define each of these statements.

For the balance sheet, the arithmetic condition is that assets must equal liabilities, plus owners equity.

BALANCE SHEET
ASSETS = LIABILITIES + OWNERS EQUITY

For the income statement, the arithmetic condition is that sales minus all costs equals a profit (or loss).

INCOME STATEMENT
SALES -- COSTS = PROFIT (LOSS)

For the cash flow statement, the arithmetic condition is that cash inflows minus cash outflows equals net cash flow.

CASH FLOW STATEMENT
CASH INFLOWS -- CASH OUTFLOWS = NET CASH FLOW

Actual financial statements appear more complicated because these major groupings are shown in more detail. Also, all three statements can assume many different specific formats because every business is different in some way. These differences are often very pronounced between different industries. But even within the same industry, one company may decide to present a balance sheet or income statement that is very different in format from another business in the same industry.

Single versus Double Entry Accounting

Despite these differences, all firms must follow the same basic rules of accounting.
But there are some choices when it comes to recording transactions. The two principal choices is whether a business chooses to use single versus double entry accounting and whether it decides to record

transactions on cash versus accrual basis.

You can think of your checkbook as a single entry accounting system. You record deposits (inflows) and checks written (outflows) only once in your check register. Periodically, you compute a "balance" of what's left over... your net cash flow.

However, your checkbook doesn't tell you if your business made a profit. Nor does it provide a picture of your assets and liabilities. Plus, as most of us unfortunately know, it's easy to make a mistake that can go undetected for some time. Double entry systems give you profit or loss information and balance sheet information about your business. But only at a cost. In a double entry system, you need to record each transaction twice.. once how the transaction impacts assets, and once how the same transaction impacts liabilities and owner's equity. This double entry procedure insures that the accounting equation is always in balance.

Cash versus Accrual Accounting

When transactions are actually "recorded" depends on whether you are using a cash or accrual method of accounting. <u>Exhibit 6</u> illustrates the differences between cash versus accrual systems of accounting. In a cash system, transactions are recorded whenever real cash changes hands. For instance, a sale isn't a sale until you actually receive the money for the product or service...even if you delivered the product or service months before getting paid. The same is true of costs or expenses. You don't incur expenses until you pay for them.

Under an accrual system of accounting, you record sales and costs when they are legally accrued. For instance, let's assume you receive a sales order and you deliver the product in April. However, you aren't paid for the sale until June. The sale is still recorded in April since that's when it was legally accrued. The same is true for expenses. Suppose receive a bill from a consultant for work done in July. You don't pay her until September. However the expense was accrued in July and that's when it will be recorded as an expense on your income statement. That's also when it will impact your balance sheet as an increase in the "accounts payable" section of your liabilities. However, your cash flow statement won't be affected until September when you actually pay the expense.

EXHIBIT 6
CASH VERSUS ACCRUAL ACCOUNTING

	SALES (INFLOWS)	EXPENSES (OUTFLOWS)
ACCRUAL METHOD	ACCOUNTED FOR WHEN SALE IS MADE	ACCOUNTED FOR WHEN EXPENSE IS INCURRED
CASH METHOD	ACCOUNTED FOR WHEN CASH IS COLLECTED FOR SALE	ACCOUNTED FOR WHEN CASH IS PAID FOR EXPENSE

Chapter Seventeen
Finance Arithmetic

If accounting is concerned mainly with actual or historical numbers, finance is concerned primarily with numbers that concern the future. The fundamental job of finance is to determine the financial resources that will be used/needed to run a business in the future. This future may be a week from now, a month, a quarter, a year, or a decade or more. It all depends on the circumstances. The length of time considered will also depend on circumstances. For instance, a business that is failing may need to look at its financial future on a week-to-week basis, even day-to-day. A well established business may need to consider the financial implications of decisions taken today over a two-or-three year basis.

Many business cases provide some accounting and financial data. One of your first analytic steps should be some crude but often revealing assessment of the organization's financial health. Several simple tools are available for this quick assessment. They include liquidity tests, turnover ratios, profitability measures, and a few other useful operating ratios. Let's look at each of these.

Liquidity Tests

Liquidity tests reflect in varying degrees the ability of an organization to cover or finance its short-term operations.

The Current Ratio is one popular liquidity test. It shows how much larger or smaller current assets (CA) are compared to current liabilities (CL). You simply divide current assets by current liabilities. The resulting number indicates to what extent short-term assets are available to finance short-term liabilities. The rule of thumb for many industries is that current assets should be about twice the size of current liabilities.

$$\frac{CA}{CL} = \text{Current Ratio} = \text{"APPROXIMATELY"} \ 2$$

For example, a "low" current ratio of one may indicate a liquidity crisis. However, "high" current ratios are not necessarily good. For instance, a current ratio of five or six may indicate that the organization is not utilizing its resources efficiently to generate additional business.

The Liquidity Ratio, (also called the "Quick Ratio" or "Acid Test") provides a more conservative look at an organization's ability to cover its current liabilities. The liquidity ratio equals cash plus accounts receivables (AR) plus other current assets that can be converted quickly into cash (e.g., marketable securities) divided by current liabilities. The rule of thumb or norm for many industries is a liquidity ratio (LR) of one.

$$\frac{\text{CASH + AR + OTHER CURRENT ASSETS QUICKLY CONVERTIBLE TO CASH}}{\text{CURRENT LIABILITIES}} = LR = 1$$

Substantial deviation below one may indicate a cash crisis, while a large liquidity ratio of, for example, three or above, suggests a fat, cash rich organization and perhaps the inefficient utilization of resources.

A third measure of liquidity is <u>Working Capital (WC)</u> which is simply Current Assets minus Current Liabilities.

$$CA -- CL = WC$$

Taken by itself, this number is not very informative. What one needs is some notion of the future growth in working capital compared to projected sales growth and inflation. For example, is working capital growing faster than the rate of inflation? If sales are expected to rise quickly, will working capital increases be sufficient to cover this growth in operations?

Turnover Ratios

A number of turnover ratios allow you to discover approximately how fast a company pays its bills, how fast its customers pay their bills to the company, and how fast the company is "turning over its inventory." A similar ratio for cash tells you how many days of cash an organization has at its disposal. This latter ratio is especially useful for small companies where the stream of sales is declining and/or uncertain. For example, under the worst conditions, (no incoming funds) how long can the company survive before going bankrupt?

The <u>Accounts Payable Turnover</u> shows you the number of days the company takes on average to pay its bills. The formula is accounts payable divided by cost of goods sold with the result multiplied by 365 days.

$$\frac{\text{ACCOUNTS PAYABLE}}{\text{COST OF GOODS SOLD}} \text{ (365 days)} = \begin{array}{l} \text{Average Number Of} \\ \text{Days To Pay Bills} \end{array}$$

The formulas for *Accounts Receivable Turnover, Inventory Turnover, and Cash Turnover* are very similar. They are:

$$\frac{\text{CASH}}{\text{NET SALES}} \text{ (365 days)} = \begin{array}{l} \text{Average Number Of} \\ \text{Days Of Cash} \\ \text{Available At The} \\ \text{Existing Rate Of} \\ \text{Operations} \end{array}$$

$$\frac{\text{ACCOUNTS RECEIVABLES}}{\text{NET SALES}} \text{ (365 days)} = \begin{array}{l} \text{Average Number Of} \\ \text{Days Your Customers} \\ \text{Take To Pay You} \end{array}$$

$$\frac{\text{INVENTORY}}{\text{COST OF GOODS SOLD*}} \text{ (365 days)} = \begin{array}{l} \text{Average Number Of} \\ \text{Days Of Inventory} \\ \text{Available To Company} \end{array}$$

*Assumes that changes in "purchases" are positively related to changes in Cost of Goods Sold. The proper expression of the ratio is between cash outflows for accounts payable and actual purchases. But since information on purchases is generally not provided in public financial statements, the practice is to use CGS as a proxy variable for purchases.

How do you interpret what these ratios mean? By themselves the numbers are almost meaningless without:

1.   some idea of an industry norm;

2.   comparative calculations for other years in order to see if, for example, Accounts Receivables Turnover has increased or declined significantly.

However, within a given year, the ratios can be compared with one another to some extent. For instance, you might become suspicious if you saw an organization with an extremely low accounts payable turnover, say 10 to 15 days, i.e., it pays its bills very fast, but at the same time saw a very high accounts receivable turnover, say 150 days or more. Is the difference between the two turnovers producing a cash squeeze? Can cash be freed by extending your accounts payable period? Will creditors get angry? Or can you reduce your own collections period and thereby increase cash?

Other Useful Ratios

I find two other ratios particularly helpful for producing a quick initial analysis.

First, the *Debt Equity Ratio* indicates the extent which outside creditors have committed capital funds to your business. Conversely, it shows the extent to which owners are committed, financially speaking, to the business. Like most of these ratios, several variations exist. I usually calculate the D/E Ratio by dividing long-term liabilities by owners' equity. The rule of thumb is .5: 1, although considerable variation exists across industries.

$$\frac{\text{LONG-TERM LIABILITIES}}{\text{OWNERS' EQUITY}} = \text{D/E RATIO} = \text{APPROXIMATELY .5}$$

Where a .5 debt equity ratio is the industry norm, creditors may become concerned if total long-term liabilities become more than half of owners' equity, thus hampering an organization's ability to raise capital investment funds using debt.

Second, the *Assets to Sales Ratio* shows you how many assets in dollar terms are needed to generate an extra dollar of sales. For instance, high fixed costs industries, like railroads and automobiles, require several dollars of assets to generate an incremental dollar of sales. By contrast, some industries with high variable costs, like most electronics businesses, often require less than a dollar's worth of assets to produce a dollar of sales.

$$\frac{\text{TOTAL ASSETS}}{\text{NET SALES}} = \text{DOLLARS Of ASSETS NEEDED TO PRODUCE \$1.00 OF SALES}$$

Besides determining if the business activity is a low or high fixed cost operation, one is also interested in the change of the assets to sales ratio over time. Is it taking an organization more or less assets to generate an extra dollar of sales over time?

In fact, the calculation of a variety of ratios over time provides a dynamic picture of an organization's financial evolution. The table on the following page presents selected ratios over a fourteen-year period for the XYZ Company. Can you explain each item in the left column? Can you interpret and explain the data for each ratio?

Profitability Measures and the Evaluation of Investment Alternatives

Several profitability measures exist which an analyst can use to evaluate different investment alternatives. Four popular measures of profitability are presented here. Two of these measures, *Return on Investment and Payback* are easy to calculate. The third and fourth measures, *Net Present Value and Internal Rate of Return* are more complicated, requiring either tables for hand calculations or access to a computer or sophisticated calculator.

Several different return on investment (ROI) formulas exist to calculate the profitability of an investment. The particular formula you select depends upon your interest (i.e., as a stockholder, top management, or a line manager). The ROI formula presented here reflects the interests of stockholders in that it includes the tax effect.

$$ROI = \frac{\text{AFTER TAX NET INCOME}}{\text{OWNERS' EQUITY}}$$

EXHIBIT 7
X Y Z Company
Selected Balance Sheet and Operating Ratios

	Dec. 31 1962	Dec. 31 1964	Oct. 31 1969	Oct. 31 1971	Oct. 31 1973	Oct. 31 1976
(R) Current ratio	2.5	2.0	3.0	4.1	4.6	5.5
($) Net Working Capital	$305.	438.	1360.	2035.	2699.	3769.
(R) Acid Test Ratio	2.6	1.0	1.0	.6	1.5	1.9
(%) Current assets to total assets	79.0	78.8	74.7	74.0	68.0	72.2
(%) Total fixed assets to total assets	20.0	20.3	24.0	25.9	31.6	26.0
(R) Net worth to debt	3.0	1.8	4.2	2.2	2.6	3.1
(%) Net worth to total assets	79.3	60.6	81.0	55.0	73.2	77.7
(days) Receivables turnover*	29.0	21.0	13.0	41.0	39.0	51.0
(days) Inventory turnover**	120	120	123	120	178	135
(%) Total assets to net sales	48.6	42.9	46.9	59.8	60.8	68.0
(%) Fixed assets to net sales	9.0	9.9	10.0	15.6	21.0	17.8
(%) Operating profit to net worth	42.3	59.8	32.1	20.3	9.9	15.1
(%) Net profit to net worth	25.0	18.6	20.3	12.7	4.9	7.0

*Accounts receivable x 360/net sales.

**Average inventory x 360/cost of goods sold.

Another way to evaluate investment alternatives is to look at relative profitability in terms of the number of years it takes to recoup your initial investment. The measurement of this recoupment period is called the *Payback*. You can calculate it by dividing the net investment over the life of the investment by the net annual return.

NET $$$ INVESTMENT
--------------------------------- = Years To PAYBACK = Number of years to
NET ANNUAL $$$ RETURN (in years) cover initial
investment

Neither ROI nor Payback adjust for the particular timing of cash outflows and inflows for particular investment alternatives. More accurate analysis of investment alternatives requires taking into account the timing of cash flows simply because a dollar received today (present value) is worth more to you than a dollar you will receive tomorrow, or next year, or ten years from now (future value).

Two different measures of discounted cash flow are often used by analysts in order to include the effect of time: 1) net present value (NPV); and, 2) internal rate of return (IRR).

The calculation of the net present value of an investment provides the *actual dollar* values for cash inflows and outflows that occur over the life of the investment, i.e., until you sell the business, the equipment wears out, etc. These cash flows are discounted back to the present by some alternative yield rate, i.e., what you could get by putting the money into some other investment, treasury bills, a savings account, etc.

The formula for NPV is:

$$NPV = (\text{The Initial Investment}) + \frac{\text{CASH FLOW No.1}}{(1 + I)^1} + \frac{\text{CASH FLOW No.2}}{(1 + I)^2} + ...\text{etc.}$$

where "I" equals the relevant "interest rate," desired yield, or required rate of return.

You can avoid lengthy hand calculations of the preceding formula by using special present value tables if:

1. All cash inflows are to be received at one time in the future, (e.g., two years out, ten years out, etc.), use Table 1 in Part Eight. An example of a typical problem and calculation of present value using this table is shown in Part Eight.

2. All cash inflows are even or equal, (e.g., $300 each year for five years), use Table 2 in Part Eight. An example of the NPV calculation using this table is provided in Part Eight.

Uneven net cash flows received at different points in time usually require considerable hand calculation or access to a computer or sophisticated calculator.

The difference between "discounted" cash inflows and your original investment (plus any discounted cash outflows if your investment occurs over time) is the net present value. If the discounted cash inflows equal your original investment, the net present value equals zero. Usually, investment proposals are not acceptable unless the NPV equals zero or is positive (i.e., greater than zero).

The Internal Rate of Return (IRR) calculates the yield rate or required rate of return for an investment alternative which equates the investment outflows with the cash inflows (i.e., NPV equals zero).

Consequently, the same formula that applies to NPV also applies to IRR except NPV = 0 and you are solving for "I".

$$0 = - \text{(THE INITIAL INVESTMENT)} + \frac{\text{CASH FLOW NO. 1}}{(1 + I)^1} +$$

$$\frac{\text{CASH FLOW NO. 2}}{(1 + 1)^2} + \qquad \text{... ETC.}$$

Again, you can use the present value tables in Part Eight when dealing respectively with a single cash inflow or even cash inflows. The procedure is simply reversed. For example, assume you make a $10,000 investment and will receive $3000 each year for five years. You can approximate the discount factor in Table 2 by dividing the initial investment by the yearly cash inflow ($10,000/$3000 = 3.333). Then find where 3.333 falls in the five year row of Table 2 (between 15% and 16%). Interpolating reveals the IRR equals 15.24%.

The main value of the IRR method is that it allows comparison of several investment alternatives without setting a "hurdle" rate or alternative investment rate as required in the NPV calculation. Establishing such a "cost of capital" rate is often very difficult in practice.

Projection of Financial Statements

In order to apply some measure of profitability, you must project what profits will result from alternative courses of action. Three kinds of projections (or pro forma analyses) are particularly useful:

1. Income Statement Projections or Profit and Loss (P&L) projections;
2. Balance Sheet projections; and,
3. Cash Flow projections.

There are two basic kinds of financial projections: 1. standalone or unlinked projections; and 2. integrated or linked projections. Both may be produced manually or by electronic spreadsheets. Standalone projections are technically <u>incorrect</u> but may suffice for "quick and dirty" analysis. They certainly are quicker and easier to produce than integrated projections. Nearly all the financial projections you will see in business school will be standalone projections.

By contrast, integrated projections are technically correct and, consequently, preferred for real world application. However, they are much more difficult to generate because a significant degree of accounting knowledge is required "to link" the financial statements together so the balance sheet "ties out" or balances without applying some arbitrary "fudge factor" or "plug" number to force things to balance.

Integrated projections "link" by formulas certain items on the P&L projection to the Balance Sheet projection and the Cash Flow projection. For instance, "cash" is an item on the balance sheet and the cash flow statement. Cash is also partly produced or affected by what happens on the income statement. Consequently, the three statements are "linked" together, just as everything in your business is linked in some way to something else.

The value or power of integrated financial projections is that they provide a simulated or dynamic model of your business. True "what if" analysis becomes possible. As one or more things change in your projections (e.g. rent, cost of goods, cost of capital, etc.), you can see how everything else is affected on all three financial projections, plus any other projected budgets (manpower, R&D, marketing, etc.) you have linked to the model.

In addition, you can also see the immediate impact on any number of output or analytic measures (breakeven, payback, ROI, inventory turnover, etc) if formulas have been written which also link these measures to the specific items that produce them in your financial projections.

You may wonder why standalone projections are still used so widely? There are two reasons. First, the fact that they are technically incorrect is still not widely appreciated by most business school professors. Second, until the emergence of the electronic spreadsheet, the creation of integrated financial models simply wasn't practical. If you are interested in learning more about integrated financials, I suggest my book on Entrepreneurial Finance and related software, Ronstadt's Financials. Given the wide use of standalone projections, what follows is a description of how they are produced.

Profit and Loss Pro Formas

You can generate a standalone P&L projection with nothing more than an estimate of future sales and a Profit and Loss Statement for the current period. The basic approach is to determine past expense loads (as a per cent of sales) and project these expenses either at their past percentage levels so they "vary" proportionately to the sales increase.

If you have additional information about future production, sales, and other overhead charges, you may be able to determine if cost of goods sold and other operating expenses will increase, decrease, or remain at their former levels as a percent of sales. The same estimates can be made for interest and other non-operating expenses. Will some "fixed" costs increase slightly, becoming semi-variable? Will some variable costs increase in a non-linear fashion with sales?

Once you answer these questions and determine total expenses, the appropriate tax rate can be applied to obtain after tax profits.

Balance Sheet Pro Formas

The projection of a balance sheet also depends on knowing or estimating a sales forecast, plus applying ratio levels as they existed in the past. For example, assume next year's sales are forecasted to increase from $1,200,000 to $1,500,000 and that last year's balance sheet showed a cash balance of $66,667. Ratio analysis revealed cash turnover was twenty days in the past:

$$\frac{\$66,667}{\$1,200,000} (360 \text{ DAYS}) = 20 \text{ DAYS}$$

If 20 days of cash are appropriate for the future, the cash balance for next year at the new sales level is:

$$\frac{\$1,500,000}{360 \text{ DAYS}} (20 \text{ DAYS}) = \$83,334$$

The procedure for estimating accounts receivables, inventory, accounts payable, debt to equity, etc. is similar.

Since assets must equal total liabilities, you may select any one item on the balance sheet as a "plug" figure for your entry. Usually long-term debt or cash is used as the plug figure.

Note: If a historical (actual) balance sheet exists for an ongoing business, you can also generate a projected balance sheet by using a percentage method. First, calculate each item on the historical balance sheet as a percentage of total assets. Then apply these same percentages to the projected balance sheet.

Cash Flow Pro Formas

A rough estimate of future cash flows can be a powerful and revealing aid to decision making. At the same time, the procedure for doing a cash flow is relatively simple.

First, determine from the cash situation what you feel is the relevant period for the cash flow (be it a week, a month, a year, etc.). In most instances, cash flow analysis that is longer than a month doesn't make much sense, except for reporting purposes. For instance, I can show you situations where a positive profit and a positive cash flow result at the end of a year but where negative cash flows exist for prolonged periods during the year which would effectively cause the bankruptcy of the business.

Second, calculate all cash inflows for this period, adding them to the existing cash balance. Remember, cash inflows are not sales (i.e., invoices) unless they are "cash sales." Cash inflows are the amount of accounts receivables you expect to collect during the period plus any cash inflows from loans you have obtained, or current portions of long-term notes due to you.

Third, calculate all cash outflows for the same period. Cash outflows are payments you must make over the relevant period for material purchases (that portion of accounts payable due), wages, direct factory overhead, selling, G & A, etc.

Fourth, determine the net cash flow by subtracting cash outflows from total cash inflows.

Fifth, (optional) if necessary, calculate the net cumulative cash flows for successive time periods using the same procedure as noted above.

Cash flow analysis is especially useful when sales are increasing or decreasing rapidly. As sales change, so do expenses. The key question for the survival of an organization, however, is how are cash receipts building up relative to cash payments as sales and expenses rapidly rise or fall. Unless a manager takes appropriate action, an organization can produce a cash shortage by growing too fast. On the other hand, a sales decline can also produce a cash shortage if expenses and cash outflows are not reduced to offset the projected decline of cash receipts (or the rate of cash inflows is not otherwise increased . . . e.g., reducing the accounts receivable period).

The topic of cash flow is crucial to business decision making. Given this importance, I highly recommend the following reading on "Cash Flow In A Small Plant" which presents an alternative way to derive cash flow requirements.

CASH FLOW IN A SMALL PLANT*

SUMMARY

The prime objective for any business is to survive. That means, a firm must have enough cash to meet its obligations. This reading shows the owner-manager how to plan for the movement of cash through the business and thus plan for future requirements.

INTRODUCTION

"Business is booming. This month alone, the sales volume has risen over 50 percent.

Many proud owner-managers equate growth in sales volume with the success of their enterprise. But, many of these so-called "successful" businesses are becoming insolvent because they do not have enough cash to meet the needs of an increasing sales volume. For, without cash, how can the business pay its bills, meet its payroll requirements, and purchase merchandise for the increased sales demand?

A business must have enough cash to meet its legal obligations and avoid becoming insolvent. This is a primary business objective that may override other objectives, such as sales volume. What good is additional sales volume if you're out of business?

Sufficient cash is one of the keys to maintaining a successful business. Thus, you must understand how cash moves or flows through the business and how planning can remove some of the uncertainties about future requirements.

CASH FLOW

Cash Cycle. In any business there is a continual cycle of events which may increase or decrease the cash balance. The following diagram is used to illustrate this flow of cash.

Cash is decreased in the acquisition of materials and services to produce the finished goods. It is reduced in paying off the amounts owed to suppliers; that is, accounts payable. Then, inventory is sold and these sales generate cash and/or accounts

receivable; that is, money owed from customers. When customers pay, accounts receivable is reduced and the cash account increases. However, the cash flows are not necessarily related to the sales in that period because customers may pay in the next period.

Net Working Capital. Current assets are those resources of cash and those assets which can be converted to cash within one year or a normal business cycle. These include cash, marketable securities, accounts receivable, inventories, etc. Current liabilities are obligations which become due within one year or a normal business cycle.

These include accounts payable, notes payable, accrued expenses payable, etc. You may want to consider current assets as the source of funds which reduce current liabilities.

---

*The author of "Cash Flow in a Small Plant" is Danny S. Litt, Corporate Budget and Planning Director for Norris Industries, Incorporated. It is reprinted with permission from the Small Business Administration, Management Aids No. 229 for small manufacturers, Washington, D.C.

One way to measure the flow of cash and the firm's ability to maintain its cash or liquid assets is to compute working capital. It is the difference between current assets and current liabilities. The change in this value from period to period is called **net working capital.** For example,

	1991	1992
Current Assets	$110,000	$200,000
less Current Liabilities	-70,000	-112,000
Working Capital	40,000	88,000
Net Working Capital Increase (Decrease)		$48,000

Net working capital increased during the year, but we don't know how. It could have been all in cash or all in inventory. Or, it may have resulted from a reduction in accounts payable.

Cash Flow Statement. While net working capital shows only the changes in the current position, a "flow" statement can be developed to explain the changes that have occurred in any account during any time period. The cash flow statement is an analysis of the cash inflows and outflows.

The ability to forecast cash requirements is indeed a means of becoming a more efficient manager. If you can determine the cash requirements for any period, you can establish a bank loan in advance, or you can reduce other current asset accounts so that the cash will be made available. also, when you have excess cash, you can put this cash into productive use to earn a return.

Exhibit 8
CASH FLOW CYCLE

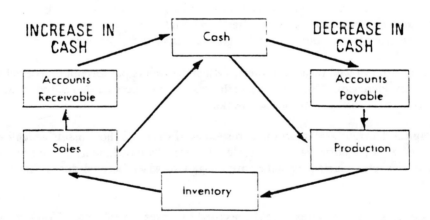

The change in the cash account can be readily determined if you know net working capital and the changes in current liabilities and current assets other than cash.

Let   **NWC**   be net working capital
            CA   be the change in current assets other than cash
            CL   be the change in current liabilities
            cash   be the change in cash

Since net working capital is the difference between the change in current assets and current liabilities,

$$\textbf{NWC} = \textbf{CA} \text{ (other than cash)} + \textbf{cash} - \textbf{CL}$$
$$\textbf{cash} = \textbf{NWC} - \textbf{CA} \text{ (other than cash)} + \textbf{CL}$$

This relationship states that if we know net working capital (**NWC**), the change in current liabilities (**CL**), and the change in current assets less cash (**CA** less cash), we can calculate the change in cash. The change in cash is then added to the beginning balance of cash to determine the ending balance.

Suppose you forecast that sales will increase $50,000 and the following will correspondingly change:

Receivables	increase by $25,000
Inventory	increase by $70,000
Accounts Payable	increase by $30,000
Notes Payable	increase by $10,000

Using net working capital of $48,000, what is the projected change in cash?

$$\begin{aligned} \text{cash} &= \textbf{NWC} - \textbf{CA} \text{ (other than cash)} + \textbf{CL} \\ &= 48{,}000 - 25{,}000 - 70{,}000 + 30{,}000 + 10{,}000 \\ &= -7{,}000 \end{aligned}$$

Conclusion: over this time period, under the condition of increasing sales volume, cash decreases by $7,000. Is there enough cash to cover this decrease? This will depend upon the beginning cash balance.

Sources and Application of Funds. At any given level of sales, it is easier to forecast the required inventory, accounts payable, receivables, etc., than net working capital. To forecast this net working capital account, you must trace the sources and application of funds. Sources of funds increase working capital. Applications of funds decrease working capital. The difference between the sources and applications of funds is the net working capital.

The following calculation is based on the fact that the balance sheet is indeed in "balance." That is, total assets equal total liabilities plus stockholders' equity.

$$\begin{matrix} \text{current} & & \text{noncurrent} & & \text{current} & & \text{long-term} & & \\ \text{assets} & + & \text{assets} & = & \text{liabilities} & + & \text{liabilities} & + & \text{equity} \end{matrix}$$

Rearranging this equation:

$$\begin{matrix} \text{current} & & \text{current} & & \text{long-term} & & & & \text{noncurrent} \\ \text{assets} & - & \text{liabilities} & = & \text{liabilities} & + & \text{equity} & - & \text{assets} \end{matrix}$$

Since the left-hand side of the equation is working capital, the right-hand side must also equal working capital. A change to either side is the net working capital. If long-term liabilities and equity increase or noncurrent assets decrease, net working capital increases. This change would be a source of funds. If noncurrent assets increase or long-term liabilities and equity decrease, net working capital decreases. This change would be an application of funds.

Typical sources of funds or net working capital are

- . Funds provided by operations
- . Disposal of fixed assets
- . Issuance of stock
- . Borrowing from a long-term source

To obtain the item, "funds provided by operations," subtract all expense items requiring funds from all revenue that was a source of funds. You can also obtain this result in an easier manner; add back expenses which did not result in inflows or outflows of funds to reported net income.

The most common nonfund expense is depreciation, the allocation of the cost of an asset as an expense over the life of the asset against the future revenues produced. Adjusting net income with depreciation is much simpler than computing revenues and expenses which require funds. Again, depreciation is not a source of funds.

The typical applications of funds or net working capital are

- . Purchase of fixed assets
- . Payment of dividends
- . Retirement of long-term liabilities
- . Repurchase of equity

The following is an example of how sources and applications of funds may be used to determine net working capital.

Statement of Sources & Applications of Funds

Sources of Funds:	
From Operations	
Net Income	$ 10,000
Add Depreciation	15,000
	25,000
Issuance of Debt	175,000
Issuance of Stock	3,000
Total Sources:	$203,000
Applications of Funds:	
Purchase of Plant	$140,000
Cash Dividends	15,000
Total Uses:	155,000
Net Working Capital	
Increase (Decrease)	$48,000
(203,000- 155,000)	

Statement of Changes in Financial Position. This statement combines two statements previously discussed: the statement of sources and application of funds and the changes in working capital accounts. This statement can be converted into a cash flow statement by solving for cash as the unknown, as shown below.

<u>**Cash Flow Statement**</u>

Sources of Funds	$203,000	
Applications of Funds	155,000	
Net Working Capital		$ 48,000
Less:		
Increase in Receivables	25,000	
Increase in Inventory	70,000	-95,000
Plus:		
Increase in Accounts Payable	30,000	
Increase in Notes Payable	10,000	40,000
Cash Flow		$ -7,000

PLANNING FOR CASH FLOW

Cash flow can be used not only to determine how cash flowed through the business but also as an aid to determine the excess or shortage of cash. Suppose your analysis of cash flow forecasts a potential cash deficiency. You may then do a number of things, such as:

. Increase borrowings: loans, stock issuance, etc.

. Reduce current asset accounts: reduce receivables, inventory, etc.

. Reduce noncurrent assets: postpone expanding the facility, sell off some fixed assets, etc.

By using a cash flow statement you can determine if sufficient funds are available from financing activities, show funds generated from all sources, and show how these funds were applied. Using and adjusting the information gained from this cash flow analysis will help you to know in advance if there will be enough cash to pay

. Bills to suppliers
. Bank loans
. Interest
. Dividends

Careful planning will insure a sufficient amount of cash to meet future obligations on schedule which is essential for the "successful" business.

PLANNING AID

The following example is presented to help you develop a cash flow analysis. Of course, all names are disguised.

During the next month, Irene Smith, owner-manager of Imagine Manufacturing, expects sales to increase to $10,000. Based on past experience, she made this forecast:

Net income to be 9% of sales	$ 900
Income taxes to be 3.2% of sales	320
Accounts receivable to increase	5,000
Inventory to increase	2,000
Accounts payable to increase	3,000

Her beginning cash balance is $3,000 and she plans to purchase a piece of equipment for $1,500. What is her cash flow?

Cash Flow Analysis

Sources of Funds:	
Net Income	$ 900
Depreciation	1,000
	1,900
Application of Funds	
Addition to Fixed Assets	$ 1,500
Payment of Taxes	320
	1,820
Net Working Capital	
Increase (Decrease)	80
Working Capital Accounts	
Less Change in	
Inventory	$-2,000
Accounts Receivable	-5,000
Plus Change in	
Accounts Payable	3,000
Cash Flow	-3,920
Plus Beginning Cash Balance	3,000
Equals Ending Cash Balance	-920

Assuming Irene's forecast is correct, she has a cash need of $920 next month. If she cannot borrow the additional funds, she must either reduce sales, which may reduce profits, or find another source of cash. She can now use her cash flow analysis to try to determine a source of funds or a reduction in the application of funds. An easy solution is to postpone the purchase of the equipment. This would increase her cash flow by $1,500, more than enough for a positive cash balance at the end of next month.

Chapter Eighteen
Production Arithmetic

Historically, production arithmetic has been concerned with ways to measure and improve output. This concern with productivity has led researchers to examine and measure the time it takes to produce products and services (e.g., time-motion measurements), and the best or optimum number of tasks to produce something. More recently, this concern has expanded to include:

a. the amount of time (particularly development time) it takes to commercialize new products, as well as,

b. the best (most efficient) ways to provide inputs, particularly components so they arrive "just in time" (JIT) in order to minimize inventory costs, and

c. the most efficient ways to improve the **quality** of a product or service

In real life, the identification and ordering of alternatives, events, or tasks in some systematic way is often more complicated than evaluating the alternatives themselves. However, I believe you should be aware of three methods that are associated with the area of production and operations management. They are particularly useful for analyzing complex operating alternatives that may confront managers dealing with ways to produce products or services.

All three methods involve diagramming techniques. The first is Process Flow Diagramming and Capacity Analysis. A second approach to alternative analysis is Decision Tree Diagramming and Probability Assessment. A third set of methods is project flow diagramming (Gantt Chart Scheduling, Critical Path Method, PERT, etc.).[1]

Process Flow Diagramming and Capacity Analysis

Process Flow Diagramming and Capacity Analysis are relevant for any organization that produces a product or a service whether the organization is involved in unit (job shop), batch, or continuous production.

The objective of process diagramming is to identify all inputs and trace the route taken by these inputs as they are converted into outputs. In short, the process flow is identified by noting each key 6 t task," the "**flows**" between tasks, and "**storage** or inventory points" throughout the process.

The key that makes process flow diagramming a powerful tool is the identification or calculation of some common **unit of capacity** for each task and storage point throughout the process.

The identification of **the bottleneck task** becomes possible by comparing the capacities of all elements of the process. The task with the lowest capacity is the bottleneck or pacing element, and the final product

---

[1] Numerous books provide a clear explanations of Gantt Charting, Pert Diagramming, and the concept of "critical path." Consequently I have chosen not to cover them here. For an excellent yet simple treatment, I highly recommend Chapter 12, "Producing Goods" of Business, 2nd Edition, by Ricky W. Griffin and Ronald J. Ebert, Prentice Hall, 1991, pp.318-322.

cannot be produced at a rate faster than the slowest element for very long.

This kind of process/capacity information allows an analyst to judge investment proposals by their impact on a bottleneck element (as well as disregard proposals that do not affect the bottleneck element, a problem which often occurs when careful process/capacity analysis is not done). With each increase in capacity, a different task or storage element may become the new bottleneck. Also, additions to capacity often come in lumpy or non-divisible amounts that are larger than the incremental capacity you may need. Consequently, you must calculate the incremental return of each additional or "extra" machine, storage area, etc., in order to be certain you are not providing too much of the wrong kind of capacity.

How does one diagram a process? **Exhibit 9** provides an illustration where triangles are used to show inventory (storage) areas and circles designate different tasks. Actual capacities for each element in the process are also shown. Because Task B has the lowest capacity, it is the slowest or pacing element. The rate of output of the process will eventually be no greater than 1000 units per day. For instance, finished goods inventory will not exceed its capacity since final parts shipping is also operating at 1000 parts shipped per day. However, Work-In-Process (WIP) Inventory will build up until its total capacity (10,000) parts is reached in 10 days (i.e., the difference between the in/out rate is 1000 parts "in" per day, so WIP is 10,000 parts/1000 parts = 10 days).

At this point, Task A will be forced to reduce its output of 1000 parts per day. In turn, this lower rate of output will cause a build-up of raw materials inventory until its capacity is reached (also 10 days). with each decision branch of the tree and, in a sense, "discount" these net benefits by the probability of occurrence.

The operation of the process at 1000 parts per day may still not present a problem if inventory carrying changes are relatively small and the delivery rate can be reduced without the loss of business. But what if our raw materials are perishable? What if inventory carrying costs are high? What could happen?

Exhibit 9
Sample Process Flow Diagram and Capacities

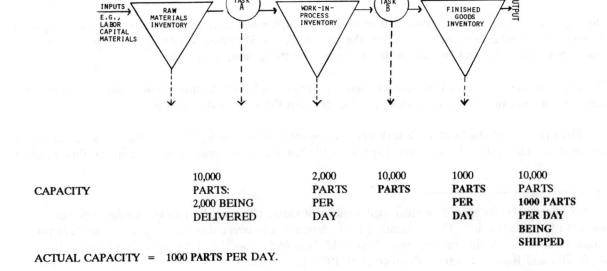

| CAPACITY | | 10,000 PARTS: 2,000 BEING DELIVERED | 2,000 PARTS PER DAY | 10,000 PARTS | 1000 PARTS PER DAY | 10,000 PARTS 1000 PARTS PER DAY BEING SHIPPED |

ACTUAL CAPACITY = 1000 PARTS PER DAY.

First, we would probably see long lines of vehicles waiting to make raw material deliveries. One response is to increase raw materials inventory in order to speed up delivery. This addition may be very expensive while only temporarily solving our delivery queuing problem. Without the benefit of careful process/capacity analysis we may not realize that increases are needed in Task B and Finished Goods Inventory. In short, the wrong course of action is sometimes easy to recommend and accept.

Decision Tree Diagramming and Probability Assessment

Often, managers are faced with decisions that are alternative or sequential in nature. For instance, if one decision path is followed, it gives rise to other possible decision alternatives, and so on.

Generally, you can diagram these decision alternatives and the events that make up each alternative. The resulting diagrams are called decision trees.

One benefit of constructing a decision tree is that the process of diagramming alone forces a decision maker to order his/her thoughts about the array of competing alternatives under consideration.

However, the purpose of decision diagramming is more than systematically arranging all the major alternatives and their component events. The technique also allows a decision maker to adjust outcomes by the probabilities of the events occurring. Consequently, you can calculate the net marginal or incremental benefits associated with each decision branch of the tree and, in a sense, "discount" these net benefits by the probability of occurrence.

The execution of the technique requires:

1. knowing or being able to assign probabilities for the various events;

2. adjusting (i.e., multiplying) cash flows associated with each group of alternative events by their probabilities, starting at the end points of the decision diagram, and working backwards to the original decision fork;

3. calculating the expected value of event forks to serve as new end points as you work back toward the original alternatives.

Steps 2 and 3 are very mechanical. (Exhibit 10 provides a diagram, sample problem, and calculations).

The key and usually difficult task in real life is determining the probabilities associated with each event. Yet a range of realistic estimates can often be made and many ingenious means have been devised to make them. Two simple aids in this regard are worth mentioning:

First, if you know the probability (P) of one event occurring is .6, then the probability of its alternative is simply (1.0 - P) or a .4 chance of occurring.

Second, if you calculate the net benefit of one decision branch, you can calculate a breakeven probability for another branch. This calculation states in effect what kind of probability you must assign to another alternative to produce the same breakeven benefits as the known branch. You may then ask yourself if the breakeven probability seems realistic to you.

EXHIBIT 8
SAMPLE DECISION TREE

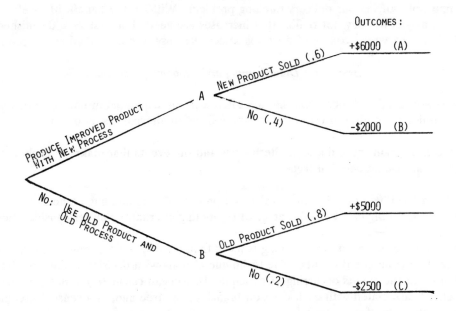

OUTCOMES:

NEW PRODUCT SOLD (.6) → +$6000 (A)

No (.4) → -$2000 (B)

OLD PRODUCT SOLD (.8) → +$5000

No (.2) → -$2500 (C)

PRODUCE IMPROVED PRODUCT WITH NEW PROCESS

No: USE OLD PRODUCT AND OLD PROCESS

(A) YIELDS A HIGHER CONTRIBUTION THAN OLD PRODUCT BECAUSE IMPROVEMENTS ALLOW HIGHER SALES PRICE AND LOWER PRODUCTION COSTS,

(B) NEW MATERIAL INPUTS AND PROCESS CHANGES PRODUCE LOWER PRODUCTION COSTS THAN OLD PROCESS,

(C) A SLIM CHANCE EXISTS THAT A COMPETITOR MAY PRODUCE THE IMPROVED PRODUCT AND SELL IT TO OUR CUSTOMER,

Sample Problem and Calculation of Decision Tree Problem

Situation: A manager must decide whether or not to produce a slightly improved product which requires a modified process for a one-time sale to a single customer. Existing equipment can be used and must be rearranged to handle the use of a few new material inputs. Capital investment is zero.

The manager forecasts the outcomes (contribution dollars or relevant costs or losses) shown at the endpoints of the decision tree. From experience, the manager subjectively assigns the probabilities (in parentheses) for each of the four events.

Sample Problem and Calculation of Decision Tree Problem

Calculation: The manager calculates the expected value for decision points A & B:

Expected Value for
Improved Product: A = $6000 (.6) + $-2000 (.4) = $2800.

Expected Value for
Old Product: B = $5000 (.8) + $-2500 (.2) = $3500.

Decision: Assuming there are no major qualitative considerations, the manager should stick with the old product/process since it has the higher expected value, $3500 vs. $2800 for the improved product.

PART SEVEN
CASES, SAMPLE ANALYSIS, AND READINGS
■ ■ ■ ■ ■ ■
Chapter Nineteen

John Hendrick:
How I Overcame The Handicap Of A College Education*

When I graduated from Yale in 1937 with a degree in English literature, I was fortunate enough to be scooped up for a training course operated by one of our best known and most highly regarded industrial firms. At the age of 23, this represented to me a success of major proportions, and I went off happily to slay dragons. Now, at the age of 40, I can evaluate with a certain amount of perspective some effects of a college education.

The training course was great fun. Six of us trainees, Harvards, Yales and Princetons, traveled together for 18 months to a dozen different plants operated in as many states. Nice social connections always seemed to materialize, often sponsored by some friendly executive in our company. We were young, unmarried, on the loose, and the time went fast. Even some of the things we were learning about were intensely interesting. When this pleasant phase was completed, they split us up and I landed in one of the company's sales offices in Chicago — in the Estimating Department. Three years later, my earning power had increased to $125.00 per month, and I had learned to add and subtract fairly well.

It must have been about this time that I sat down and wrote myself a long thoughtful letter. I ran across it the other day in some old papers, and it saddened me to recall how this boy had searched his soul trying to bring to light what was going on and where he was headed. He seemed to be most puzzled that the whispered insinuations from the early training days indicating that he was top executive material and might be President of the Corporation before too many years did not seem to be materializing. But then, patience, Rome was not built in a day. So the big job and big pay hadn't come through yet; all would be well. And still, there were those letters from the other boys in the training course indiscreetly advising that they too had been more or less promised the Presidency before long. Where was this leading?

Had the boy taken a closer look at his draft number before he wrote this plaintive question, he would have known the answer right away. Five years later he had gone from Apprentice Seaman to Lieutenant Commander, had commanded ships in both war areas, and could definitely add. He had also met a girl and married her. While in the Service, jobs weren't often discussed; the present simply floated between the past and the future. The war over, it was time to get a job — probably the old job.

When I went to the General Office in Pittsburgh at company invitation, I was warmly received by the now Vice-President, whom I had known as a branch manger. This gentleman assured me that according to the law, nothing had changed. My job in the estimating department at Chicago was still waiting for me and best of all, my raises had been kept up while I was away in the Service for five years. I was now to get $250.00 per month, $10.00 less than they were offering new college graduates starting.
That's when I politely declined and went back to Philadelphia, to my wife and two year old girl, having seen the latter for the first time only three weeks before. And that's when I got thinking about things

---

and began to argue with the other boys who were lying around and began to develop my own thoughts. As I argued and griped and recriminated and tried to get used to the idea of going to work, it gradually dawned on me that I no longer cared about the standing or prestige of the firm I was to be attached to. I was 32 years old now, and I had the feel of responsibility and of doing something strictly on my own, and further, the wonderful satisfaction of having some of my wartime operations turn out well.

It was during this time and during these arguments that my feelings regarding college education as a handicap to personal progress evolved into a theory. I found myself explaining to anyone who would listen that when I had graduated from Yale I was being controlled by forces of prejudice, snobbery, social acceptance, rivalry, ambition, and they all stemmed from lack of information and understanding; my classmates had brought these forces to bear on me and I on them. Friends, neighbors and relatives had exerted a silent pressure on all of us unknowingly; and without realizing it, I had in those days yearned desperately to be associated with this or that giant industrial firm. There was no alternative if you were going into business.

These arguments now brought out another point which I was beginning to discern. Several boys I had grown up with or known in High School had their own businesses and seemed to be doing fine. Oh sure, there were those five years "wasted" in the Service, but that didn't account for everything because these boys had started their concerns well before the war. Where was I during the period when they were starting. Why, in the Estimating Department, of course, learning to add and subtract and waiting for the call! Was I dumb, lazy, incompetent? Well, maybe, but I couldn't see where Charlie Bianchi with his six cement mixer trucks and road building equipment was so much smarter. Anyway, he wasn't that smart in high school, and he hadn't had two nickels to rub together for capital. Now he was rapidly putting together a substantial contracting business and building himself a large house on the hill. The war? Yes, of course, but that still didn't quite explain Charlie and his growing operation and me lying around wondering — not even knowing what I wanted to do.

It all came clear one night when I was arguing and describing how Charlie had not been able to go to college, but instead after working in a restaurant had bought a second-hand dump truck. That's when it dawned on me that BECAUSE I went to college, I could NEVER buy a second-hand dump truck, not even a brand new one with someone else to drive it. When I ran across an old friend, I could not afford to explain that I was the owner of a dump truck. No, I was "with" the ABC Corporation. Not necessary to explain that they were the largest producers of this and that in the world. I was "with" them, and my friend was "with" someone just like them.

Recognition came fast then and the evidence piled up irrefutably. All of the boys I knew who had succeeded in making their own business were noncollege; none of my college mates, at least to my knowledge, had started anything. I was convinced that here lay the secret. But I was still bothered as to how Charlie Bianchi had suddenly become smart enough to make a thriving business out of nothing. During those trying weeks, I gradually became convinced that Charlie was no smarter than he had ever been. His main asset was that he was doing something, not just thinking about it or worrying about it.

I decided to kick all my pretensions in the face, lower my standard of living and make the big plunge on my own. Two weeks later, I went to work for the XYZ Corporation. This was not entirely my fault since they had offered me a job, and I had no more idea than the man in the moon what my own enterprise was to be. Also, my wife had intimated that we could not stay with her parents indefinitely.

This job lasted two years when it was brought to a halt by certain words and figures written on a pink slip. But I had learned something; I had learned what I could do. I was in better touch with industry and I knew in a general way where my interests lay. And now I had a son to consider.

While I was thinking things out, we ran out of money and I went to work for the largest corporation I had ever worked for. This pink slip did not take so long — one year. In the next six months, I had eleven job offers and turned them all down. We moved to a poor street where we rented. I drew unemployment insurance because my wife was finding things difficult with the two children and no income. We gave up entertainment and our friends, and my wife with all her loyal support came close to giving me up. During this period, I made a feeble attempt to operate a sales promotion. It had to be put to bed before it got fairly started. We were not too far from cracking up.

Then I got an idea; a brand new idea. It required working with my hands and getting them dirty for the first time. A $5,000.00 loan financed it, and the first year, working alone in new surroundings near Boston, I made $2,000.00. That was five years ago. Now we have a well-equipped shop which supports 33 people in our manufacturing type business. My income is very satisfactory, there are no debts of any description; my wife and I have been able to travel and enjoy ourselves and the tradition smashing idea is the sole source of our income.

Good you say? If you haven't had the experience, you just can't know how really good it is. And if you are the one who can't break through the social fences which have been set up by your college education, you probably never will know.

J.H. Hendrick
Wellesley, Mass.
1955

POST SCRIPT

What I wrote in 1955 seems even more true to me today. Of course, there never was any intention to prove that a college education is a "bad thing." Every kind of education is an asset, a "good thing" if integrated into the overall picture without allowing it to dominate other significant factors.

Sure, go to college by all means. Don't settle for less. But don't let your college education rule your life and exclude the excitement of enterprising your own private project.

ASSIGNMENT QUESTIONS

1. Why did Hendrick perceive his college education as a handicap to his entrepreneurial career?

2. When, in a person's life, is it easiest to start an entrepreneurial career?

3. What is the best type of preparation for an entrepreneurial career?

Chapter Twenty
The Story Of Richard West: The Making Of An Engineer*

This is a true story about a friend of mine—Richard West. I wanted to tell it because it might be helpful to those of you who manage others, and also offer a certain amount of hope to the college graduate who is trying to make the transition from the world of academia to the "real" world of profits, schedules and limited resources.

Graduation

Six years ago Richard graduated with a B.S. in engineering. He had selected a small, but relatively expensive school, because he wanted a good education. Richard was not from a wealthy family so he had to work part-time during the school year, work each summer and borrow the maximum allowable amount of money to get through school.

After graduation Richard accepted a commission in the Army to fulfill his military obligation. Fortunately, he was assigned to the engineering corps and was able to get some practical experience in his field of engineering.

First Job

After discharge from the service, Richard took an engineering trainee position with the U.S. Government. It was an interesting job, but after two years Richard realized that the opportunities in his particular specialty were limited without an advanced degree. However, he was reluctant to try to go back to school because he now had a wife, and they were expecting their first baby. Should he be content doing something less than he knew he was capable of doing? Or should he plunge further into debt and return to school for a master's degree in his specialty?

Big Decision

After considerable thought and discussion he and his wife decided that he should go back to school and get the advanced degree. Fortunately, he was able to get an assistantship and some financial aid through the federal G.I. bill. So the amount they had to borrow was not great, but they did have to "scrape along" for 18 months. Richard did well in graduate school. He received the best grades in his class, and received fine recommendations from the faculty.

The next problem was to find another job. Richard was graduating at the depth of the worst recession since the 1930's. He now had a wife and a baby and considerable debt, and there were no openings with the government agency that he had left to go to school.

Hope

Through an unusual circumstance he learned that a fine company had an opening requiring his specialty, and that it was even located in the area of the country where Richard and his wife wanted to live. He

---

*The author of this case is Dr. Theodore F. Gautschi. It is reprinted with permission from his book, <u>Management Forum</u>, Volume 3, Wellesley, MA, 1983, available from the author.

sent in his resume, visited their offices and interviewed with their key managers. Then, after what seemed an eternity, but was really only three weeks, he was offered a position doing just what he wanted to do in a location just where he wanted to do it! He quickly accepted, and started to work.

The challenges of working out new relationships and learning the business and the prospect of finally doing useful, important work were especially significant after having spent so many years in preparation. Richard was happy. He was a husband, a father and a working engineer.

Despair

But after a few months, when the newness began to wear off, Richard perceived that he wasn't being given much discretion in his work activities. In fact, his supervisor was really making all of the decisions and Richard and the other "engineers" were operating more or less at the technician level in support of the supervisor. Richard wasn't being given any projects of his own, and oftentimes when asked a question about some aspect of a design, the answer was, "You don't need to know about that." He did receive a lot of communication. However, it was all in the form of detailed directions and criticism—the supervisor was even concerned about the grammatical construction of Richard's engineering reports. But the supervisor never had time to discuss any alternatives, or even his own design approach—he was just too busy getting the work out.

There was always a large backlog of work because the supervisor and his "helpers" just couldn't grind out the designs fast enough to satisfy their customers. Also, they didn't have time to make valid estimates, so they were usually facing cost and schedule overruns as well.

Doubt

Needless to say, Richard was not happy! Was this the payoff for all of those years of study and the accumulation of a significant debt, and those years of "scraping by" while in graduate school?

It got to the point where Richard just put in his eight hours at work each day and no more. He never discussed his work with his wife, or anyone. His job was becoming something to be endured rather than to be enjoyed. He often seemed tired and listless. In a sense he probably felt that he had been "ripped off" by the system. There were times when he even daydreamed about opening a restaurant or becoming an artist.

Renewed Hope

In the midst of all this despair, Richard's supervisor left the company, and a new supervisor was brought in to take his place. That was over six months ago.

Fulfillment

The new supervisor is a complete contrast to the old one. He treats Richard and the others as professionals and now *they* are responsible for the various tasks. The new supervisor perceives his job as one of coaching Richard and the others, one of helping them to perform at a higher professional level, one of interfacing with customers to work out more realistic cost estimates and task schedules. The whole environment has changed. Now Richard is involved, he talks about his work, he often works a little late to complete some aspect that he is interested in, he is full of energy and life is exciting! He is even thinking about taking some additional courses at night school.

The future is still unknown—but now it at least offers Richard the possibility of accomplishing the things that he had hoped to do.

As for the team, schedules are now being met, their technical quality has improved and there is even some talk about applying some advanced techniques to improve their quality and productivity even further.

Retrospect

Now a few questions for *you* managers.

- Do I sometimes forget the importance and significance of each person on the team and operate in a Theory X mode like the first supervisor?

- Do I view my job basically as "a one-person operation with helpers," or do I view it as an opportunity to maximize the contributions of each member to the organizational objectives?

- Am I concerned about the individual growth of the various team members, or am I too busy with production activities?

- Do I give too much detailed direction and do I not delegate enough discretion to my subordinates?

- Are the people working with me concerned and involved—or are they simply enduring the job?

"When the administrator feels himself to be the sole driving agency, and finds himself chiefly engaged in arousing those who are apathetic and coercing those who are antagonistic, there is something vitally wrong with the administration. An executive should find himself engaged chiefly in directing the energies which create themselves naturally in all parts of the business, and in finding the proper outlet for the eager upward striving of the ranks below."   E.D. Jones, 1925

Richard West: Ten Years Later*

Some of you may remember Richard West. We've been tracking his career since 1976 when he was 29 years old. Then, Richard had just finished a tour of duty in the U.S. Army and was working in the federal government's highway department. After graduate school, he started an engineering job.

Richard has been through a lot during the last 10 years. He is now 40 and runs his own company, which employs 20 people. Although many would envy his position, getting where he is today hasn't been easy. The years have been filled with choices and trade-offs. And he still has worries, although they are quite different from the ones he had 10 years ago.

Richard's career path is an interesting one. Let's review it and learn from his choices and decisions.

A rocky start with a first job

Richard realized after a few months at his first job that he didn't have much responsibility in his work activities. (Many of you will recognize this as a Theory X or mechanistic environment.) He was unhappy, and felt that he had been ripped off by the system. He seldom worked more than eight-hour days.

In the midst of this despair, Richard's supervisor left the company and a new supervisor, who was very different from his predecessor, took over. He treated Richard and the other employees as responsible professionals. The whole work environment changed for the better, and so did Richard's attitude.

By 1980, Richard's outlook changed somewhat. Still with the same company, he was number two in terms of seniority on a staff of 15 engineers in his department. However, he believed that his percentage of the financial pie would remain fixed as long as he continued to work as an engineer with his company—unless something drastic happened. This was a frustrating situation for an ambitious 34-year-old engineer who had a master's degree and an engineering license. He also had the responsibilities and pressures of all the expenses that must be incurred to support the "good life," including sending his three children through college.

Similar to four years earlier, he began to feel as though he had been ripped off by the system. However, this time the reason was different. He was happy in his work, but he didn't think he was paid what he was worth for doing it.

Richard and I discussed his problems at this point. There were no simple solutions. As we talked, we identified the following interrelated factors:

- Richard could reduce his frustration by reducing his standard of living to be compatible with what he could earn doing what he wanted to do. But the question lingered: would that be the best thing for him?

- He could change employers in order to increase his salary. However, this had the potential of increasing his frustration because the 10% or so increase in salary would soon be absorbed.

---

*The author of this case is Dr. Theodore F. Gautschi. It is reprinted with permission from his book, <u>Management Forum</u>, Volume 3, Wellesley, MA, 1983, available from the author.

- The only way he could increase his income significantly, at least in the short run, was to do something drastic such as going into business for himself, or sharing the risks and rewards in a small but growing firm through stock options, for instance.

- A good long-term approach would be to become an outstanding technical contributor or to move on to the management ladder. Both approaches would require more education, dedication, hard work, and some luck.

Shortly after our discussion, Richard moved to a small firm that specialized in his technical area. He was soon promoted to project engineer and then to project manager, where he was responsible for a number of project engineers. He also enrolled in an MBA program at a local college. He began to realize that it was much more productive to make contributions than to criticize the system.

That was seven years ago. As I told you earlier, Richard now has his own engineering business employing 20 people. He and his partner started the business about three years ago. It broke even financially within the first nine months, which is a testimonial to Richard's management and technical capability. Currently, they have three engineering subsidiaries in their group and are planning to start a fourth soon.

It has not been easy. Both partners had to mortgage everything they had in order to get started. Fortunately, Richard completed his MBA degree, and learned a great deal about planning, organizing, leading, and controlling. Richard is trying to treat his employees the way he wanted to be treated when he worked for other companies. He gives them responsibility, listens to them, and tries to provide rewards that are related to results.

Richard still has problems, but they are different than those he had 10 years ago. Ten years ago he was worried about being able to do meaningful work and receiving adequate compensation for doing it. Now he is worried about the future direction that his company should take. He is also concerned about being able to identify and keep qualified and productive employees. He spends a great deal of time thinking about the business.

It will be interesting to talk with Richard 10 years from now. I wonder if he'll think he made the right choices, and what he would do differently if he had the chance.

Chapter Twenty-One
Vermont Tubbs, Inc*

In early August 1971, Mr. C. Baird Morgan, Jr. was reviewing his two years as president of Vermont Tubbs, Inc., a leading manufacturer of snowshoes located in Wallingford, Vermont (population 800). While sales and profit had increased, he knew he had several unresolved problems. In addition, a number of attractive opportunities for expansion and diversification had come up recently and Mr. Morgan thought he should decide which, if any, to pursue. Finally, during the past year, he had rejected an average of one inquiry a week to purchase Vermont Tubbs and he wondered if now was not the time to consider some of the more attractive feelers.

After he received his MBA from the University of Pennsylvania, Wharton School of Business Administration in 1964, Baird Morgan taught mathematics in a small private boys school near Philadelphia. After three years he found he had lost his zeal for teaching so he moved to Vermont:

> I did things backwards. I moved and then looked for a job. Since I enjoyed flying, I helped organize Northern Airways, a regional carrier located in Burlington, Vermont. I was their marketing manager for two years, but all the time I was looking for a company to buy on my own. I was single, independent, not afraid of hard work or long hours and did not want to work for someone else.

> Unfortunately, Vermont is a popular place and a lot of other guys also wanted to do what I was doing, so I had a lot of competition. Furthermore, the few people who had businesses to sell all wanted cash in full.

> I had met Harold Underwood, the president of Tubbs, shortly after I arrived. He seemed to prefer to fish and hunt rather than own a business so I tried to buy the company. Finally with luck, we agreed. I borrowed $10,000 from my father, borrowed $20,000 on a personal note, mortgaged the rest from Harold Underwood and Vermont Tubbs was mine.

Morgan owned 2/3 of the stock, Mr. Morgan, Sr. the other 1/3. The Board of Directors consisted of: Mr. Morgan, Mr. Morgan, Sr. and the Corporate Attorney.

Company History
Vermont Tubbs, Inc. was founded about 100 years ago in Norway, Maine as W.F. Tubbs, Inc. In 1928 it was bought by American Fork and Hoe, Inc. (now True Temper, Inc.) and moved to Wallingford, Vermont and the name changed. During World War II, Tubb's production of snowshoes reached over 100,000 units (pairs) per year, sold entirely to the
U.S. Government for use in Scandinavia, the Alps and the Himalayas. After the War, production fell drastically and Tubbs was spun off and sold. Thereafter, the company passed through several owners until it went bankrupt in 1958. Mr. Harold Underwood, a local gasoline station owner, was a creditor and received the business in full settlement of his claim (about $250). Mr. Underwood ran the business successfully. According to Mr. Morgan, production during the last year
of Underwood's ownership was approximately 9,000 units (pairs). (Production during 1970-1971 was

----

approximately 15,000 units and 20,000 units were projected for 1971-1972.)

Product

In one form or another, snowshoes have been used throughout the world for over 2,500 years. Snowshoes are devices worn with boots to support the wearer while walking on the surface of snow. They consist of a light, bent-wood frame laced usually with rawhide strips. The wearer's boot is attached to the center section of the snowshoe with a binding which allows the heel to be raised while walking. Expert snowshoers can walk quite fast with them. (See Exhibit 1 for additional information on snowshoes.)[2]

Market[3]

According to Mr. Morgan, snowshoeing has become phenomenally popular in recent years. He attributed this popularity to three causes:

1. Increased emphasis on physical fitness
2. The "Ecology Movement" bringing people back to nature
3. Disenchantment with Alpine (downhill) skiing

Alpine skiing and snowmobiling got people involved in outdoor winter sports. But skiing can cost anywhere from $400-$600 per person per season. At that price the average family of four or five can't afford to ski so they look around for an alternative. Snowshoeing is fun, easy to learn and inexpensive. For as little as $100[4] you can be in business for a lifetime. Being out alone in the woods and fields is a wonderful experience.

Part of our success, of course, has been simply being in the right place at the right time. The market is probably growing at a rate of 30% per year. But we know we are also doing better than that. We have recruited a terrific sales network and are putting much more effort into customer orientation. As a result we are knocking the daylights out of competition.

Competition

Mr. Morgan knew of no reliable market survey of the snowshoe industry. There were a few domestic manufacturers and several foreign competitors. Snocraft Division of Garland Industries, located in Saco, Maine, had the reputation of being the largest and best manufacturer. Tubbs, he thought, was considered to produce nearly as good a shoe and would shortly have as large a market share. In fact, Mr. Morgan felt Tubbs' shoes were now as high quality as Snocraft's shoes. Other manufacturers were smaller, generally produced a lower quality shoe, and usually used discount store outlets. He believed the total market was $2,500,000 which might be divided as follows:

---

[2] All exhibits are located at the end of the text portion of the case.

[3] For background data on recreation in the U.S., see Exhibit 2.

[4] Includes boots, jacket, cap and gloves, in addition to snowshoes.

Snocraft	20.0 %	market share	
Faber (Canada)	17.0	"	"
Tubbs	16.0	"	"
Ross Brothers (Canada)	11.0	"	"
Bastion Brothers (Canada)	11.0	"	"
Snotread (Plastic)	11.0	"	"
Swanson & Swanson (Japan)	7.0	"	"
Chestnut (Canada)	7.0	"	"
	100.0 %		

Tubbs sales in the previous two years had not been analyzed to determine where the company had picked up sales, from whom sales might have been taken, or where competitors might have taken sales from Tubbs. But Mr. Morgan thought he had a good feel for the relative volume of his major customers.

In addition to snowshoes, competitors usually had other product lines. For example, Ross Brothers produced canoes while Snocraft produced children's skis, sleds, toboggans and some hardware products. They also operated a small sawmill.

Distribution
Mr. Morgan believed improved distribution to be the most important improvement made since 1969. Mr. Underwood almost exclusively had sold directly to dealers (i.e., retail sporting goods stores and mail-order houses) primarily in New England. He had no sales force and used reps and jobbers only infrequently. When he took over, Mr. Morgan recruited an aggressive team of 11 reps outside New England while maintaining the existing network within New England. The reps in turn sold to numerous dealers and 10 jobbers depending on the geographic nature of their territory. Tubbs shoes were now sold nationwide including Alaska. He estimated that next year over 50% of his sales would be through jobbers.

Except for a few house accounts which were sold by Mr. Morgan personally, reps received commissions on direct sales to dealers in their areas. The commission was on a sliding scale from 8% to 5% depending on volume. Exhibits 3 and 4 show dealer and rep price lists and dealers' terms of sale respectively.

Pricing
In previous years, Tubbs snowshoes were priced slightly below Snocraft. For 1971-72, factory retail, price[5] had been increased in all shoes to match Snocraft model for model. At the same time, quantity discounts to dealers (see Exhibit 3) had been increased somewhat to provide a slightly larger margin for the Tubbs dealer than Snocraft. Tubbs shoes were not fair traded and no effort was made to set retail prices. Tubbs retailed shoes at the factory for about $40, while dealers usually charged between $30 and $35.

Typically, the largest and best jobbers and dealers ordered in the late spring (May and June) for delivery commencing in late summer. Smaller firms ordered on a random basis as the snow begins to fall during the late fall and early winter. Almost no orders were received during March and April; few deliveries were made between March and August. Invoices were dated December 10, which was normal practice for winter sporting goods. According to Mr. Morgan, some customers would take the dating whether or not it was offered.

Advertising
Traditionally, snowshoe manufacturers did little or no advertising. Tubbs advertised during the summer

---

[5]Factory retail prices were not suggested retail, but were set to meet Snocraft and to discourage factory sales in favor of dealer sales.

months (the buying season for dealers in <u>Sporting Goods Dealer</u>; it did not advertise in any other magazine. However, prior to 1969, Tubbs had been the subject of several feature articles in <u>Vermont Life</u>, <u>The Boston Globe</u>, and other publications.

On the other hand, Tubbs had created an 18" x 24" poster for dealers to display. It had also prepared a promotional brochure to show all models sold by Tubbs and to describe the conditions under which each should be used. Exhibit 1 shows <u>part</u> of that brochure. Mr. Morgan knew of no competitor who provided these services.

Mr. Morgan felt a booth at a national trade show was too expensive: a 10-foot booth cost $700, while manning and other expenses could cost another $1,300. Rather, he attended the shows himself and tried to contact all his important dealers, reps, and jobbers. He felt he was able to give them personalized attention and to spend more time with them this way and could emphasize the importance of ordering early to avoid shipping delays.

Brand Image

Since Tubbs was not a registered trademark, Mr. Morgan had tried to develop a brand image. He had designed a new logo and written a use and care manual to be provided with each new pair of shoes. Finally, Tubbs shoes were finished with a high-gloss urethane varnish which Morgan thought improved their appearance in comparison to competitors. Mr. Morgan felt these steps (particularly the brochure and manual) helped the customer and differentiated Tubbs products from those of competitors:

> Up until a few years ago, we sold primarily to professionals: the Vermont Fish and Game Department, the U.S. Forest Service, etc. These people had lived on snowshoes and knew how to care for them and select the correct model. The new customer hardly knows what snowshoes are, so we have to teach him. Traditionally, shoes were sold by weight: if you weigh 185 pounds buy this snowshoe; 205, buy that snowshoe. We think that is hogwash. We sell based on several factors: usage, terrain, snow conditions, degree of maneuverability. This is a complete break from the Canadian and Snocraft approach.

Tubbs produced nine models, one size each (except Michigans, which had three models). Snocraft produced eight models, five of which had multiple sizes.

Bindings

Like skis, snowshoes required bindings which were sold separately. Tubbs manufactured its own bindings from both leather and neoprene, including one of its own design. Morgan believed that neoprene was superior to leather (it did not stretch when wet) but customers preferred leather:

> We're doing ourselves a disservice selling leather, but it is what the customers demand. I think if we doubled the price of leather bindings, they would still sell.

Bindings were sold at retail for between $5 and $8.

Production

When Mr. Morgan took over, he only had a skeleton force:

> Harold Underwood laid off his workers during the summer, so I essentially had to start from scratch. I remember the exhilarating feeling when we hit 100 units per week. Now we are at 300 aiming for 400. To achieve our production goals, I keep a steady force throughout the year. Even with level production, shipments last winter fell about six weeks behind orders.

The manufacturing process for snowshoes had changed little over the centuries. A piece of wood was bent into either an oval or a racket shape then laced, usually with rawhide thongs (strips).

The bending process put such strain on the wood that the slightest imperfection caused the wood to break, and even the best wood broke occasionally for no apparent reason. Tubbs purchased only the highest quality white ash available: straight grained, absolutely no knots. Mr Morgan said, "This wood is of such high quality it is above the highest grade in the grading manuals."

Lacing traditionally used untanned cowhide called rawhide. Tubbs purchased hides from tanneries which in turn had purchased from slaughterhouses. The tanneries removed the hair and flesh, soaked them in a lime solution, then stretched and dried them. Tubbs found that only certain hides were suitable and that even in the best hide certain portions did not have adequate strength or consistency.

Mr. Morgan personally handled the purchasing of both wood and rawhide.

There were essentially three steps in this manufacturing process: woodworking, lacing and finishing. All were performed in a two-story cement-block building just across the railroad tracks from the center of Wallingford. Exhibit 5 shows photographs of the plant and both floors; Exhibit 6 shows a floor plan of the plant.

After a week or two of air drying, white ash boards (approximately 1" x 8" x 84" up to 144")[6] were planed to 13/16" thickness. They were then rip sawed into 13/16" strips and then cross-cut to the maximum usable length for each board. For example, the strip used in one of Tubbs shoes was 85" long while the next longer was 92" long. A board 89" long would be cut into strips and the strips cross-cut to 86" to fit the smaller shoe. After being cut to length, a shallow scoop or trench was cut on a band saw from what would be the toe of the shoe. This "toeing" process partially relieved the stress of bending.[7]

After toeing, strips were placed in a steam chamber for at least one hour to soften the fibers and make them more flexible. One at a time strips were removed and bent around a wooden mold (see Exhibit 7 for a photograph of this shaping mold in use). This operation took about one minute per strip. Each model shoe had a unique mold. After a few minutes on the mold, the newly-shaped frames were transferred to a rack (capacity: 28 frames) and dried slowly in a kiln @ 120° for at least 48 hours. About 10 racks could be filled per day. At the end of the drying operation the wood had a moisture content of about 7%. After drying each frame was mortis to accommodate cross bars.

Operations described thus far were performed in the lower floor of the factory. Completed frames were carried upstairs to be sanded (see Exhibit 7), drilled, riveted and assembled with their cross bars. The tails (i.e., ends) were then trimmed off square to the correct length and sanded smooth. After the logo was placed on the crossbars, the frames were placed in a bath of a wood sealer to maintain a constant moisture content.

---

[6] Hardwoods like ash are not normally sold in standardized lengths and widths. Hardwood lumber mills cut logs to get the maximum useable wood rather than standard sized boards.

[7]The ends of bearpaw models were tapered to facilitate bending and overlapping the heel sections.

Lacing

Completed frames were then passed to the lacing room where either rawhide or neoprene webs were woven onto the frame. While Tubbs and other manufacturers recommended neoprene as an excellent substitute for natural rawhide, neoprene was requested by 20% of Tubbs customers.

Hides were soaked overnight in a bath to make them pliable and then cut on a machine into laces approximately 1/4" wide. (Neoprene sheets were cut similarly.) Each day's supply of laces was cut by the plant superintendent from about 7:00-10:00 a.m.

Each frame was clamped into place on a "lacing jack".[8] The center portion was always laced first. As lacing this section required great strength, it usually, but not always, was performed by men, while women usually laced the heels and toe sections (heel and toe lacing was also performed at home by about 15 local women). Fully laced shoes were dried overnight.

Lacing with neoprene was unpopular and many lacers refused to work with it. Neoprene was not as soft and pliable as rawhide and was much harder on the hands of lacers.

Finishing

Completed frames were dipped in a high gloss urethane varnish and dried. Finished shoes were paired (since the final shape of a shoe varied somewhat depending on vagaries of how the frames cured and the lacing dried) and packaged into bundles of five units. During the off season, bundles were stored both in an adjacent railroad boxcar (which was rented from Vermont Railways for $100 per year) and a nearby warehouse. At its peak, Tubbs inventory was about 5000 units.

Shipping

Orders were filled on a first-come, first-serve basis. Commenting on the backlog of orders during the prior winter, Mr. Morgan commented:

> Because production got so far behind orders, we had to be pretty strict. But at the end of each day's production there were usually broken bundles (i.e., bundles less than five units) so we could ship some small orders ahead of other larger orders. The decisions of who gets what are tough: they don't teach you how to do that in an MBA program!

Production Organization

Tubbs employed 35 workers of whom, as stated previously, about 15 worked at home. Plant workers were evenly divided over and under 40 years old. There was no union.

The plant superintendent, Hadwin Young, was 41 years old and had 19 years' experience at Tubbs. Mr. Morgan described Mr. Young as "extremely capable," "a hard worker," and "fantastic with people." In addition to his overall plant duties, he was in charge of the lacing operations.

The downstairs foreman, or manager of wood operations, was Stanley Stewart who had just recently left the GE Rutland plant (which produces aircraft engines) after 18 years, recently as a foreman. He said he "got tired of the big-company politics."

As Mr. Morgan described his philosophy of supervision:

---

[8]See Exhibit 7.

We are all working supervisors. I don't have enough desk work to keep myself busy, so I fill in wherever I'm needed in the factory. The foremen work alongside everyone else, too.

Recruiting had always been difficult for Tubbs. Rutland, Vermont was only 10 miles away and a four-lane superhighway connected the two towns. Among others, GE, Howe Richardson Scale, True Temper, and Moore Business Forms had large plants in Rutland. Each had a union and their jobs paid significantly more than Tubbs could afford. In addition, Mr. Morgan said the wood industry was traditionally low paying. Tubbs paid $1.85-$2.75/hour for hourly work while lacers received a piecework rate:

    Bodies: rawhide: $1.00/pair; neoprene: $1.65/pair
    Toe and Heel: rawhide: $0.85/pair; neoprene: $1.10/pair

Mr. Morgan estimated that the best lacers could lace 20 pair per day of either rawhide bodies or toes and heels, while the best neoprene lacers laced 14 bodies or 16 toes and heels.

Foremen received $165/week and $145/week, respectively. Fringe benefits included vacation, normal holidays and a Blue Cross Major Medical plan. Factory hours were
7.00 a.m. - 4:00 p.m., one shift, although some personnel set their own hours according to their own requirements. Mr. Morgan had not found reliable personnel to man a second shift.

Production Control
Each morning at about 6:30 a.m., Morgan, Young and Stewart met to plan the day's production. Since some shoes were harder to shape than others and still others were harder to lace, scheduling was best performed daily, Mr. Morgan felt. Based on what orders were due to be shipped and the status of frames in process (which determined the lacing requirements) the models and quantities of shoes to be shaped were determined. According to Mr. Morgan, there were no major bottlenecks in the manufacturing operation although he felt his plant was too crowded for truly efficient operation.

Daily lacing reports[9] and bending reports were kept to compare output against that for any period desired as far back as a year. There was no formal cost accounting system in effect and individual models did not have standard costs. Commenting on this situation, Mr. Morgan stated:

I believe our average cost per unit is around $13.40 for direct costs plus about $4.00 for overhead. Since models vary in how difficult they are to bend and lace, standard costs are hard to pin down. Even more important, since our raw materials vary so much in quality, the waste factor is highly unpredictable. Finally, our raw materials have such wide cost fluctuations, standard costs are meaningless.

Only about two pair of shoes per day were considered to be "seconds": warped or discolored or otherwise imperfect units. Seconds were sold from the factory at $20 per pair.

Repairs
Broken lacings on customers' shoes were repaired by one woman at home. Prices ranged from $2.00 for a single lace to $19.50 for a completely new lacing job. Broken frames could not be repaired. Normally repairs were not accepted from September 1 to February 1, although Morgan hoped to be able to accept some the following winter.

---

[9]See Exhibit 8. The bending report was similar.

Chapter Twenty-One

Critical Problems

When asked about his critical problems, Morgan said:

> Well, right now we have only a one-week supply of rawhide. If we don't find any more, I don't know what we'll do. No one knows what makes a good hide: we don't; our suppliers don't. They get hides from dealers who collect them from slaughterhouses. By the time they get to the tanner (our supplier) their origin has long since disappeared.
>
> The problem with natural raw materials is variety. Each animal is different: where it was raised, what it was fed, its size, etc. If the hide is too thick, it is hard to use; if it is too thin or flabby, it stretches and doesn't lace well.
>
> We simply don't know where to go to get reliable, uniform hides. There are only two tanners in the country from whom we can get acceptable quality hide. Most tanners deal in large volumes and their export business takes most of their volume.
>
> Even when we can find hides to buy, we have a huge waste factor, anywhere from 25-60% because their quality varies so widely. There is virtually no waste with neoprene but there is lower demand for neoprene-laced shoes and we have problems finding lacers willing to work with it.

Finding an adequate supply of wood was also difficult. White ash was being used more and more by furniture manufacturers. Since the ash used by Tubbs was of such extremely high quality, finding a source of supply was extremely difficult. Furthermore, in two years the cost had risen from $250 to $400 per thousand board feet. Mr. Morgan said:

> The $64,000 question is how to reduce waste wood, too. Ash is the only wood we have found which will take the strain of bending and be sturdy enough to stand the punishment of use. Even with ash, we lose between 25% and 50%. We tried oak but it warps and becomes brittle and breaks. No one has been able to suggest a suitable alternative. We presently haul our waste to the dump.
>
> One of my bad dreams is synthetics. Eventually, wooden shoes will probably disappear like wooden boats. Chris Craft and Old Towne Canoe both swore they would never change. But they did. Someone is bound to come up with a synthetic. If we are not first and beat, we will get aced.
>
> We have tried alternatives: aluminum is too soft and can't stand the punishment. Laminated wood can't take the compound bending in the toes of our shoes[10]. I hate to have all our eggs in one basket but I haven't found an alternative.

Finance and Control

Accounting operations were performed by Mrs. Arlene Doty who had been hired about a year earlier. She prepared invoices, handled accounts payable, payroll, accounts receivable and general ledger posting in addition to other routine chores. (Mr. Morgan called her a "jack-of-all-trades.") She was assisted in peak periods by Mrs. Morgan who was also Mr. Morgan's secretary (Morgan was married in 1969 after he

---

[10]The toes of certain models are raised like a ski tip. The toe is bent all at once creating a compound bend: the toe and the raising.

purchased Tubbs). All checks (except payroll) were countersigned by Mr. Underwood, the former owner.[11]

An outside accountant provided semi-annual financial statements (see Exhibits 9 and 10). He reviewed operations periodically with Mr. Morgan.

Banking relations with a local bank were excellent. Tubbs had a $150,000 line of credit which was used to support the inventory built up during the spring and summer. Typically the loan was paid up by the end of the year. The loan was secured by inventory. Monthly statements of models and numbers of units on hand as well as an accounts receivable ageing were provided to the bank.

Mr. Morgan stated:

> Except for my accountant, I really work in a vacuum. I never really know whether I'm doing the right thing or not. I thought of getting someone else in here if we diversify, but my accountant pointed out he would probably want a piece of the action. I'm not willing to give up any yet.

Bristol Chemical Diversification Opportunities

In order to try to get his "eggs" out of one basket, Mr. Morgan had been looking for some time for diversification opportunities. In the spring of 1971 Mr. Bristol, president of Bristol Chemical Co., had approached him. Mr. Bristol had been forced to move away for medical reasons and wondered if Tubbs could buy out his company. Bristol was located in Burlington, Vermont, 80 miles from Wallingford, and manufactured the varnish Tubbs used on its snowshoes. It also produced the "Fall Line Ski Wax"® which was considered by many to be the best ski wax in the world. The U.S. Olympic Ski Team used it exclusively. Other products included "Leath-R-Seal"® a popular boot preservative, as well as specialized coatings for swimming pools and asphalt tennis courts. For the previous year, Bristol had sales of $101,000. Officer salaries and net profit combined were $22,000. The corporation had net assets of approximately $43,000, liabilities of approximately $41,000. Morgan thought that he could bring in Bob Penniman to manage Bristol. Penniman was a tool and die engineer and one of the country's experts in ski waxes.

To help Mr. Bristol, Tubbs had advanced $50,000 on a short-term basis in late June. While this advance held the purchased option for Tubbs and was revocable, Morgan knew he must decide soon whether to complete the purchase. He felt Bristol would broaden his product line, improve cash flow and provide needed engineering know-how. But he wondered if the time was appropriate.

Cross-Country Skis

For some time Morgan and Patrick Dule[12] had discussed the possibility of marketing cross-country skis under the Tubbs label. Dule, one of the nation's foremost skiers (a member of the U.S. Olympic Team), had selected an excellent Scandinavian ski manufacturer who did not have a U.S. distributor. Morgan felt that under the Tubbs name and with Dule's endorsement, sales of $100,000 and a gross profit of $25,000 could be reached the first year. He thought that cross-country skiing was a complementary sport to snowshoeing and attracted somewhat the same kind of customer. It was also one of the fastest growing winter sports. (For background on cross-country skiing see Exhibit 11.)

---

[11]Under the provisions of the mortgage with Mr. Underwood, two signatures were required through 1972. The mortgage contained no other unusual provisions.

[12]Disguised name.

Another Plant
In connection with his concerns about the size of his present plant, Mr. Morgan had found a building for sale in Middletown Springs, Vermont, a town about 8 miles (15 minutes drive) away. Located on a two acre plot, the building contained 6,000 sq. ft., two boilers and about $5,000 of miscellaneous woodworking equipment. It had an apartment whose rental income completely paid for land taxes. The plant was for sale for $13,700.

Snowshoe Furniture
While rummaging through some old files, Morgan had found some old plans for a line of "snowshoe furniture" Tubbs had once produced (see Exhibit 12). This furniture had been used by Admiral Byrd at the South Pole and pieces were occasionally returned to Tubbs for relacing. Morgan felt that with a simple advertising campaign in Yankee magazine, Maine Times and other similar publications, Tubbs could reintroduce this furniture for indoor or outdoor use. Later he might be able to distribute the line through his existing network of sporting goods dealers and eventually to furniture outlets. Although marketing furniture might be very different from snowshoes, Mr. Morgan felt the line might help reduce waste by using shorter strips and perhaps some sticks broken in the shaping step of making snowshoes. Also, presumably furniture would improve cash flow.

Plastic Snowshoes
Finally, Mr. Morgan wondered if he should pursue the question of plastic snowshoes:

> One of the advantages of living in Vermont is Yankee ingenuity. I have a friend who has studied snowshoes carefully and has promised to design a die for me to produce plastic frames. It will cost $15,000. I asked my jobbers and dealers about the idea of a plastic shoe to retail for about $20 and they were enthusiastic. But when I asked how many they would order, they only came up to 2,000 shoes.

Summarizing his feelings, Mr. Morgan said:

> Maybe I shouldn't worry: We're making money and I haven't gotten stuck yet. But I still don't know where next week's hides will come from and as I said before, I hate to have all our eggs in one basket.

> A friend came in one day last week scouting for a conglomerate. He told me, "Gee, Baird, we're paying 18-24 times earnings. You should consider coming along." Still, I told him I wasn't ready to sell out. My father did that and grew awfully unhappy working for a conglomerate.

Exhibit 1
VERMONT TUBBS, INC.

S N O W S H O E S — for fun and health

Snowshoes have been used in some form for 2500 years or more, their origin lost in antiquity. There is evidence of a primitive form being used in Asia and Northern Europe and Arctic regions. But only in North America has the snowshoe survived in time. The North American Indians through necessity developed this means of locomotion to such a degree that even today modern technology would be hard put to improve the design. The forest Indians found the short broad shoe best for woods and brush because of easier maneuverability and the plains Indians found the long narrower shoe best for hunting and tracking the buffalo. Minor variations in these basic designs evolved through the years and this fine heritage of craftsmanship has left us many choices. So your choice of snowshoes will be a matter of personal preference.

SELECTING SNOWSHOES

In selecting the pair of snowshoes which is "right" for you, you should take into consideration several factors:
1. Terrain—flat, open, trails, brush
2. Snow conditions—light powder, deep, crusty
3. Usage—hunting, back packing, forestry, general recreation
4. Weight and height
5. Experience

Rawhide or Neoprene

Rawhide is still a favorite among sportsmen and recreational snowshoers. With the new finish that Tubbs had developed, the rawhide shoe is more abrasion resistant and consequently less prone to wear and sagging. The distinctive Tubbs overlay pattern on the toe and heel, give a better all around purchase than the traditional fine weave style or the neoprene.

Neoprene is a synthetic material which represents the first material change in the manufacture of snowshoes in several hundred years. While not as aesthetically appealing as rawhide, neoprene resists snow build-up and consequently is comparatively lighter than rawhide under wet snow conditions. Neoprene is impervious to gasoline, oil, rodents and will generally give better wear. Professional woodsmen prefer the neoprene shoe because of its durability and low maintenance.

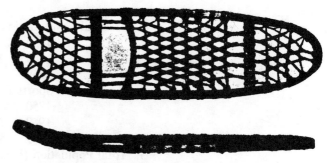

Green Mountain Bear Paw—10 x 36

This shoe, designed by Tubbs, is the most versatile shoe on the market. Its unique design makes it easy for the beginner and is a favorite of the Vermont Fish & Game Department. It is designed for New England snow conditions and is best in the woods and the brush. Very popular with hunters, it will support weights up to 200 lbs.

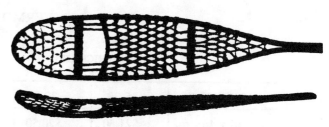

Cross Country—10 x 46

Basically this is the same design as the Green Mountain Bear Paw with the addition of a tail. The tail offers less drag than the Bear Paw models and acts as a stabilizer, much like a fin on a boat. The Cross Country is easy to walk on and is well suited to all conditions. It is popular with professional and recreational snowshoers and will support up to 225 lbs.

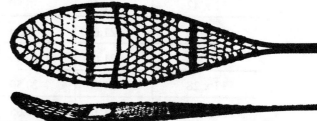

Michigan

The Michigan type is an excellent all-purpose snowshoe. Developed by the Indians, the Michigan was used for both back-packing and hunting. It supports weight better than any other model but is more difficult to master for the beginner. It is suggested for all snow conditions and for all terrain, save for thick brush.
12x48 is usually used by women
13x48 is for men weighing between 140-200
14x48 is for taller men or those weighing over 200

Exhibit 2
VERMONT TUBBS, INC.
Selected Data on Recreation in the U.S. 1950-1969

1. Personal Consumption Expenditure for Recreation
   1950 $11.1   Billion
   1960   18.3   Billion
   1969   36.3   Billion
2. Purchases of Sports Equipment (boats, aircraft, etc.)
   1950 $ 869   Million
   1960   2106   Million
   1969   4219   Million
3. Total Population (incl. Armed Forces abroad)
   1950 152.3   Million
   1960 180.7   Million
   1969 202.6   Million

Source: Statistical Abstract of the U.S., 1971, p. 200, 308, 5 Exhibit 3

Exhibit 3
VERMONT TUBBS, INC.
PRICE LIST

SNOWSHOES	DEALER PRICE LIST EFFECTIVE APRIL 1, 1971			JOBBER PRICE LIST	FACTORY RETAIL PRICE[13]
	5-29	30-99	100		
10 x 46	$21.60	$20.50	$18.40	$18.40	$40.00
12 x 48	21.60	20.50	18.40	18.40	40.00
13 x 48	21.60	20.50	18.40	18.40	40.00
14 x 48	22.25	21.15	18.60	18.60	41.00
12 x 42	21.60	20.50	18.40	18.40	40.00
10 x 36	21.60	20.50	18.40	18.40	40.00
13 x 33	21.60	20.50	18.40	18.40	40.00
13 x 28	21.60	20.50	18.40	18.40	40.00
14 x 25*	211.10	20.05	18.00	18.00	37.00
10 x 56	23.40	22.20	19.00	19.00	43.50
8 x 40	21.60	20.50	18.00	18.00	40.00

*Not available in neoprene

[13]Shown for illustrative purposes only. Factory retail prices are not suggested retail prices. Individual dealers set their own prices. (See text).

Exhibit 3 (Cont.)
VERMONT TUBBS, INC.
PRICE LIST: BINDINGS

PRICE BINDINGS	DEALER PRICE LIST EFFECTIVE APRIL 1, 1971		JOBBER PRICE	FACTORY RETAIL	LIST
	1-50	Over 50			
H	$3.60	$3.25	$3.10		$5.95
Howe	5.70	5.10	5.00		7.95
A Mens	3.00	2.50	2.40		4.95
A Women	3.00	2.50	2.40		4.95
Tubbs	5.70	5.10	4.40		7.95

Varnish $1.15 Minimum 1 Dozen Pints $1.00 Pint

Exhibit 4
VERMONT TUBBS
1971-1972 PROGRAM

TERMS

1% 10 Days-Interest at the rate of 1 1/2% monthly, or 18% per year, will be charged on Past Due accounts.

DATING

Winter dating is available for shipment after April 1, 1971 with billing at 1971-72 prices. Terms are 1% December 10, 1971, subject to credit standing. ANTICIPATION is 1% per month.

WARRANTY

VERMONT TUBBS products are guaranteed against defects in material and/or workmanship for one year from date of shipment.

FREIGHT

F.O.B.   Wallingford, Vermont

DEALER PRICE

The initial order establishes the quantity discount for the year.

REPAIRS

Repair service will be provided throughout the year. Estimate sheets are available upon request.

RETURN OF MERCHANDISE

No merchandise returns will be accepted without prior written authorization. A 10% handling charge will be made on all unauthorized returns. A handling charge equal to 10% of the purchase price will be made where the original order was filled correctly and arrived in good condition.

STANDARD PACKS

Snowshoes are packaged throughout the off season in units of five (5). While any quantity of any style of snowshoes is available, initial orders made in units of 5 can be shipped more expeditiously.

Exhibit 5
VERMONT TUBBS, INC.

Recent photograph
of plant

Upstairs:
Lacing and Inventory

Downstairs:
Woodworking
operations

Exhibit 6
VERMONT TUBBS, INC.

Approximate dimensions
of building: 25' X 50'

Floorplan Downstairs

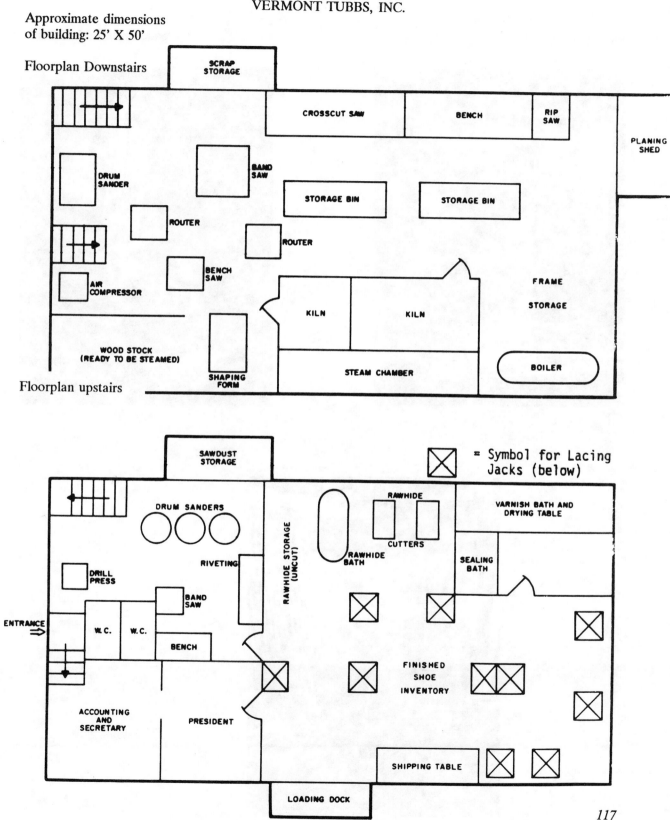

Floorplan upstairs

Exhibit 7
VERMONT TUBBS, INC.

Shaping mold in use

Sanding unfinished frame

Lacing jack in use

Exhibit 8
VERMONT TUBBS, INC.
LACING FOR WEEK ENDING January 30, 1971

BODIES

NAME	COX	NESBITT	REOIMHBALD	LERZO	PERRY	TARBELL	DAY	SENECAL	DAILY TOTALS	CUMULATIVE
MON	14 10x36 5 14x48 3 12x42	9½ 10x36 1 12x48 2½ 10x46	—	12 pr.	14 10x36	16 10x46	8 10x56	12 10x46	105	105
TUES	6 13x28 14 10x36	6 10x46 8 12x48	—	3½ 13x32 2 13x48 4½ 10x46	14½ 10x36	5 10x56 10 10x26	10½ 12x42 2 10x56	—	88½	193½
WED	4 13x28 17 10x46	12½ 13x33 2½ 10x46	—	1 13x33 4 10x36	13½ 10x46	14½ 10x46	—	12 10x36	81	274½
THURS	3 10x46 9 13x53 10 8x40	11 13x33	9½ 10x56	9 10x36	14 12x42	6 10x46	8 10x56	—	79	349½
FRI	3 8x40 19 10x46	—	1 10x56 8½ 12x42	—	—	16 10x46	7½ 10x56	3 10x36 5 13x33 5 12x42	69½	419
SAT	12 10x46	15½ 10x36 6 13x33	—	—	—	9 10x46	—	—	42½	461
TOTAL										

Exhibit 8 (cont.)
VERMONT TUBBS, INC.

LACING FOR
WEEK ENDING January 30, 1971

TOE & HEEL

NAME	PERRON	REYNOLDS	KENNEDY E.	JOHNSON	BROWN	BULLOCK	WARREN	BAKER	STEWART	KENNEDY D.		
MON	14½ 10x46 / 5½ 14x48	10 10X46	—	11 10x36	9½ 10x36	9 13x28 / 1 10x56	12 12x48 / 4½ 10x36	3½ 10x56 / 6½ 10x46 / 1 13x48	—	SENECAL 12 10x46	106	106
TUES	—	10 10x46	8½ 10x36	10½ 10x36	8½ 10x36	10 10x56	5½ 8x40 / 2 10x56 / 9 12x42	5 10x46 / 2 13x48 / 3½ 12x42	—	12 10x46	76	182
WED	6½ 10x40 / 1 10x36 / 10½ 12x42	10 10x46	10 10x36	10½ 10x36	8½ 10x36	—	1½ 8x4 / 7 10x46 / 8 12x46	—	—	2 10x46 / 1 10x56 / 3½ 13x33	92	274
THURS	18 10x46	10 10x36	10 10x36	10 10x36	8 10x36	10 10x56	4 10x46 / 4 14x48 / 8½ 13x33	1 13x33 / 4 10x36	—	—	87½	361
FRI	10 12x42 / 19 10x46	—		10½ 13x33	½ 10x36 / 8½ 13x33	10 10x56	7½ 10x56	—	3 10x36 / 5 13x33 / 5 13x42	2½ 13x33	72½	433½
SAT	—	10 10x46	—	—	—	—	—	5 10x56 / 3 12x48 / ½ 12x42	1½ 10x46 / 1½ 13x33 / 1 12x48	—	23½	457
TOTAL												

Exhibit 9

VERMONT TUBBS, INC.

Comparative Balance Sheets 6/30/70, 6/30/71

Assets	1970	1971
Current Assets		
Cash	$ 3,945.69	$ 16,058.28
Accounts Receivable (net)	5,270.34	24,576.64
Inventory	55,869.75	64,369.00
Advance to Bristol Chemical	-0-	50,000.00
Other	349.32	69.86
Total Current Assets	65,435.10	155,073.78
Fixed Assets (net)		
Land	3,000.00	3,000.00
Building & Improvements	50,547.32	49,129.89
Machinery & Equipment	39,553.62	34,303.22
Vehicle	1,833.33	2,907.61
Office Equipment	-0-	187.03
Total Fixed Assets	94,934.27	89,527.75
Other Assets (incl. Goodwill $1,000)	1,211.52	1,159.72
TOTAL ASSETS	$161,580.89	$245,761.25
Liabilities and Capital		
Current Liabilities		
Accounts Payable	$ 6,710.50	$ 13,795.10
Accrued Taxes	2,592.67	2,396.53
Accrued Wages	-0-	1,013.85
Notes Payable: Bank	10,000.00	50,000.00
Notes Payable: H. Underwood (current Portion)	5,572.09	6,430.50
Total Current Liabilities	24,875.26	73,635.98
Long Term Liabilities		
Due Officers & Stockholders	3,395.00	7,394.75
Notes Payable: C.B. Morgan, Sr.	2,000.00	15,000.00
Notes Payable: H. Underwood, Inc.	96,582.77	89,727.37
Total Long Term Liabilities	101,977.77	112,122.12
TOTAL LIABILITIES	126,853.03	185,758.10
Capital		
Capital Stock	30,000.00	30,000.00
Retained Earnings	4,727.86	30,003.15
Total Capital	34,727.86	60,003.15
TOTAL LIABILITIES & CAPITAL	$161,580.89	$245,761.25

Exhibit 10

VERMONT TUBBS, INC.

Comparative Income Statements F/Y 1970, 1971

	1970	1971
Sales:		
Snowshoes	$180,436.22	$283,932.13
Bindings	27,669.44	52,912.75
Repairs	1,734.23	2,276.47
Sawdust & Supplies	-0-	2,304.58
Deduct: returns & allowances	(1,378.49)	(3,481.18)
Net Sales	208,461.40	337,994.75
Cost of Sales		
Inventory 7/1/70	37,229.62	55,869.75
Add: Lumber	31,499.40	26,293.02
Rawhide, leather, bindings, neoprene	61,531.24	107,099.72
Operating Supplies	10,832.24	14,067.58
Labor	59,691.79	85,767.40
Depreciation	7,728.23	9,321.12
Taxes & Licenses	5,414.83	7,162.57
Heat & Lights	4,464.43	5,196.58
Freight (in)	1,930.26	2,676.03
Other (incl. repairs)	5,354.07	2,435.03
Deduct: Inventory 6/30/71	(55,869.75)	(64,369.00)
Total Cost of Sales	169,806.36	251,519.80
Gross Profit	38,655.04	86,424.95
General and Administrative		
Salary: Officer	3,600.00	10,000.00
Salary: Office	3,666.50	5,545.22
Commission	6,293.59	9,277.03
Travel & Promotion	1,741.46	1,033.25
Telephone	1,009.31	2,320.78
Interest	8,488.07	10,407.67
Advertising	2,397.76	1,821.59
Office Expense	1,465.73	2,936.00
Repairs	-0-	1,606.62
Legal & Audit	2,551.26	1,687.51
Insurance	3,537.18	5,057.09
Bad Debts	-0-	3,653.60
Other	447.07	2,300.84
Total G&A	35,197.93	57,647.20
Profit on Operations	3,457.11	28,777.75
Other Income (cash discounts)	1,270.75	1,225.40
NET PROFIT	$ 4,727.86	$ 30,003.15

Exhibit 11
VERMONT TUBBS, INC.
Wall Street Journal: 4/1/71 on Cross-Country Skiing

"NATURE WALK ON SKIS: 'TOURING' ENTHUSIASTS SPURN DOWNHILL RACING"
by David McLean

SUGARBUSH VALLEY, Vt. — So here you are at one of the country's swingingest ski areas, and what's more fun than clamping on your $155 Head 360s, riding the lift to the top of the slope and schussing downhill at seventy-seven miles an hour like the real ace you are?

Well, to a growing number of folks, there is something more fun. That's clamping on your $37.50 Bonna skis, walking across the road and trudging at three miles an hour over the snow-blanketed golf course at the foot of the hill like the real plodder you are.

Not for you the fancy gear, the downhill thrills and the broken legs in casts. you pass up all that because you're in on the newest thing in skiing, a vigorously noncompetitive form of it called ski touring. It caught on in this country last year-partly, its exponents say, because of the crowds and commercialism of downhill, or alpine, skiing. It uses the same kind of equipment as cross-country skiing, but that form of skiing is organized, and competitive.

"Suddenly everyone is tuned in to the newest thing," says Ski magazine. Resorts around the country have marked off touring areas and now are renting touring gear. In Stowe, Vt., the famous Trapp family offers a touring area around Mount Mansfield. Here in Sugarbush, the Sugarbush Inn has access to 45 miles of touring trails. In the West, touring now is established at such well-known Colorado areas as Steamboat Springs, Vail, and Snowmass.

MODESTY IN ALL THINGS

Fans say there's a lot to be said for ski touring. For one thing, it's inexpensive. You don't need costly arctic wear-blue jeans and a sweater or two will do- because ski touring is hard work that generates a lot of body heat. You don't need skis of space-age materials with sophisticated bindings because you are going slow and rarely risk a serious fall. You don't need a $10 lift ticket because most trails are free.

Touring boots are more like shoes. They don't have to be as sturdy as downhill boots, designed to immobilize the ankle in a viselike grip. A simple toe clamp binds the touring boot to the ski, leaving the heel free. On downhill skis, a more costly and complex heel-and-toe binding is used.

The touring techniques probably is the oldest in skiing. It's a sort of sliding walk on long, narrow wooden skis that cut easily through fresh snow. You plant a touring pole into the snow and shift your weight to the foot opposite to slide forward. The "feel" for this step doesn't come naturally to most people, even to experienced downhill skiers, but it doesn't take much time to learn.

To climb hills about all the technique a novice need master is the simple herringbone walk (ski tips pointed outward, ski edges dug in) or a sidestep.

Exhibit 11 (cont.)

VERMONT TUBBS, INC.

Wall Street Journal: 4/7/71 on Cross-Country Skiing (cont.)

DOWNHILL TECHNIQUE

But when a beginning ski tourist does take a downhill trail, he faces the same problem as an alpine tyro: how to stop. Until you've developed your balance, you simply stop by falling or preferable, by sitting down. Instructors advise novices to try to slow down by grabbing low-hanging tree branches or bushes.

Ski touring enthusiasts liken the activity to other quiet pursuits like ice fishing, hiking and bird watching. "It has limitless possibilities," says Janet Nelson, a ski writer who has taken up touring. "You see the birds and the trees, and they're a greater pleasure than you realized. You see things that you don't see in summer hiking. I think I like the nature and the quiet best."

"It's not a hassle," says Suzanne Meister, a novice ski tourist, after her first afternoon of touring here at Sugarbush. "It's a joy to be outside. It's not horribly dangerous. I buy the idea that you can have fun as a beginner, and you can't in alpine skiing."

SALES BOOM

Sporting goods makers, distributors and dealers have observed the sharp surge of interest in touring. G.H. Bass & Co., a shoe manufacturer in Wilton, Maine, imported a "couple of hundred" cross-country skis in the winter of 1969-70 for distribution around the country. In the winter just ended, Bass reports, orders ran into the thousands. "It's fantastic," a spokesman says. "We couldn't keep up with the demand."

Harry Vallin, owner of Scandinavian Ski Shops in New York, expects to have sold about a thousand pairs of touring skis by the end of the current season, double his seasonal sales two years ago.

"I think it will be as popular or more popular than alpine skiing at some point," says Richard Falcone, president of Garcia Ski & Tennis Corp., Teaneck, N.J. Mr. Falcone says his company is in the "throes of negotiating" the import of touring equipment to add to its line of alpine ski gear.

Reprinted by permission of The Wall Street Journal.

Exhibit 12
VERMONT TUBBS, INC.
Proposed Line Of Snowshoe Furniture

Chapter Twenty-Two
The Passkey Restaurant and Lounge

Student Assignment

The Passkey case covers issues spanning a number of course areas including marketing, accounting, production operations, entrepreneurship, small business management, finance, and business policy. Read the case and use the information provided in this book to develop an analysis and presentation. Your assignment questions are:

1. What are the prospects for The Passkey?
2. What elements will determine how successful The Passkey will be?
3. What would you advise Mr. Aquilano to do now?

■ ■ ■ ■ ■ ■

The Passkey Restaurant and Lounge

In early June, 1973, Mr. David Aquilano was reviewing the results of his first year in business. He had just received his financial statements from his accountant and the results were not encouraging (see Exhibits 1 and 2).

Mr. Aquilano wasn't sure what he should do now. The venture's original concept did not appear to be working as originally planned by him. He had several alternatives to consider if he wished to remain in business. However, he couldn't help wondering if he shouldn't also start thinking about selling his business and minimizing his losses.

David Aquilano: Background

David Aquilano was born in 1919 in San Jose, California of Mexican-American parentage. His family later moved to East Los Angeles where he grew up during the Depression. David had four other brothers and two sisters. Since he was the eldest child, he was expected to help provide support for the family. Mr. Aquilano commented on these early years to the case writer.

> "In 1933, I managed to graduate from junior high school. I entered high school later that year, but dropped out before the school year was over. The main reason I left was that I couldn't get into a college preparatory course. The particular high school was, at the time, about 85% Negro, 6% Mexican-American, 4% other minorities, and the balance were Anglos. The school felt that 95% of all graduates would end up in the trades and industry, so we were limited to the school's industrial program. I had only one course that could be called 'academic,' namely, English.

In 1934, I joined the Conservation Corps Camp and was sent to a camp in California. I was discharged from the C.C. Camp in 1935 to attend school. While in the C.C. Camp, I had investigated the possibility of entering a private school where I could take a college preparatory course. I was finally accepted by St. Augustine High School on a scholarship. I worked nights to pay for my books and help support my family.

In 1937, I graduated in the upper 10% of my class and was granted a scholarship by Loyola University. I majored in sociology and personnel administration, and I graduated with honors in 1941.

After serving in World War II, David Aquilano worked for a number of large companies, mainly in personnel administration (see Exhibit 3 for his resume). However, he decided to make the break with "big industry" in 1969 and start his own company in the Los Angeles area. Commenting on this experience, Mr. Aquilano said,

> "I joined three graduate engineers and a marketing specialist in the formation of a small electronics firm. The company got off to a fairly good start; however, two of the engineers could not afford to tighten their belts and embezzled company funds.

> The company, although undercapitalized, managed to survive and earn a modest profit. My interest was purchased in 1971. However, I retained possession of several items of electronic equipment which I now lease."

The Decision to Enter the Restaurant Business

During the Fall of 1971, Mr. Aquilano and his wife, Janet, decided to enter the restaurant business. Their motivation for this decision came mainly from the experience of a former friend and associate with two new restaurants that were organized around a new concept. The restaurants, called the "Giveaways," combined fast food sales of pizzas and hamburgers with sales of stereo cartridge tapes and records, aimed at the youth market. The key promotion under this concept was to offer a free small pizza or hamburger when any 8-track cartridge or LP album was purchased.

Both Giveaways Restaurants were quite successful, and reinforced by their success, Mr. Aquilano began searching throughout the South and Southwest for possible sites.

> "I realized that running a restaurant wasn't an easy business. But I had some experience during my high school and college years. I did everything from washing dishes to fry cook. And I felt I had the administrative experience to run a successful operation. We had $10,000 to invest, and I felt I could get a loan to cover other start-up costs, working capital, as well as some reserve or contingency funds."

The Selection of the Passkey Restaurant and Lounge

> "We were looking for a relatively small city with a large college population. The rationale for this kind of location was that rent and advertising costs would be considerably cheaper than in a large metropolitan area. Also, competition from other discount tape and record outlets would be less severe. However, the task of finding a restaurant that had all of the favorable aspects that we were seeking (yet where profits were marginal due to poor management) was astronomical. Various locations in California, Arizona, Nevada, Oklahoma, Texas, and Louisiana were evaluated and rejected.

Finally, in early 1972, Mr. and Mrs. Aquilano found an ongoing restaurant located in a small city in Texas (population 70,000). The restaurant, called The Passkey, met their requirements of regional economic stability, potential growth, proximity to a university with over 10,000 students, and reasonably inexpensive media for advertising. The restaurant also was located near a new commercial complex. Exhibit 4 shows a map of the area.

EXHIBIT 1
THE PASSKEY
PROFIT AND LOSS STATEMENT
May 31, 1973
(unaudited)

INCOME:		
Sales	145379.14	
Vending Machine Income	2628.53	
Interest	111.25	
Misc. Income	80.86	148199.78
COST OF SALES:		
Merchandise	76351.79	
Materials-Supplies	5059.23	
Outside Labor	2504.88	83915.90
		64283.99
Closing Inventory		9307.13
Gross Profit		73591.01
EXPENSES:		
Salaries*	33876.61	
Taxes & Licenses	1461.67	
Auto Expenses	2070.63	
Utilities	4507.56	
Advertising & Promotion	2744.32	
Linens	796.65	
Maintenance & Repairs	3380.15	
Insurance	2534.73	
Freight	146.81	
Rent	15724.50	
Interest	1245.11	
Legal & Accounting	1242.00	
Payroll Taxes	2356.93	
Relocation Expenses	3412.10	
Consulting Fees	200.00	
Subscriptions & Dues	104.00	
Travel Expenses	608.93	
Appraisal Cost	400.00	
Office Expenses	1191.59	
Depreciation	894.47	78898.76
Net Profit (Loss)		(5307.75)

Source: company records.

*Casewriter's note: These are actually all wages and salaries except
Mr. Aquilano's salary.

EXHIBIT 2
THE PASSKEY
BALANCE SHEET
Y/E May 31, 1973
(unaudited)

ASSETS

Cash in Bank	3318.45	
Petty Cash	640.00	
Employee's Loans	146.70	
Inventory	9307.13	
Prepaid Rent	2887.50	
Donation Reserve	231.00	16530.78

FIXED ASSETS

Furniture & Equipment		8595.08	
Leasehold Improvements	7461.90		
Depreciation Reserve	(677.83)	6784.07	15379.15

OTHER ASSETS

Organization Expenses	900.00		
Amortization Depreciation	(216.64)	683.36	
Utility Deposits		435.00	1118.36
			33028.29

LIABILITIES

CURRENT LIABILITIES

Payroll Taxes	429.81	
Sales Tax	671.06	
Accounts Payable	3541.58	4642.45

LONG-TERM LIABILITIES

Notes Payable	17829.11	
Loan Payable—Mr. & Mrs. Aquilano	5864.48	23693.59

Capital Stock	10000.00	
Net Income-(Loss)	(5307.75)	
Stockholder's Equity		4692.25
		33028.29

Source: company records.

EXHIBIT 3
THE PASSKEY
RESUME OF DAVID AQUILANO
Eugene Drive
Sherman Oaks, California 91366
Telephone: (213) 996-XXXX

Experience:

Fifteen years of business experience at the director and manager level in medium size and large corporations. Have actively participated in making those decisions and plans necessary to obtain optimum profits and growth of the company. Have been directly responsible for the administration of industrial Relations, Personnel Administration, Advertising, Recruitment, Wage and Salary, Corporate Insurance, Group Medical, Group Life, Employee Relations, Manpower Training, Management Development, Policy and Procedures, Organizational Structure, Manpower Forecasts, Labor Relations, Plant Protection, Industrial Security. In addition, have had direct line experience in Systems Training, Digital Computer Technology (IBM) and man-machine relationships. This experience has been obtained from 1951 to 1969 with the following companies:

Hughes Aircraft Company
Daniel, Mann, Johnson and Mendenhall
The Rand Corporation
System Development Corporation
Guidance Technology, Inc.

Education:

Loyola University
Administration and Sociology
Bachelor of Arts Degree (Cum Laude) 1941
Loyola University Graduate School (full-time)
UCLA Graduate School (full-time) 1950-1951

Military
Service:

United States Army, Lieutenant 1943-1946

Personal:

Excellent health, athletic
Married, three children.

In addition, the brick building was less than three years old, air conditioned, had modern fixtures and equipment, and a lovely paneled interior. The total floor area was in excess of 4,000 square feet. Ample parking in front and along the side of the structure was available.

Opened in 1969, the restaurant had a different name and focus during its first two years of operation. Called "The Sparrow Lounge," it focused on a bar trade and was, according to the owner, moderately successful. Exhibit 5 provides a summary of operations that the owner gave to Mr. Aquilano.

During 1971, the owner, Mr. Johnson, decided to change the operation's name to The Passkey, "to give it a more clubby atmosphere because several college fraternities were beginning to frequent the lounge regularly."

Mr. Johnson decided to sell or lease The Passkey in early 1972. He was a lawyer and had several other businesses in addition to The Passkey. He felt the latter operation was simply not worth the time he was putting into it. He also had another business venture which looked more attractive to him.

Mr. Aquilano felt the restaurant had operated on a marginal basis due to poor management. While sales exceeded $122,000, he believed the gross profits had not kept in line with overall national standards or percentages. However, David Aquilano believed The Passkey could be more than a marginal operation. An income statement was generated by a consultant based upon what Mr. Aquilano felt were realistic assumptions about The Passkey's future potential (see Exhibit 6).

Mr. Johnson was asking $200,000 for the property, but Mr. Aquilano thought Johnson would take $180,000. The Aquilanos felt they should not risk purchasing the property outright because this was their first venture in the restaurant business and the possibility of staying in business was uncertain. Also, they felt that buying the building at that point would saddle them too heavily in terms of an upfront cash investment. Finally, they did not believe the restaurant's existing floor plan would best suit their purposes. The customer area was completely open and, as Mr. Aquilano later described, "like the inside of a barn or a large, undivided cafeteria room. It simply wasn't providing a feeling of an informal, intimate atmosphere. Consequently, we knew we would have to make improvements by dividing up the space." (Exhibit 7 shows the layout of The Passkey after these leasehold improvements were made.)

The Aquilanos preferred to lease The Passkey. However, they were concerned about losing control of the site should the business become quite successful. Consequently, they sought and obtained a fifteen year net lease from Mr. Johnson. The rent of $1335 per month was steep now, but would be very reasonable in later years given projected rates of inflation. Also, the Aquilanos felt the location was simply worth it to them and represented an excellent place to test the new concept which they believed would lift the restaurant's overall return beyond its marginal performance of the past three years.

Mr. Aquilano divided his "turnaround" program into three phases:

Phase I: The immediate objective is to reorganize the work force, establish workable standards, control costs, investigate where the dollars from the sales are going, improve the quality of the food, and communicate the change of ownership and improvements to the public.

Phase II: Continue the evaluation of the two Giveaway Restaurants which were placed in operation less than 18 months ago. One was located in Colorado Springs and the second in Austin, Texas. Both restaurants were doing extremely well, as far as Mr. Aquilano knew.

Mr. Aquilano noted:

"What makes the two establishments unique is not their physical structure (one is 2700 sq. ft., the other in Austin is 3,000 sq- ft., both in fairly modern structures - former Lum's buildings), but their method of merchandising their food (pizzas, hamburgers, etc.) and beverages. They continuously run promotional sales, informing the public that in the event a pizza or hamburger is purchased, they may get up to a dollar discount on stereo cartridges (tapes) or records.

The prime factor is the combination of selling a total product that appeals to the fastest growing economic group in America."

Phase III: Start and complete lease improvements. Set up record shop. Start advertising and sales campaign. See projections for twelve month operation.

First Year Operations

During the early Spring of 1972, Mr. Aquilano obtained the long-term loan he needed and the deal with Mr. Johnson was completed.

The restaurant operated seven days a week, 11:00 a.m. until 1:00 a.m., but didn't open until 4:00 p.m. on Sundays.

As noted in the preceding plan, the Aquilanos decided to delay introducing the music/pop art side of the business until several serious problems were solved with the operation of the restaurant, and they teamed more about the food/drink side of the business.

The restaurant continued to sell sandwiches, pizzas, hamburgers, etc. Mr. Aquilano stated his average "ticket" or transaction was about $1.25 for food and $1.00 for drinks.

The currently popular music, as well as the decor, made for an informal atmosphere but one which was nice enough to take a date. In fact, The Passkey was one of the few places in town to go on a "nice but inexpensive" date.

Near the bar, the Aquilanos kept four "foosball" machines (similar to mechanical hand hockey games) which they inherited from the former owners. Many younger people (16-20 years of age) came in especially to play foosball. "We always had to be careful about serving liquor to the younger kids, but they were usually well behaved, ordered sodas and food, and played the games." A large billboard type menu was hung overhead, and anyone wishing food would simply have his order "called in" to the kitchen. This made it unnecessary to have waitresses.

The Aquilanos felt there was no place quite like their restaurant in town. The city had its share of Burger Kings and McDonalds, as well as a few middle-priced restaurants from place to place. These, however, did not have a bar or music, so it was not felt that they were actually in direct competition. One small block intersection did exist, however, where many college students went after classes. These

EXHIBIT 4
THE PASSKEY
MAP OF GENERAL LOCATION

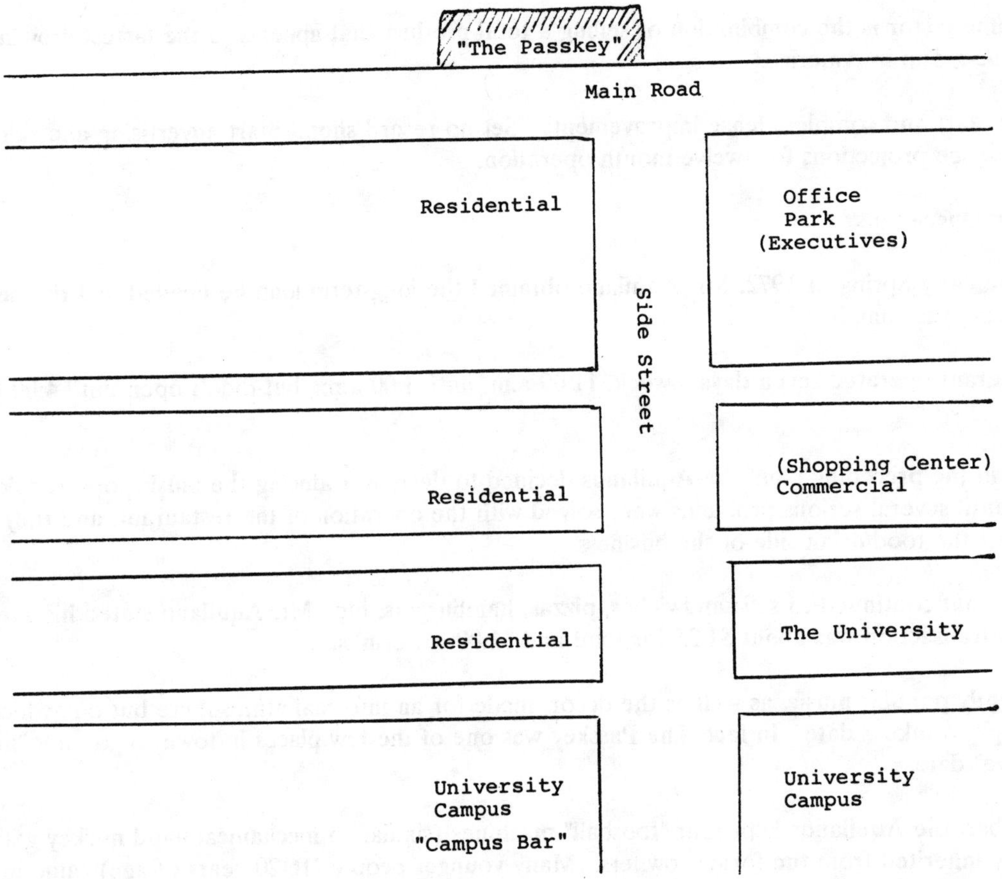

"The Passkey"

Main Road

Residential

Office
Park
(Executives)

Side Street

Residential

(Shopping Center)
Commercial

Residential

The University

University
Campus

"Campus Bar"

University
Campus

EXHIBIT 5
THE PASSKEY
THE SPARROW
STATEMENT OF PROFIT AND LOSS
For Year Ended December 31, 1970

	Food	Beer	Liquor	Franchise	Total
Sales	58,798.13	51,929.40	11,827.37	130.00	122,684.90
Cost of Sales (Schedule 1)	44,360.64	35,773.43	7,082.13	65.00	87,281.21
Gross Profit	14,437.38	16,155.97	4,745.24	65.00	35,403.69
Percent	24.55	31.11	40.10	50.00	28.85

Operating Expenses (Schedule 2)					43,418.81
Net Loss from Operations					(8,015.12)

Other Income:	Machine	6,793.05			
	Interest	68.59			
	Cover Charges	606.00	7,467.64		
Other Expense:	Interest	3,319.43			
	Cash Short	309.78	3,629.21		3,838.43
Net (Loss)					(4,176.69)

Prepared without audit

EXHIBIT 5 (Continued)
THE PASSKEY
Schedule #1
THE SPARROW
SCHEDULE OF COST OF SALES
For Year Ended December 31, 1970

	Food	Beer	Liquor	Franchise	Total
Inventory, January 1, 1970	$ 434.41	$ 366.60	$ 775.74	$322.70	$ 1,899.45
Purchases	26,855.38	24,951.56	4,442.33	65.00	56,314.27
Materials Available	$27,289.79	$25,318.16	$5,218.07	$387.70	$58,213.72
Less Inventory Dec. 31, 1970	450.00	400.00	600.00	322.70	1,772.70
Materials Used	$26,839.79	$24,918.16	$4,618.07	$ 65.00	$56,441.02
Labor	12,989.85	6,844.51	1,553.66		21,388.02
Direct Overhead:					
Payroll Taxes	971.55	512.65	116.37		1,600.57
Supplies	2,029.77	2,274.21	516.23		4,820.21
Breakage	51.61	21.97	4.98		78.56
Repairs	221.57	86.23	19.57		327.37
License		346.40	78.63		425.03
Extra Help	26.25	187.12	42.47		255.84
Depreciation	1,230.26	582.18	132.15		1,944.59
COST OF SALES	$44,360.65	$35,773.43	$7,082.13	$ 65.00	$87,281.21

Prepared Without Audit

EXHIBIT 6
THE PASSKEY
PRO FORMA INCOME STATEMENT
May 1, 1972 - April 30, 1973 period

	12 Months
Sales	261,450.00
Cost of Goods Sold	173,775.00
Gross Revenue	87,675.00
Operating Expenses	72,111.00
Wages and Salaries	41,936.00
Rent	16,020.00
Advertising	6,000.00
Other Overhead	4,850.00
Interest	2,475.00
Depreciation	830.00
Profit Before Owner	
Draws Salary	15,564.00
Owner's Salary	12,000.00
Net Profit	3,564.00

EXHIBIT 7
THE PASSKEY
RESTAURANT LAYOUT

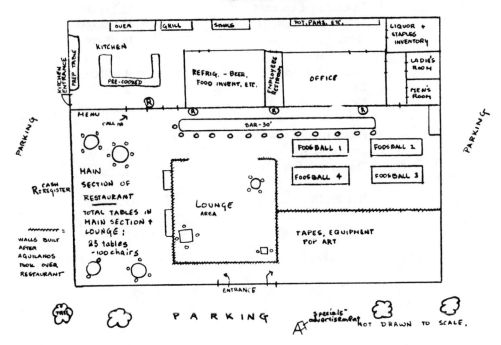

EXHIBIT 7
THE PASSKEY
RESTAURANT LAYOUT

were strictly beer drinking places and did not serve anything more than snack foods. Also, many students went to the modern, nicely decorated Student Union at the university which was right on campus and sold beer.

During the first nine months of operation, the Aquilanos made the following changes:

1. Strict theft controls were instituted and some personnel replaced. They discovered the cost of goods sold was inordinately high. After keeping close watch on their inventory and control methods, they thought that one or more of their employees was stealing from them. Their greatest loss was at the bar. They thought that their bartenders were giving free drinks to friends, a double instead of a single and/or not putting the money in the register. Also, food was missing from inventory.

2. They re-evaluated their prices and raised them slightly. (See Exhibit 8 for a sample menu and prices.)

3. They made many leasehold improvements to the structure, i.e., a big sign out front, lighting, enclosing the lounge area to reduce the vast spaciousness of the building interior in order to make it more intimate. They also created the room where the music equipment and tapes were to be sold. These, along with the organizational costs, were one-time costs which they did not anticipate for the following year.

4. Instead of renting the foosball machines, they purchased them for $450 each. They recouped their investment in the foosball machines within a month, and the revenue coming in from the machines was nearly all profit. A few people played the machines during lunch but most of the activity was at night.

5. They reevaluated the efficiency of their bar and corrected some inefficiencies by purchasing a more varied line of glasses, another cash register, etc.

6. After being in business for a few months, they found that their practice of paying for inventory deliveries direct from the cash register with cash caused many bookkeeping problems. That practice was stopped, and thereafter, all payments were made by check.

7. In addition to their other inventory control problems, they found that they were not keeping strict enough account of drinks and food which they allowed their employees to take as part of their compensation. Consequently, they instituted some rules to limit and keep track of these expenses.

8. Accounting procedures had always been troublesome to them as neither of them had the time to do it. They contracted an accounting firm who put them on a computerized system with monthly reports of financial statements.

Lunch time business was discovered to be much better than expected due to the people who worked at the nearby office complex. Also, business was very good weekends during the football and basketball seasons. However, mid-day was slow, especially during dinner hours, but business jumped again as the regular bar crowd came in during the evening or, on the weekends, when the younger people came in with dates. Consequently, attempts were made to increase business during the slow hours. Although only moderately successful, some of the things tried were:
    1.   free hors d'oeuvres, 5-7 p.m., Monday-Friday;
    2.   1/2 price beer and liquor 5-7 p.m., Monday-Thursday;
    3.   Two drinks for the price of one, 5-7 p.m., Monday-Thursday.

During the Spring of 1973, Mr. Aquilano began selling records, tapes, stereo-cartridge equipment, and some pop art products at The Passkey. Sales were considerably less than anticipated, however, the

EXHIBIT 8
THE PASSKEY
ORIGINAL AND REVISED FOOD MENU AND PRICES

ORIGINAL MENU and REVISED MENU

ORIGINAL MENU	Individual 10"	Large 13"	Giant 15"	REVISED MENU	Small 8"	Med. 10"	Large 13"	Giant 15"
Cheese	1.00	1.35	2.05	Cheese	.90	1.35	2.15	2.70
Black Olive	1.30	1.80	2.35	Black Olive	1.20	1.75	2.65	3.60
Mushroom	1.30	1.80	2.35	Mushroom	1.20	1.75	2.65	3.60
Bell Pepper	1.30	1.80	2.35	Bell Pepper	1.20	1.75	2.65	3.60
Onion	1.30	1.80	2.35	Onion	1.20	1.75	2.65	3.60
Jalapeno	1.30	1.80	2.35	Jalepeno	1.20	1.75	2.65	3.60
Salami	1.40	1.95	2.70	Salami	1.30	1.85	2.85	3.70
Sausage	1.40	1.95	2.70	Sausage	1.30	1.85	2.85	3.70
Meat Ball	1.40	1.95	2.70	Meat Ball	1.30	1.85	2.85	3.70
Bacon	1.40	1.95	2.70	Bacon	1.30	1.85	2.85	3.70
Pepperoni	1.40	1.95	2.70	Pepperoni	1.30	1.85	2.85	3.70
Ea. Added Vegetable	.15	.25	.35	Ea. Added Vegetable	.15	.20	.25	.30
Ea. Added Meat	.25	.35	.45	Ea. Added Meat	.20	.25	.35	.45

Daily Specials:
Red Bean w/Rice (w/Garlic Bread) 1.45
Filet of Fish (w/Fries & Salad) 1.25
Spaghetti (w/Garlic Bread & Salad) 1.25

ORIGINAL MENU (continued):

Hot Roast Beef 1.05	Salami & American		1.05
Hot Meat Ball 1.05	Baked Ham & American		1.05
Baked Ham .95	Baked Ham & Swiss		1.05
Salami .95	Salami & Swiss		1.05
Sausage .95	Cheese A .60	$	.65
Buzzard Burger			1.05
Hamburger			.75
Cheeseburger			.85
Fish Sandwich			.70
French Fries			.30

REVISED MENU (continued):

Hot Roast Beef	1.15	Sausage	1.10
Hot Corned Beef	1.65	Cheese	10¢ extra
Hot Meat Ball	1.15	Chef's Salad	1.55
Jumbo Po-Boy	1.65	Dinner Salad	.50
Baked Ham	1.15	Cheese A .65 $	.70
Salami	1.10		
Buzzard Burger			1.10
Hamburger (special $1.00 w/french fries)			.80
Cheeseburger			.90
Fish Sandwich			.75
French Fries			.30
1/2 Po-Boy & Salad			1.10
Jumbo Burger	1.05	Coffee	.15
Cajun Burger	1.10	Milk	.20

Aquilanos were not sure:

1. if they had promoted the music side of the business adequately (See Exhibit 9 for advertising samples);
2. if they had given the project sufficient time to catch on.

Nevertheless, the stereo-cartridge and stereo equipment portion of the business was so slow that Mr. Aquilano was beginning to feel that perhaps it should be discontinued. Only a few tapes and record albums were being sold each day. It was financially prohibitive for the Aquilanos to stock and maintain a large inventory of stereo equipment. Also, all transactions were on a cash basis. The Aquilanos would "special order" the equipment. However, they felt that the equipment business would have to at least triple before it would be worth continuing.

With regard to the tapes, it might be possible that the combination of music and pop art, even though it worked in other places, just might not work here, and the owners, as much as they might want to be in that business, might prepare themselves for the possibility that the need for that type of mix may not exist in their town. Of course, it was possible that the reason for their delayed success in the music portion of their business was because they delayed putting it in at the beginning and the word just hadn't gotten around yet.

At the same time, the Aquilanos felt the restaurant, bar, and game portions of their business were improving. If they decided to discontinue the music/pop art project, they could possibly do something more profitable with that portion of the building where the tapes were now located. They considered the following alternatives in the event they discontinued the tape business:

1. rent the tape room to a business which would be compatible with their business, i.e., a package store - or even put in a package store themselves, (this was legal in their town);

2. move the games into the tape area, seal it off - cutting down on the noise the foosball machines made - and make a more quiet, intimate cocktail lounge where the games had been located. Several bar "regulars" had complained about the noise;

3. make the tape area into a dancing area and bring in music - either taped or live;

4. use the tape room as a lounge and make the existing lounge for dancing;

5. add more tables and increase the menu to include steaks, etc. to encourage the dinner crowd. They had researched this last alternative and felt that there would be relatively low start-up costs. All they would need additionally would be the grill ($300). Of course, the waitress question would have to be rethought, as well as the best arrangement of space; or,

6. add more tables, but limit the menu and push the lunch business.

Mr. Aquilano felt he could expand volume considerably with little or no additional bartenders, kitchen staff, or other indirect labor (e.g., office help, maintenance). At the same time, he felt he couldn't easily reduce the number of employees given the nature of his operations. He explained this situation:

"For example, I have one grill man during lunch. He may be making 7 or 8 hamburger orders at any given moment during the lunch period. Even if he were making only 1 or 2 orders, I'd still need him. But the point is he could be working on 15 to 20 orders before I'd worry about getting another grill and grill man. The same is true for bartenders and the other work stations in this operation.

EXHIBIT 9
THE PASSKEY
AD SAMPLES

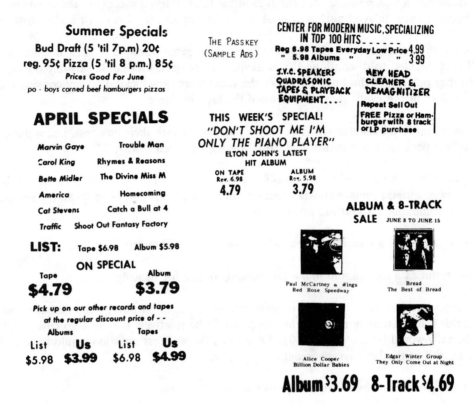

Sample Case Analysis

Stop! You have just finished reading "The Passkey" case. Now, before proceeding to read the analysis in Chapter Twenty-Three, outline your own analysis of The Passkey case.

Then compare your analysis to the one in the book. You will learn considerably more about your present ability to analyze a case if you first try to analyze The Passkey on your own.

When you read the analysis, remember just because your approach is probably different, doesn't mean it is wrong or inferior to the analysis presented here. The important thing is to ask how your analysis can be improved. In fact, you should also ask how the sample analysis can be improved?

The subsequent analysis is sufficient to serve as a basis for a comprehensive classroom presentation or an input for a written case report.

■ ■ ■ ■ ■ ■

Chapter Twenty-Three
Sample Case Analysis
of
The Passkey Restaurant and Lounge Case

Assigned Questions:

1. What are the prospects for The Passkey?
2. What elements will determine how successful The Passkey will be?
3. What would you advise Mr. Aquilano to do now?

Some Unassigned Questions (but likely to be asked in class):

1. What is the existing financial health of The Passkey?
2. What is the sales breakeven of continuing with the existing concept? The cash breakeven?
3. Should Mr. Aquilano buy the property from Mr. Johnson?
4. What do you think of the original concept? Is it viable?
5. How do you rate the Aquilanos as entrepreneurs?

Some Explicit Case Issues:

1. Viability of original concept (fast food and tapes) versus developing "new concept" for the business.
2. Pros and cons of existing deal made with Mr. Johnson.
3. The Aquilanos as entrepreneurs.

Some Implicit Case Issues:

1. Aquilanos' goals - are they changing? Do they intend to pursue a "high potential" new venture vs. a marginal (though perhaps very secure) "Ma and Pa" operation?
2. Is a "General Manager's Perspective" missing?
3. What are the principal marketing, production, finance, and administrative issues?

Question No. 1 - What are the Prospects for The Passkey?

Past performance has been disappointing. Comparing actual versus forecasted sales (Exhibits 1 and 6) shows that The Passkey has achieved only 57% of its original forecast.

Also, wide divergence exists between expense levels shown in the Aquilanos' P&L (Exhibit 1) versus forecast expenses (Exhibit 6) and the previous owner's experience (Exhibit 5). One reason for these differences is that the Aquilanos are expensing some items as "operating" expenses that are associated with start-up costs (i.e., relocation expenses, appraisal expenses, probably part of office expenses). They also seem to be including some personal expenses not directly or completely associated with the business (e.g., auto expenses, travel expenses).

Another reason for the difference between the expense levels is different accounting approaches. The usual accounting convention is to include direct labor and direct overhead into the "cost of goods sold" or in the case of restaurant operations, the "cost of sales." Mr. Johnson has followed this approach in Exhibit 5. However, both the industry and the Aquilanos followed another approach which yielded a statement that recognized the "fixed" nature of most restaurant "direct" labor and overhead for monthly and even yearly accounting periods (without substantial changes in the operating process or volume). The truly "variable" components of cost of sales are mostly raw materials (merchandise) and small amounts of labor and other materials and supply over relevant ranges of volume changes. For instance, Exhibit 10 shows the industry breakdown for "drinking and eating places," taken from Dun & Bradstreet's "Cost of Doing Business."

Exhibit 11 shows an adjusted P&L and balance sheet for The Passkey which

1. focuses on restaurant receipts since "other income" items have essentially no expenses incurred against them;
2. accounts for the error in Exhibit 1 of adding closing inventory back into gross profit.

The revised P&L shows a much larger loss than originally shown in Exhibit 1, especially for the food and beverage operations. Cost of sales (e.g., variable costs) are also about three percentage points higher than the industry average, yielding a contribution to fixed costs of 42%.

Incorporating the larger net loss into a revised balance sheet raises some additional points and questions. For example, the revised balance sheet indicates that the Aquilanos must have made an additional loan to the operation, beyond the $5864 shown in Exhibit 2. How did they do this? The combined amount of these loans ($15,172) is sizeable. Of course, the cash for these loans could have come from savings, sale of personal assets, or loans from relatives. But more likely, the cash came from The Passkey operation itself.

Students familiar with restaurant operations will realize that a number of ways exist to siphon off cash. Mr. Johnson was probably skimming profits from The Sparrow since he states that the operation was "marginally successful" yet showed Mr. Aquilano an income statement (Exhibit 5) showing a loss.

Assuming cash is being skimmed, where it is being taken could be important for evaluating the viability of the original concept. For instance, if cash is being taken from the bar or the kitchen, the concept may be doing better than supposed. But there isn't any evidence to indicate that cash is being drained intentionally from either the bar or food operations. On the other hand, the case does state that Mr. Aquilano purchased the game machines outright and that they paid for themselves in a month. Consequently:

$435. x 12 months x 4 machines = $21,000,
versus $2628 of vending income shown in case Exhibit 1.

If this observation is true, the game machines provide not only a source of cash, but are also a significant factor in the restaurant's overall business volume. For example, The Passkey will have to generate at least an additional $50,000 in food and drink sales to replace the lost "contribution" provided by the games:
($21,000/.42 = $50,000
where .42 is The Passkey's contributing margin taken from Exhibit 11).

Considering the importance of "game income," we can evaluate the business using some simple breakeven calculations and projections of the P&L statement.

First, Exhibit 12 estimates the fixed costs that The Passkey is likely to experience over the following year. Actually, three levels of fixed costs are estimated given different advertising and promotion strategies. The assumption is that if Mr. Aquilano continues with the tape/record business, he will require a substantial increase in advertising. Also, if he decides to drop the tape/record business, he may still need to increase advertising if he makes substantial changes in the operation (e.g., adds a dinner menu, provides dancing, etc.)

EXHIBIT 10
INDUSTRY AVERAGES
COST OF DOING BUSINESS - PROPRIETORSHIPS*

	Drinking Places	Eating Places
C.G.S.	*55.5%*	53.4%
Merchandise	52.4	45.6
Labor	1.7	4.4
Materials/Supplies	0.8	1.9
Gross Margin	44.5	46.6
Selected Op. Exp.		
Salaries & Wages'	10.3	15.4
Rent	2.9	4.1
Interest	1.0	0.8
Taxes	*5.0*	3.5
Repairs	*1.5*	1.4
Depreciation	2.7	2.8
Profits on Business		
Receipts	9.6	8.0

Excludes owner's salary

*Source: Dun & Bradstreet. *Cost of Doing Business: Partnerships and Proprietorships.*

EXHIBIT 11
REVISED P&L

	$	%
Sales Receipts	145379	100%
Cost of Sales	83916	58
Gross Margin	61463	42
Total Expenses	78899	54
Net (Loss) from food and drink	(17436)	(12)
Other Income	2820	2
Net (Loss)	(14616)	(10)

REVISED BALANCE SHEET

Assets		Liabilities	
Current		**Current**	
Cash	3318	Payroll Taxes	430
Petty Cash	640	Sales Tax	671
Empl. Loans	147	A.P.	3542
Inventory	9307		4643
Prepaid Rent	2888		
Reserve	231	**Long Term**	
	16531	Note —	17829
		Loan — Aquilano's	5864
Fixed Assets			23693
Furniture	8595	Addit. Loan:	
Net Improvements	6784	Aquilano's	9308*
	15397	Capital Stock	10000
Other	1118	Net Loss	(14616)
	33028		33028

*plug

EXHIBIT 12
FIXED COSTS FOR DIFFERENT ADVERTISING
AND PROMOTION PROGRAMS

Fixed Costs

Other Wages	34000
Tax & Lic.	*1500*
Auto	2100
Utilities	4500
Linens	800
Maintenance/Repairs	3400
Insurance	2500
Rent	15700
Interest	1200
Legal & Acct.	1200
Payroll Tax	2400
Dues	100
Office*	*600*
Depreciation	900
Fixed Costs Subtotal	82900

	Low As Is	Medium Double	High Triple
Fixed Costs Subtotal	82900	82900	82900
Advertising & Promot.	2700	5400	8100
Total Fixed Costs:	85600	88300	91000

*About 1/2 of 1973 since $1191 + 5059 is 4.3% of sales and more than twice industry average. Consequently, I assume some nonrecurring purchases have been included in 1972/73 figures.

Exhibit 13 takes these fixed cost levels and calculates profit and cash breakevens for three different contribution margins - the contribution margin experienced by The Passkey during 1972/73 and two industry averages.

The breakeven sales ranges for profit and cash breakevens are shown below.

	Sales at low fixed cost level		Sales at high fixed cost level
for profit breakeven:	$183,691	versus	$216,667
for cash breakeven:	$175,107	versus	$207,142

These breakevens are, in effect, being realized now for the low fixed cost levels, when the equivalent sales volume ($50,000) of game income is added to the existing sales level of $145,000.

Exhibit 14 projects P&L outcomes for different growth and expense levels. The result is quite encouraging when all "other income" is included in the projections.

The year 1972/73 has been a learning one for the Aquilanos. Assuming they have gained control of theft and other problems affecting material purchases, they may improve their gross margin considerably and further lower their breakeven. Yet, like unexpectedly finding a chicken in the pot, these results seem rather fortuitous for the Aquilanos, and certainly not attributable to the original concept nor perhaps even their food operation.

Question 2 - What elements will determine bow successful The Passkey will be?

A.) The games and related bar activity during the evening hours are critical elements in the operation at this point. Operating improvements that effectively increase luncheon volume will be helpful, but probably will not drastically improve profitability.

A brief example demonstrates this situation. The Sparrow's past performance plus statements made in the case indicate that food and beverages (beer and liquor) sales are about evenly split. Consequently, for a combined sales volume of $150,000, each additional dollar of sales for beer and liquor results in 30 cents of profit (nearly twice the profit impact of food) because of the role of game income.

	Food	Drink
Sales	$75,000	$75,000
Industry Profit before Tax	8.6%	9.0%
Profit	$ 6,450	$ 6,750
Derived Game Income (% of total game income, est. @):	25%	75%
Prorated Game Income	$ 5,250	$15,750
Total	$11,700	$22,500
% of Sales	16%	30%

EXHIBIT 13
COST STRUCTURES AND BREAKEVEN CALCULATIONS

Variable Costs	The Passkey	Drinking Places	Eating Places
Cost of Sales	58%	55.5%	53.4%
Contribution Margin	42	44.5	46.6

$$\text{Profit Breakeven} = \frac{\text{Fixed Costs}}{\text{Contribution Margin}} = \frac{85,600}{.42} = 203,809$$

For Fixed Costs of: and Contribution Margins of:

			42%	44.5%	46.6%
See	85,600	=	203,809	192,360	183,691
Exhibit 13	88,300	=	210,238	198,427	189,485
	91,000	=	216,667	204,494	195,279

$$\text{Cash Breakeven} = \frac{\text{Fixed Costs} - \text{Other cash sources*}}{\text{Contribution Margin}}$$

Net Fixed Costs of:

		81,600	=	194,285	183,370	175,107
		84,300	=	200,714	189,438	180,901
		87,000	=	207,142	195,506	186,695

*Vending Income ($3000) + Depreciation ($800) + Interest and Misc. Income (200) = $4000. Consequently, net fixed costs equal $85,600 − 4000 = 81600, etc.

EXHIBIT 14
PROFORMA P&L
FOR DIFFERENT GROWTH LEVELS

	A	B	C
		Growth in Sales	
	No Growth	17%	33%
Sales	150,000	175,000	200,000
CGS (58%)	87,000	101,500	116,000
G. Margin	63,000	73,500	84,000
Other Expenses	85,600	88,300	91,000
Advertising at low, medium, high levels, respectively			
NPBT	(22,600)	(14,800)	(7,000)
		Assumes Respectively	
"Other Income"		17% Growth	33% Growth
—Cash From	21,000	24,570	27,900
Game Rev.	2,800	3,270	3,700
—Other rev. from vending interest, misc.			
Net Profit	1,200	13,040	24,600

B.) The Aquilanos themselves will invariably affect the success of the operation. Thus far, they have exhibited various strengths and weaknesses:

Strengths	Weaknesses
1) seem to be doing good job in with food and bar operations.	1) Apparent weaknesses areas of accounting and finance.
2) ability to handle personnel/administrative matters.	2) Objectives unclear.
3) ability to get into business, "to get the doors open."	3) tendency to be involved with too many different businesses
4) minimum investment upfront.	4) apparent weaknesses in marketing and site location; no evidence that they researched the Give-Away Restaurants very carefully.

C.) The evaluation of different opportunities available to them choosing the best one or combination.

Currently, The Passkey's alternatives can be divided into strategic options which influence the nature and direction of the overall business versus options that may improve existing operations regardless of any particular strategy. These strategic alternatives are:

1. Stay as is: the mixed business concept:
    a) push tapes/records
    b) another business to replace tapes/LPs.
2. Full service restaurant - dinner and waitress service
3. Limited restaurant concept - self-service
    a) push bar trade

Other important but non-strategic opportunities are:

4. Buy buildings and land instead of leasing property
5. Sell out.

Let's look at each of these options.

<u>la) Stay as is: push tapes/records</u>

.   doesn't make sense given basic weakness yet potential of present food and drink business.
·   tapes and records sales must probably triple just to break even (see Tape/LP analysis below).
·   efforts better spent elsewhere.

.   Tape/LP Album Analysis

Average Disc Sales Price:	$4.00	100%
Variable <u>Cost:</u>	2.50	63
Contribution margin:	1.50	37

<u>Fixed Costs</u>
Advertising	3,000/yr.
Labor	4,160/yr.($80./wk for 1 clerk)
Rent	1,340/yr. (about 1/12 total rent)
Utilities	250/yr. (est.)
<u>Miscellaneous</u>	<u>250/yr. (est.)</u>
Total	9,000/yr.

$$\text{BE Sales} = \frac{\text{total Fixed Costs}}{\text{Contribution Margin}}$$

$$\text{BE Sales} = \frac{\$9000}{.37} = \$24,324.$$

$$\text{BE Volume Per Year} = \frac{\$24,324}{\$5 \text{ per tape}} = 4865 \text{ tapes per year}$$

$$\text{BE Volume Per Day} = \frac{4865}{365 \text{ days}} = 13 \text{ tapes/day}$$

$$\text{BE Sales per Day} = 13 \text{ tapes/day} * \$5.00 = \$66 \text{ day}$$

What is the viability of the existing concept, i.e., combining tapes/ records with the food and drink business? Most of the pro and con arguments appear to be weighted against the concept:

Pros

- May be possible to educate college population with big advertising push - but have to do $30-$40,000 volume to make it worthwhile.

Cons

- Restaurant's name doesn't convey concept;
- Location may not be optimum vis-a-vis college population;
- Older business groups and bar "regulars" probably don't care about tapes;
- Weak advertising thus far;
- May have lost the momentum by not opening with tapes from the start;
- Aquilanos trying to do too many things (e.g., different business without requisite skills);
- Image of Passkey probably unclear to potential market. They are probably confused or wondering how this place is different from the Sparrow? versus Passkey under Mr. Johnson? versus Passkey under Aquilanos without tapes/LPs?

lb) Another business activity to replace tapes...e.g. Liquor Store

Mostly "cons" here:

- may ruin growing image as one of the nicer places to go on a date;
- another tough business with different set of skills required;
- can sell "over the bar" now;
- may just further confuse potential market about what kind of place The Passkey is;
- doesn't provide clear alternative concept or strategic direction for The Passkey.

2) Full Service Restaurant - Dinner and Waitress Service

Pros

- increase volume during slow hours (5-9 p.m.)
- upgrade image.
- provide dinner date capability.

Cons

- different products and kitchen processes required.
- must train and retain waitresses and hostesses.
- some new investment required for kitchen equipment.
- considerable extra effort required on part of Aquilanos; already working seven days/week.
- won't affect (increase) income from game machines.
- no better than industry gross and net profit margins.

3) Limited Restaurant Concept - Self Service

One particular variant of this strategy is to push the bar trade in order to maximize the high contribution income from the game machines.

Assuming time and energy are limited resources for the Aquilanos, the key elements of this strategy are:

a) keep food operations substantially the same;
b) spend efforts on improving bar/game trade.
   - utilize space now used for tapes for dancing;
   - establish a bar/disco theme;

- rename restaurant to fit theme;
- advertise and promote new image/concept at "high"
  ($8100) level.

Specific goals are a 25% improvement in total food receipts and a 75% improvement in bar receipts. These goals may seem unduly high; however, the average daily receipts for The Passkey in 1972/1973 are only $404/day ($145,379/360 days). For a facility with 4,000 square feet, this daily revenue is very low (about 10 cts. per square foot per day).

Given a 30 foot bar, the actual capacity of The Passkey is much higher. For instance, one bartender can serve at least two uncomplicated drinks per minute or 120 per hour. Consequently, the room for growth is enormous. On the food side, the last quote of the case clearly indicates that existing capacity is not a constraint. What's needed is more customers.

4) Buy versus Lease

If you look only at the monthly average, the proposal to buy is not acceptable. For instance:

Price:	$180,000	Assumes 25 year mortgage
Down Payment:	$36,000	Assumes 20% down required;
Mortgage:	$144,000	Monthly payment = $1208 at 9% interest
Monthly savings over leasing	= $127	($ 1335/mo. - $1208/mo.)

However these savings are effectively zero if we assume property taxes (paid by the property owner) are roughly $1550 per year or $130/mo.

If Property Taxes	= 0, then
Yearly savings	= $1524

From the Present Value Table (in Part Eight), $1524 (10.675)* = $16,269

*the discount factor of 10.675 assumes an 8% return is required.

Note: The proposal to buy is not acceptable even at 6% return:

$1524 (12.783) = $19,480
which is still less than the
initial investment of the
$36,000 cash down payment

However, the proposal to buy the property becomes immediately acceptable on economic grounds as soon as cash savings are included from increased depreciation. For example:

Straight Line 180,000/ 25 years = $7 200.
7200 (10.675) = $76,860.

Since this $76,860 is more than double $36,000, the proposal is acceptable. In fact, the cutoff rate would have to be as high as 20% before we'd consider rejecting this investment in favor of another investment.

Note: if you look at the proposal over 15 years (which is the term of the lease) instead of 25 years, the proposal to buy is still acceptable. Assume the worst case: you can only get a 15 year mortgage. Consequently, depreciation savings are lowered by larger net rent payments of about $1500 per year (mortgage $1460 - $1335 for the lease = $125/mo. *
12 mos. = $1500/yr.). As the calculation below shows, the investment is acceptable because the net present value of these cash flows is $48,786, which is greater than the $36,000 we "presently" have: $7200/yr - $1500 yr = $5700 yr (8.559) = $48,786. Also, the cutoff rate would be about 18% over 15 years.

The question then is whether or not the Aquilanos can raise the $36,000 investment and whether they can make 18%-to-20% better with another investment. Assuming they can raise the money, they probably can not earn such a high return without selling The Passkey and getting into another business.

5) <u>Sell Out</u>

After one year of operations, the Aquilanos have managed to survive and earn a living from The Passkey. The discouraging results of the tape/record business seem to have disappointed David Aquilano to the point where he is considering selling the business. However, the potential of the business without the tapes/LP operation appears relatively attractive for a family business. The question, of course, is whether or not this is the kind of business venture that David Aquilano wants? His personal goals are not clearly stated. Some indication exists that as an entrepreneur he has been looking for high potential new ventures -- first in electronics, and later in the novel fast food/ music business which he possibly hoped to use as a model to replicate at other locations.

It appears Mr. Aquilano would not gain much by selling out at this time. Yet, he has very little downside risk for staying with the business, at least for the short term.

Also, selling the business while being locked into a 15 year lease will not be easy. One wonders about the legal advice the Aquilanos had when they made their agreement with Mr. Johnson. Two extreme events are possible, each with a different outcome.

<u>EVENT</u>	<u>OUTCOME OR PREFERRED DECISION</u>
A) The business is a great success	Probably will want to own facility
B) The business is a flop	Will want out of lease. If locked into 15 year lease, will need to find buyer willing to assume it.

A much better option would have been a short-term lease with an option to buy or at least options to renew.

<u>Question #3 - What would you advise Mr. Aquilano to do now?</u>

      1)   Get a good accountant and a good lawyer.
      2)   Buy property as soon as possible, if possible.
      3)   Concentrate activities around bar/game operations. In this regard:
          a)   Get rid of tape/record business;
          b)   Maintain and improve lunch business, but limit efforts;
          c)   Refrain from putting in a dinner operation;
          d)   Strong effort to push evening bar trade, dancing, disco theme;

e)   Change name to indicate new theme and concentration around bar, lounge, disco activities, for "date" market.

How to Present Your Analysis in Class

Try to start with Question #3.

- List recommendations.
- Proceed to support from analysis of questions 1 and 2.

Question 1: What are prospects?

- Seem poor, but actually okay.
- Focus on Exhibits 1, 5 and 6.
- Bring in Industry Performance Figures.

Question 2: What are key elements for success?

- Bar/game trade.
- The Aquilanos and choice of options (list them).
- Strategic choice versus other opportunities.

PART EIGHT
REFERENCE MATERIALS FOR
CASE ANALYSIS

■ ■ ■ ■ ■ ■

The need often arises during case analysis for present value tables, industry ratios, and various conversion factors, including currency equivalents. Much time can be saved if the case analyst has easy access to this information. Consequently, I have summarized what I believe are some of the most commonly needed items.

Present Value Tables and Sample Calculations

Table 1 provides present value factors for a future single payment. Table 2 presents present value factors for yearly payments. I have included two sample problems and calculations using these tables.

Sample Calculation for a Present Value Problem Requiring a Single Future Payment.
(See Table 1)
You have the opportunity to receive $5,000 now from a real estate investment. However, you can remain invested in the same venture, and in three years you will receive $8,000. You don't trust the stock market, so you plan to put the money into a savings account yielding 6% if you do not stay with the real estate investment.

From Table 1, the present value factor for a 6% return in three years is 0.840. The present value equals: $8,000 (0.840) = $6,720. This $6,720 is obviously greater than the $5,000 you can also receive now. Consequently you are better off remaining invested in the real estate venture.

Also, if you put your $5,000 into a savings account, its *future value* in three years, compounded at 6%, is $5,955, which is also less than $8,000.

Sample Calculation for a Present Value Problem with Yearly Payments. (Table 2)

You have an opportunity where for a $10,000 investment, you can receive $3,000 a year for four years. You require at least an 8% rate of return. From Table 2, the present value factor for $1 at 8% over four years is 3.312. Consequently the present value for $3,000 per year is $3,000 x (3.312) = $9.936.

Since $9,936 is less than $10,000, the proposal is not acceptable.

Table 1

PRESENT VALUE TABLE FOR FUTURE SINGLE PAYMENTS

Years Hence	1%	2%	4%	6%	8%	10%	12%	14%	15%	16%	18%	20%	22%	24%	25%	26%	28%	30%	35%	40%	45%	50%
1	0.990	0.980	0.962	0.943	0.926	0.909	0.893	0.877	0.870	0.862	0.847	0.833	0.820	0.806	0.800	0.794	0.781	0.769	0.741	0.714	0.690	0.667
2	0.980	0.961	0.925	0.890	0.857	0.826	0.797	0.769	0.756	0.743	0.718	0.694	0.672	0.650	0.640	0.630	0.610	0.592	0.549	0.510	0.476	0.444
3	0.971	0.942	0.889	0.840	0.794	0.751	0.712	0.675	0.658	0.641	0.609	0.579	0.551	0.524	0.512	0.500	0.477	0.455	0.406	0.364	0.328	0.296
4	0.961	0.924	0.855	0.792	0.735	0.683	0.636	0.592	0.572	0.552	0.516	0.482	0.451	0.423	0.410	0.397	0.373	0.350	0.301	0.260	0.226	0.198
5	0.951	0.906	0.822	0.747	0.681	0.621	0.567	0.519	0.497	0.476	0.437	0.402	0.370	0.341	0.328	0.315	0.291	0.269	0.223	0.186	0.156	0.132
6	0.942	0.888	0.790	0.705	0.630	0.564	0.507	0.456	0.432	0.410	0.370	0.335	0.303	0.275	0.262	0.250	0.227	0.207	0.165	0.133	0.108	0.088
7	0.933	0.871	0.760	0.665	0.583	0.513	0.452	0.400	0.376	0.354	0.314	0.279	0.249	0.222	0.210	0.198	0.178	0.159	0.122	0.095	0.074	0.059
8	0.923	0.853	0.731	0.627	0.540	0.467	0.404	0.351	0.327	0.305	0.266	0.233	0.204	0.179	0.168	0.157	0.139	0.123	0.091	0.068	0.051	0.039
9	0.914	0.837	0.703	0.592	0.500	0.424	0.361	0.308	0.284	0.263	0.225	0.194	0.167	0.144	0.134	0.125	0.108	0.094	0.067	0.048	0.035	0.026
10	0.905	0.820	0.676	0.558	0.463	0.386	0.322	0.270	0.247	0.227	0.191	0.162	0.137	0.116	0.107	0.099	0.085	0.073	0.050	0.035	0.024	0.017
11	0.896	0.804	0.650	0.527	0.429	0.350	0.287	0.237	0.215	0.195	0.162	0.135	0.112	0.094	0.086	0.079	0.066	0.056	0.037	0.025	0.017	0.012
12	0.887	0.788	0.625	0.497	0.397	0.319	0.257	0.208	0.187	0.168	0.137	0.112	0.092	0.076	0.069	0.062	0.052	0.043	0.027	0.018	0.012	0.008
13	0.879	0.773	0.601	0.469	0.368	0.290	0.229	0.182	0.163	0.145	0.116	0.093	0.075	0.061	0.055	0.050	0.040	0.033	0.020	0.013	0.008	0.005
14	0.870	0.758	0.577	0.442	0.340	0.263	0.205	0.160	0.141	0.125	0.099	0.078	0.062	0.049	0.044	0.039	0.032	0.025	0.015	0.009	0.006	0.003
15	0.861	0.743	0.555	0.417	0.315	0.239	0.183	0.140	0.123	0.108	0.084	0.065	0.051	0.040	0.035	0.031	0.025	0.020	0.011	0.006	0.004	0.002
16	0.853	0.728	0.534	0.394	0.292	0.218	0.163	0.123	0.107	0.093	0.071	0.054	0.042	0.032	0.028	0.025	0.019	0.015	0.008	0.005	0.003	0.002
17	0.844	0.714	0.513	0.371	0.270	0.198	0.146	0.108	0.093	0.080	0.060	0.045	0.034	0.026	0.023	0.020	0.015	0.012	0.006	0.003	0.002	0.001
18	0.836	0.700	0.494	0.350	0.250	0.180	0.130	0.095	0.081	0.069	0.051	0.038	0.028	0.021	0.018	0.016	0.012	0.009	0.005	0.002	0.001	0.001
19	0.828	0.686	0.475	0.331	0.232	0.164	0.116	0.083	0.070	0.060	0.043	0.031	0.023	0.017	0.014	0.012	0.009	0.007	0.003	0.002	0.001	
20	0.820	0.673	0.456	0.312	0.215	0.149	0.104	0.073	0.061	0.051	0.037	0.026	0.019	0.014	0.012	0.010	0.007	0.005	0.002	0.001	0.001	
21	0.811	0.660	0.439	0.294	0.199	0.135	0.093	0.064	0.053	0.044	0.031	0.022	0.015	0.011	0.009	0.008	0.006	0.004	0.002	0.001		
22	0.803	0.647	0.422	0.278	0.184	0.123	0.083	0.056	0.046	0.038	0.026	0.018	0.013	0.009	0.007	0.006	0.004	0.003	0.001	0.001		
23	0.795	0.634	0.406	0.262	0.170	0.112	0.074	0.049	0.040	0.033	0.022	0.015	0.010	0.007	0.006	0.005	0.003	0.002	0.001			
24	0.788	0.622	0.390	0.247	0.158	0.102	0.066	0.043	0.035	0.028	0.019	0.013	0.008	0.006	0.005	0.004	0.003	0.002	0.001	0.001		
25	0.780	0.610	0.375	0.233	0.146	0.092	0.059	0.038	0.030	0.024	0.016	0.010	0.007	0.005	0.004	0.003	0.002	0.001	0.001			
26	0.772	0.598	0.361	0.220	0.135	0.084	0.053	0.033	0.026	0.021	0.014	0.009	0.006	0.004	0.003	0.002	0.002	0.001				
27	0.764	0.586	0.347	0.207	0.125	0.076	0.047	0.029	0.023	0.018	0.011	0.007	0.005	0.003	0.002	0.002	0.001	0.001				
28	0.757	0.574	0.333	0.196	0.116	0.069	0.042	0.026	0.020	0.016	0.010	0.006	0.004	0.002	0.002	0.002	0.001	0.001				
29	0.749	0.563	0.321	0.185	0.107	0.063	0.037	0.022	0.017	0.014	0.008	0.005	0.003	0.002	0.002	0.001	0.001	0.001				
30	0.742	0.552	0.308	0.174	0.099	0.057	0.033	0.020	0.015	0.012	0.007	0.004	0.003	0.002	0.001	0.001	0.001					
40	0.672	0.453	0.208	0.097	0.046	0.022	0.011	0.005	0.004	0.003	0.001	0.001										
50	0.608	0.372	0.141	0.054	0.021	0.009	0.003	0.001	0.001	0.001												

Table 2

PRESENT VALUE TABLE FOR ANNUITIES

Years (N)	1%	2%	4%	6%	8%	10%	12%	14%	15%	16%	18%	20%	22%	24%	25%	26%	28%	30%	35%	40%	45%	50%
1	0.990	0.980	0.962	0.943	0.926	0.909	0.893	0.877	0.870	0.862	0.847	0.833	0.820	0.806	0.800	0.794	0.781	0.769	0.741	0.714	0.690	0.667
2	1.970	1.942	1.886	1.833	1.783	1.736	1.690	1.647	1.626	1.605	1.566	1.528	1.492	1.457	1.440	1.424	1.392	1.361	1.289	1.224	1.165	1.111
3	2.941	2.884	2.775	2.673	2.577	2.487	2.402	2.322	2.283	2.246	2.174	2.106	2.042	1.981	1.952	1.923	1.868	1.816	1.696	1.589	1.493	1.407
4	3.902	3.808	3.630	3.465	3.312	3.170	3.037	2.914	2.855	2.798	2.690	2.589	2.494	2.404	2.362	2.320	2.241	2.166	1.997	1.849	1.720	1.605
5	4.853	4.713	4.452	4.212	3.993	3.791	3.605	3.433	3.352	3.274	3.127	2.991	2.864	2.745	2.689	2.635	2.532	2.436	2.220	2.035	1.876	1.737
6	5.795	5.601	5.242	4.917	4.623	4.355	4.111	3.889	3.784	3.685	3.498	3.326	3.167	3.020	2.951	2.885	2.759	2.643	2.385	2.168	1.983	1.824
7	6.728	6.472	6.002	5.582	5.206	4.868	4.564	4.288	4.160	4.039	3.812	3.605	3.416	3.242	3.161	3.083	2.937	2.802	2.508	2.263	2.057	1.883
8	7.652	7.325	6.733	6.210	5.747	5.335	4.968	4.639	4.487	4.344	4.078	3.837	3.619	3.421	3.329	3.241	3.076	2.925	2.598	2.331	2.108	1.922
9	8.566	8.162	7.435	6.802	6.247	5.759	5.328	4.946	4.772	4.607	4.303	4.031	3.786	3.566	3.463	3.366	3.184	3.019	2.665	2.379	2.144	1.948
10	9.471	8.983	8.111	7.360	6.710	6.145	5.650	5.216	5.019	4.833	4.494	4.192	3.923	3.682	3.571	3.465	3.269	3.092	2.715	2.414	2.168	1.965
11	10.368	9.787	8.760	7.887	7.139	6.495	5.937	5.453	5.234	5.029	4.656	4.327	4.035	3.776	3.656	3.544	3.335	3.147	2.752	2.438	2.185	1.977
12	11.255	10.575	9.385	8.384	7.536	6.814	6.194	5.660	5.421	5.197	4.793	4.439	4.127	3.851	3.725	3.606	3.387	3.190	2.779	2.456	2.196	1.985
13	12.134	11.343	9.986	8.853	7.904	7.103	6.424	5.842	5.583	5.342	4.910	4.533	4.203	3.912	3.780	3.656	3.427	3.223	2.799	2.468	2.204	1.990
14	13.004	12.106	10.563	9.295	8.244	7.367	6.628	6.002	5.724	5.468	5.008	4.611	4.265	3.962	3.824	3.695	3.459	3.249	2.814	2.477	2.210	1.993
15	13.865	12.849	11.118	9.712	8.559	7.606	6.811	6.142	5.847	5.575	5.092	4.675	4.315	4.001	3.859	3.726	3.483	3.268	2.825	2.484	2.214	1.995
16	14.718	13.578	11.652	10.106	8.851	7.824	6.974	6.265	5.954	5.669	5.162	4.730	4.357	4.033	3.887	3.751	3.503	3.283	2.834	2.489	2.216	1.997
17	15.562	14.292	12.166	10.477	9.122	8.022	7.120	6.373	6.047	5.749	5.222	4.775	4.391	4.059	3.910	3.771	3.518	3.295	2.840	2.492	2.218	1.998
18	16.398	14.992	12.659	10.828	9.372	8.201	7.250	6.467	6.128	5.818	5.273	4.812	4.419	4.080	3.928	3.786	3.529	3.304	2.844	2.494	2.219	1.999
19	17.226	15.678	13.134	11.158	9.604	8.365	7.366	6.550	6.198	5.877	5.316	4.844	4.442	4.097	3.942	3.799	3.539	3.311	2.848	2.496	2.220	1.999
20	18.046	16.351	13.590	11.470	9.818	8.514	7.469	6.623	6.259	5.929	5.353	4.870	4.460	4.110	3.954	3.808	3.546	3.316	2.850	2.497	2.221	1.999
21	18.857	17.011	14.029	11.764	10.017	8.649	7.562	6.687	6.312	5.973	5.384	4.891	4.476	4.121	3.963	3.816	3.551	3.320	2.852	2.498	2.221	2.000
22	19.660	17.658	14.451	12.042	10.201	8.772	7.645	6.743	6.359	6.011	5.410	4.909	4.488	4.130	3.970	3.822	3.556	3.323	2.853	2.498	2.222	2.000
23	20.456	18.292	14.857	12.303	10.371	8.883	7.718	6.792	6.399	6.044	5.432	4.925	4.499	4.137	3.976	3.827	3.559	3.325	2.854	2.499	2.222	2.000
24	21.243	18.914	15.247	12.550	10.529	8.985	7.784	6.835	6.434	6.073	5.451	4.937	4.507	4.143	3.981	3.831	3.562	3.327	2.855	2.499	2.222	2.000
25	22.023	19.523	15.622	12.783	10.675	9.077	7.843	6.873	6.464	6.097	5.467	4.948	4.514	4.147	3.985	3.834	3.564	3.329	2.856	2.499	2.222	2.000
26	22.795	20.121	15.983	13.003	10.810	9.161	7.896	6.906	6.491	6.118	5.480	4.956	4.520	4.151	3.988	3.837	3.566	3.330	2.856	2.500	2.222	2.000
27	23.560	20.707	16.330	13.211	10.935	9.237	7.943	6.935	6.514	6.136	5.492	4.964	4.524	4.154	3.990	3.839	3.567	3.331	2.856	2.500	2.222	2.000
28	24.316	21.281	16.663	13.406	11.051	9.307	7.984	6.961	6.534	6.152	5.502	4.970	4.528	4.157	3.992	3.840	3.568	3.331	2.857	2.500	2.222	2.000
29	25.066	21.844	16.984	13.591	11.158	9.370	8.022	6.983	6.551	6.166	5.510	4.975	4.531	4.159	3.994	3.841	3.569	3.332	2.857	2.500	2.222	2.000
30	25.808	22.396	17.292	13.765	11.258	9.427	8.055	7.003	6.566	6.177	5.517	4.979	4.534	4.160	3.995	3.842	3.569	3.332	2.857	2.500	2.222	2.000
40	32.835	27.355	19.793	15.046	11.925	9.779	8.244	7.105	6.642	6.234	5.548	4.997	4.544	4.166	3.999	3.846	3.571	3.333	2.857	2.500	2.222	2.000
50	39.196	31.424	21.482	15.762	12.234	9.915	8.304	7.133	6.661	6.246	5.554	4.999	4.545	4.167	4.000	3.846	3.571	3.333	2.857	2.500	2.222	2.000

Useful Conversion Factors

Length	1 inch = 25.4 millimeters 1 foot = .305 meters 1 mile = 1.6 kilometers
Area	1 sq. inch = 6.4 sq. centimeters 1 sq. foot = .09 sq. meters 1 acre = 43,560 sq. feet I sq. mile = 640 acres
Volume	1 ounce (fluid) = .029 liters 1 gallon (fluid) = 3.78 liters
Mass	1 ounce (mass) = 28.3 grams 1 pound (mass) = .9 metric tons
Energy and Power	1 British thermal unit (BTU) = 1055 joules 1 watt hour = 3600 joules 746 watts = 1 horsepower (electric)
Temperature	fahrenheit = 1.8 celsius plus 32 celsius = 5/9 (times fahrenheit minus 32)
Liquid	2 pts. = 1 qt. = .94 liters 4 qts. = 1 gallon = 3.78 liters 32.5 gallons = 1 barrel (in the U.S.) 36 Imperial gallons = 1 barrel (in Great Britain)

Summary of Metric Measures

Linear	1 meter = 39.37 inches or = 3.28 feet 1000 meters = 1 kilometer = .621 miles 10 kilometers = 6.21 miles
Land/Square	1 sq. meter = 1550 sq. inches 1 sq. kilometer = .386 sq. miles 1 sq. kilometer = 100 hectares 1 hectare = 2.471 acres
Capacity	1 liter = 1.06 liquid quarts or .91 dry quarts 10 liters = 2.64 gallons or .28 bushels 1 kiloliter = 264 gallons or 35.3 cubic feet
Weights	10 grams = .35 ounces 1000 grams = 1 kilogram = 2.2 pounds 1000 kilograms = 1 metric ton = 2204.6 pounds

CRITICAL LIBRARY RESOURCES

These library references were provided graciously by Pepperdine University's Associate Librarian, Ms. Cindi Lundquist. Specific library call numbers and locations have been retained as a convenience for Pepperdine students and faculty.

DATABASES AVAILABLE IN MANY BUSINESS LIBRARIES

Note: At Pepperdine, the databases described below are available to current students and faculty for curriculum-related assignments ONLY. Reservations and downloading to disk may be necessary in some cases. Please call the library for reservations and times available. Database use instructions are included in User Manuals at each workstation.

ABI/Inform (CD-ROM)   **Data Courier**
Provides abstracts and indexing for journal articles in over 800 business and management journals. Subject classification and controlled indexing vocabulary are used. May also be searched by keyword, company names, SIC codes and personal names. Referred to as "PROQUEST" when used together with full-image of articles in Business Periodicals On Disk.
Coverage: 1987 to present   Updated: Monthly

Business Periodicals On Disk (CD-ROM)   **UMI**
Provides full-image, cover-to-cover, of 400 journals indexed in ABI/Inform. Referred to as "PROQUEST" when used together with ABI/Inform database.
Coverage: 1987 to present   Updated: Monthly

Dialog Business Connection (Online)   **DIALOG INFORMATION SERVICES**
Dialog Business Connection (DBC) provides menu-driven access to 25 business databases offered by Dialog. Sources include investment analyst reports, journal article abstracts, 10K and annual reports, and international company directories.

Information on specific companies (public and private), financial screening, industry & share-of-market data, and worldwide sales prospecting according to specified criteria can be easily obtained.
Coverage: Varies by type of data   Updated: Continuous

Dow Jones News Retrieval (Online)   **DOW JONES**
DJNR provides current news and information on companies (public/private, international/local), industries, investment, foreign exchange, and worldwide economic conditions. Sources include 10K and annual reports, newswires, and newspapers. Databases available through DJNR are listed in the User's Manual located near the DJNR workstations. Most databases are searched by using a series of menus. It is helpful to know the ticker symbol and exchange for publicly owned companies when searching for company financial information.
Updated: Continuous (stock prices and news updated every 15 min.)

ERIC (CD-ROM)   **SilverPlatter**
Provides abstracts for documents on education practices and research and for articles in more than 780 English language journals. Microfiche of all documents abstracted in ERIC are available in Plaza Library. The ERIC database may be searched by subject classification or descriptors, personal names, journal titles, publication year(s), type of publication (article or document), target audience, and keywords. ERIC on CD-ROM is the electronic counterpart to the print sources, Current Index to

Journals in Education (CIJE) and Resources in Education (RIE). Indexing and abstracting is provided by subject specific clearinghouses funded by the U.S. Dept. of Education.
Coverage: 1966-present; 2 disks   Updated: quarterly

LEXIS/NEXIS (ONLINE)   **Mead Data Central**
The full range of information needed for legal research support is included in the LEXIS/NEXIS service. The LEXIS service provides full-text case law, law review journals, statutes, UCC, and related material. Other services are: MEDIS - includes Medline, drug, toxicology, and other specialty files; NEXIS - includes full -text news, patent and trademark information; ASSOCIATED PRESS POLITICAL; COUNTRY INFORMATION; FINANCIAL INFORMATION - includes company, merger, investment information and stock quotes; and NAARS (National Automated Accounting Research System). Information files are organized into research libraries and are keyword searchable. Adequate time for training or familiarization with this service is advised for beginning searchers. Downloading of research results is strongly encouraged.

National Trade Data Bank (CD-ROM)   **U.S. Dept. of Commerce**
Includes complete publications from 11 government agencies such as: CIA, Bureau of Economic Analysis, and International Trade Administration. The database can be searched by agency, broad topic, program (publication title), keywords or combinations of keywords or publication title), keywords or combinations of keywords or publication item number. Potential trading partners may be identified with the Foreign Traders Index. Tabular data may be downloaded into spreadsheet format or printed. Download or print complete documents to capture necessary footnote and document information.
Updated: Monthly

ECONOMICS AND BUSINESS FORECASTING
Book Reference Sources*

BUSINESS STATISTICS. United States, Bureau of Economic Analysis. Washington, D.C.: Government
   Printing Office, annual. Payson and Plaza Ref **HF1016 B87x**

ECONOMIC INDICATORS HANDBOOK, edited by Arsen J. Darnay. Detroit, MI: Gale, 1992. Plaza
   Ref **HC103 E26 1992**.

ECONOMIC REPORT OF THE PRESIDENT. TRANSMITTED TO THE CONGRESS, FEBRUARY
   (each year); TOGETHER WITH THE ANNUAL REPORT OF THE COUNCIL OF
   ECONOMIC ADVISERS. U.S. President. Washington, D.C.: Government Printing Office,
   annual. Payson and Plaza Ref **HC106.5 A272**

HISTORICAL STATISTICS OF THE UNITED STATES, COLONIAL TIMES TO 1970.
   United States. Bureau of the Census. Washington, D.C.: Government Printing Office, 1975. 2
   vols. Payson and Plaza Ref **HA202 B87 1975**

INVESTOR'S GUIDE TO ECONOMIC INDICATORS, BY Charles R. Nelson. NY: Wiley, 1987. Plaza
   HC106.8 N38 1987

NEW PALGRAVE: A DICTIONARY OF ECONOMICS, edited by John Eatwell, Murray Milgate,
   Peter Newman, NY: Stockton Press, 1987. Payson and Plaza Ref **HB61 N49, 1987**

STATISTICAL ABSTRACT OF THE UNITED STATES. United States. Dept. of Commerce, Bureau of the Census. Washington, D.C.: Government Printing Office, Annual. Payson and Plaza Ref. **HA202 A2**

TRACKING AMERICA'S ECONOMY, by Norman Frumkin. Armonk, NY: M. E. Sharpe, 1987. Plaza **HC106.8 F78 1987**

UCLA BUSINESS FORECASTS FOR THE NATION AND CALIFORNIA. Los Angeles, University of California, quarterly. Payson and Plaza Ref **HC101 B822**

U. S. INDUSTRIAL OUTLOOK. U.S. Dept. of Commerce, International Trade Administration. Washington, D.C.: Government Printing Office, Annual. Payson, Plaza and Orange Ref **HC101 U54**

Periodicals

ECONOMIC INDICATORS, monthly. U.S. Council of Economic Advisers.

FEDERAL RESERVE BULLETIN, monthly. Board of Governors of the Federal Reserve. Pepperdine also receives periodical publications from all Federal Reserve Banks - New York, Cleveland, Richmond, San Francisco, etc.)

SURVEY OF CURRENT BUSINESS, monthly. U.S. Bureau of Economic Analysis.

■ ■ ■ ■ ■ ■

To find other related material, consult the online catalog under the following subject headings:

> S/Economic indicators
> S/Economics-Dictionaries
> S/United States--Economic Conditions--Statistics--Periodicals

Or look under the "country. agency" as author as follows:

> A/United States. Bureau of Economic Analysis
> A/United States. Dept. of Commerce

For journal articles, use the following indexes:

BUSINESS PERIODICAL INDEX. New York: Wilson, monthly with quarterly and annual cumulations.

INTERNATIONAL EXECUTIVE (Reference Guide at the end of each issue) New York: Wiley & Thunderbird, bimonthly. (Located in alphabetical order with periodicals.)

JOURNAL OF ECONOMIC LITERATURE (Book Review, Annotated Listing of New Books. Subject Index of Articles in Current Periodicals with Selected Abstracts.) Nashville, TN: American Economic Association, quarterly.

PAIS INTERNATIONAL IN PRINT. New York: Public Affairs Information Service, monthly with quarterly and annual cumulations.

■ ■ ■ ■ ■ ■

Economic statistics for the United States and other countries may also by found in the **NATIONAL TRADE DATA BANK (NTDB) database,** produced on CD-ROM by the U.S. Department of Commerce. NTDB is available at Payson, Plaza and Orange County Pepperdine Libraries and other government depository libraries.

■ ■ ■ ■ ■ ■

BUSINESS REFERENCE SOURCES
Industry Surveys

ANNUAL SURVEY OF MANUFACTURERS. Washington, D. C. U.S. Bureau of the Census. Includes information by Standard Industrial Classification on number of establishments, value of shipments, # of employees, etc. Payson and Plaza ref **HD9724 A211**

ENCYCLOPEDIA OF ASSOCIATIONS, 3 volumes. Detroit: Gale Research, Annual. Keyword index in volume 2 and geographic index in volume 3. Includes address, telephone number, officers, annual meeting dates and publications for each. Payson, Plaza and OCC Ref **HS17 G337**

INSIDE U.S. BUSINESS: A Concise Encyclopedia of Leading Industries, by Philip Mattera. Homewood, IL: Dow Jones-Irwin, 1987. Plaza **HC106.8 M337 1991**

STANDARD & POOR'S INDUSTRY SURVEYS. New York: Standard & Poor's Corporation. Basic Analysis section revised annually, Current Analysis section revised quarterly. Payson, Plaza and OCC Ref **HC106.6 S74**

STANDARD INDUSTRIAL CLASSIFICATION MANUAL. Washington, D.C.: Executive Office of the President, Office of Management and Budget, 1987. Payson, Plaza and OCC Ref **HF1042 A55** 1987

STRUCTURE OF AMERICAN INDUSTRY, by Walter Adams. New York: Macmillan, 1986. 7th edition, Plaza **HC106.8 S78 1986**

U.S. INDUSTRIAL OUTLOOK. Washington, D.C.; U.S. Department of Commerce, Annual. Payson, Plaza, OCC **HC101 U54**

VALUE LINE INVESTMENT SURVEY. New York: Value Line, Inc., weekly. Part 1 Selection and Opinion, Summary/Index and each Edition updated every 13 weeks, Part 2 Selection & Opinion, Part 3 Ratings and Reports. Payson, Plaza, OCC Ref **HG4501 V26**

■ ■ ■ ■ ■ ■

Industry Surveys
Ratios

ALMANAC OF BUSINESS AND INDUSTRIAL FINANCIAL RATIOS. Englewood Cliffs, New Jersey: Prentice-Hall, annual. Payson and Plaza Ref **HF5681 R25 T68**

ANNUAL STATEMENT STUDIES. Philadelphia: Robert Morris Associates, annual. Payson, Plaza and OCC Ref **HF5681 B2 R6**

INDUSTRY NORMS AND KEY BUSINESS RATIOS. New York: Dun & Bradstreet, Inc., annual. Payson, Plaza and OCC Ref **HF5681 R25 I525**

Periodicals

BUSINESS WEEK, INVESTMENT OUTLOOK Special Issue Annually in the first or last issue of the year, CORPORATE SCORE BOARD quarterly.

FORBES, ANNUAL REPORT OF AMERICAN INDUSTRY. Annually in the first issue of the year.

COMPANY INFORMATION
Directories

AMERICA'S CORPORATE FAMILIES, THE BILLION DOLLAR DIRECTORY. Parsippany, NJ: Dun's Marketing Services, annual. Payson, Plaza, OCC Ref **HG 4057 A147**

DIRECTORY OF COMPANIES REQUIRED TO FILE ANNUAL REPORTS WITH THE SECURITIES AND EXCHANGE COMMISSION UNDER THE SECURITIES EXCHANGE ACT OF 1934. Washington, D.C.: The Commission, annual. Payson, Plaza, OCC Ref **HG4057 A216**

DIRECTORY OF CORPORATE AFFILIATIONS. WILMETTE, IL: National Register, annual. Payson, Plaza Ref **HG4057 A217**

DUN'S BUSINESS RANKINGS. Los Angeles: Dun's Marketing Services, annual. Payson, Plaza OCC Ref **HG4057 A237**

MACMILLAN DIRECTORY OF LEADING PRIVATE COMPANIES, Willmette, IL: National Register, 1990. Payson, Plaza Ref **HG4057 A2899**

MILLION DOLLAR DIRECTORY. New York: Dun & Bradstreet, annual. Payson, Plaza, OCC
   Ref **HC102 D8**. (Includes geographic and industry 9SIC) index.)

THOMAS REGISTER OF AMERICAN MANUFACTURERS, THOMAS REGISTER CATALOG
   FILE. Vols. 1-10 Products & Services, 11 & 12 Company Profiles, 13-18 Catalogs, annual.
   Payson, Plaza, OCC Ref **T12 T6**

WARD'S DIRECTORY OF LARGEST U.S. CORPORATIONS. By the editors of News
   Front/Business Trends. Vol.1 Largest Public & Private, Vol.2 Largest
   private, Vol.3 Largest International, annual. Payson, Plaza, OCC **HG4009 W35**

   (Includes ranking within SIC industries by sales)

Directories - California

"CALIFORNIA 500". Los Angeles: California Business News, Inc. Annually in May issue of
   CALIFORNIA BUSINESS.

A MANUFACTURERS REGISTER. Los Angeles: Times Mirror Press, annual. Payson, Plaza and
   OCC Ref **T12 C15**

CALIFORNIA SERVICES REGISTER. Los Angeles: Times Mirror Mirror Press, 1987. Payson and
   Plaza Ref **HD9981.7 C2 C34**

SOUTHERN CALIFORNIA BUSINESS DIRECTORY AND BUYER'S GUIDE. Los Angeles: LA
   Chamber of Commerce, annual. Payson, Plaza, OCC Ref **HF5065 C2 S66**

History and Financial Data

HOOVER'S HANDBOOK OF AMERICAN BUSINESS. Austin, TX: Reference Press, annual.
   Payson, Plaza, Orange Ref **HG 4057 A28617**

INTERNATIONAL DIRECTORY OF COMPANY HISTORIES, vols. 1-6. Chicago, IL: St. James
   Press, 1988- Payson & Plaza Ref **HD2721 I57x**

MOODY'S MANUAL OF INVESTMENTS. New York: Moody's Investors Service. Annual
   volumes with semi-weekly NEWS REPORTS. Payson & Plaza Ref BANK AND
   FINANCE, 4 vols. **HG4961 M65**; INDUSTRIAL, **HG4961 M67**; INTERNATIONAL,
   HG4009 M66; MUNICIPAL AND GOVERNMENT, **HG4931 M58**; OTC INDUSTRIAL,
   HG4961 M7237; OTC UNLISTED, **HG4501 M582**; PUBLIC UTILITY, **HC4971 M7245**;
   TRANSPORTATION, **HG4971 M74**

STANDARD CORPORATION RECORDS. New York: Standard and Poor's Bimonthly, with DAILY
   NEWS updates. Loose-leaf in 7 binders. Payson Ref **HG4501 S76635**

STANDARD 7 POOR'S STOCK REPORTS, NYSE, AMSE 7 OTC. New York: Standard and Poor's Continuously updated.

Competitor Intelligence

BUSINESS COMPETITOR INTELLIGENCE: METHODS FOR COLLECTING, ORGANIZING AND USING INFORMATION, by William L. Sammon, Mark A. Kurland & Robert Spitalnic. New York: Wiley, 1984. Plaza **HD38.7 B87** 1984

COMPETITOR INTELLIGENCE: HOW TO GET IT, HOW TO USE IT, by Leonard Fuld. New York: Wiley, 1985. Plaza **HD38.7 F85** 1985

HOW TO FIND COMPANY INTELLIGENCE IN FEDERAL DOCUMENTS, Edition IL. Washington, D.C.: Washington Researchers, 1988. Plaza Ref **Z1223 Z7 H69 1986**

HOW TO FIND INFORMATION ABOUT COMPANIES, THE CORPORATE INTELLIGENCE SOURCE BOOK, Edition I, 2 vols. Washington, D.C.: Washington Researchers, 1991. Payson, Plaza, OCC & SFV Ref **HD2785 H68 1992-93**

MONITORING THE COMPETITION: FIND OUT WHAT'S REALLY GOING ON OVER THERE, by Leonard Fuld. New York: Wiley, 1988. Plaza **HD38.7**

GUIDES TO BUSINESS REFERENCE SOURCES

Berle, Gustav. BUSINESS INFORMATION SOURCEBOOK. New York: Wiley, 1991. Plaza and Orange Ref **HF5035 B4** 1991

Daniells, Lorna. BUSINESS INFORMATION SOURCES. (rev. ed.) Berkeley, CA: University of California, 1985. Payson, Plaza, OCC, SFV Ref **Z7164 C81 D16** 1985

Fletcher, J. INFORMATION SOURCES IN ECONOMICS. London: Butterworths, 1984. Plaza Ref **HB71 I53** 1984

Halperin, Michael and Steven J. Bell. RESEARCH GUIDE TO CORPORATE ACQUISITIONS, MERGERS, AND OTHER RESTRUCTURING. New York: Greenwood, 1992. Plaza Ref **HD2746.5 H357**

Lavin, Michael R. BUSINESS INFORMATION: HOW TO FIND IT, HOW TO USE IT (2nd ed.). Phoenix, AZ: Oryx, 1992. Law, Payson, Plaza Ref **HF5356 L36 1992**

Mayros, Van and D. Michael Werner. BUSINESS INFORMATION APPLICATIONS AND SOURCES. Radnor, PA: Chilton, 1983. Plaza Ref **HD30.35 M39**

Popovich, Charles J. BUSINESS AND ECONOMICS DATABASES ONLINE: ENVIRONMENTAL SCANNING WITH A PERSONAL COMPUTER. Littleton, CO: Libraries Unlimited, 1987. Plaza Ref **HF5548.2 P612** 1987

Schlessinger, Bernard S. THE BASIC BUSINESS LIBRARY: CORE RESOURCES (2ND ED.).

Phoenix, AZ: Oryx, 1989. Payson and Plaza Ref **Z675 B8 B37** 1989

Strauss, Diane Wheeler. HANDBOOK OF BUSINESS INFORMATION: A GUIDE FOR
LIBRARIANS, STUDENTS AND RESEARCHERS. Englewood, CO: Libraries Unlimited,
1988. Plaza Ref **HF5361 S7796** 1988

Woy, James, editor. ENCYCLOPEDIA OF BUSINESS INFORMATION SOURCES. Detroit, MI:
Gale Research, (Triennial). OCC, Payson and Plaza Ref **HF5035 E53**

INVESTMENTS BIBLIOGRAPHY
General Sources

THE BUSINESS ONE IRWIN GUIDE TO USING THE WALL STREET JOURNAL, by Michael B.
Lehman. Homewood, ILL: Business One Irwin, 1993. Payson, Plaza, Orange
Ref **HB3743 L44** 1993

DOW JONES-IRWIN BUSINESS AND INVESTMENTS ALMANAC. Homewood, ILL: Business One
Irwin, annual. Plaza Ref **HF5003 D68a**

THE SOCINVESTMENT ALMANAC: COMPREHENSIVE GUIDE TO SOCIALLY RESPONSIBLE
INVESTING, edited by Peter D. Kinder, et al. New York: H. Holt and
Company, 1992. Plaza Ref **HG4527 K525** 1992

THE SPICER AND OPPENHEIM GUIDE TO SECURITIES MARKETS AROUND THE WORLD.
New York: J. Wiley, 1988. Plaza Ref **HG4551 S645** 1988

Stocks

MOODY'S DIVIDEND RECORD. New York: Moody's Investor Service, annual. Payson,
Plaza, Orange Ref **HG4905 M795**

MOODY'S HANDBOOK OF COMMON STOCKS. New York: Moody's Investor Service, quarterly.
Payson, Plaza, Orange Ref **HG4501 M59**

O'NEIL DATABASE. Los Angeles, CA: William O'Neil & Company, weekly. Payson,
Plaza, Orange Ref **HG4916 O532**

STOCK GUIDE, Standard and Poor's Corp. New York: Standard and Poor's Corp,
monthly. Payson and Plaza Ref **HG4921 S75**

THE UNLISTED MARKET GUIDE. Glen Head, NY: Unlisted Market Service Corp., 1984.
Plaza Ref **HG4916 U54** 1984

Bonds

BOND GUIDE, Standard and Poor's Corp. New York: Standard and Poor's Corp., monthly. Payson and Plaza Ref **HG4905 S435**

MOODY'S BOND RECORD. New York: Moody's Investors Service, annual. Payson, Plaza, Orange   Ref **HG4905 M78**

MOODY'S BOND SURVEY. New York: Moody's Investors Service, weekly. Payson and Plaza Ref **HG4905 M785**

Mutual Funds

THE DOW JONES-IRWIN GUIDE TO MUTUAL FUNDS, by Donald Rugg. Homewood, Ill: Dow Jones-Irwin, 1986. Payson Ref **HG4530 R83** 1986

GUIDE TO MUTUAL FUNDS. Washington, D. C.: Investment Company Institute, 1987. Payson Ref **HG4930 G85** 1987

INVESTMENT COMPANIES, 1987 MEETING NEW CHALLENGES, by Stanley J. Freedman. New York: Practicing Law Institute, 1987. Plaza Ref **KF1078 I577** 1987

INVESTMENT COMPANIES' SERVICES. New York: A. Wiesenberger, annual. Payson and Plaza Ref **HG4497 W47**

MORNINGSTAR MUTUAL FUNDS. Chicago, IL: Morningstar, Inc., biweekly. Plaza Ref **HG4530 M8**

THE MUTUAL FUND ENCYCLOPEDIA, by Gerald W. Perritt. Chicago, IL: Dearborn Financial Publications, 1990. Payson Ref **HG4530 P432** 1990

MUTUAL FUND FACT BOOK. Washington, D.C.: Investment Company Institute, Annual. Payson and Plaza Ref **HG4930 M85**

WILLIAM E. DONOGHUE'S NO-LOAD MUTUAL FUND GUIDE, by William E. Donoghue and Thomas Tilling. New York: Harper & Row, 1983. Plaza **HG4930 D65** 1983

Commodities

COMMODITY YEAR BOOK. New York: Commodity Research Bureau, annual. Plaza Ref **HF1041 C56**

Periodicals

BARRON'S NATIONAL BUSINESS AND FINANCIAL WEEKLY. Chicopee, MA: Dow Jones. Payson, Plaza, Orange

MONEY. Chicago, IL: Time, Inc., monthly. Payson and Plaza

PENSIONS AND INVESTMENTS. Chicago, IL: Crain Communications, Inc., biweekly.
   Plaza

WALL STREET JOURNAL. New York: Dow Jones, daily except Weekends and Holidays.
   Pason, Plaza, Orange

ADVERTISING AND MARKETING
General

BEACHAM'S MARKETING REFERENCE, 2 vols. Washington, D.C.: Research Publishing,
   1986. Plaza Ref **HF5415 B379** 1986

MACMILLAN DICTIONARY OF MARKETING & ADVERTISING. N.Y.: Nichols Publishing
   Company. Payson and Plaza Ref **HF5415 B273** 1984

Advertising

ADVERTISING RATIOS & BUDGETS. Evanston, IL: Schonfeld & Associates, Inc. Plaza
   Ref **HF5801 A383**

BACON'S PUBLICITY CHECKER. Chicago: R. H. Bacon, annual. Payson and Plaza
   Ref **HD59 B3**

DIRECT MARKETING MARKETPLACE. Hewlett Harbor, N.Y.: Hilary House Publishers,
   annual. Payson and Plaza Ref **HF5415.1 D57**

STANDARD DIRECTORY OF ADVERTISERS. Skokie, Il.: National Register, annual.
   Payson Ref. **HF5804 S72**

STANDARD DIRECTORY OF ADVERTISING AGENCIES. New York: National Register, 3/yr.
   Payson Ref **HF5805 S72**

Demographics

EDITOR & PUBLISHER MARKET GUIDE. New York: Editor & Publisher, annual. Payson
   and Plaza Ref **HF5905 E38**

SIMMONS STUDY OF MEDIA AND MARKETS (microfiche). New York: Simmons Market
   Research Bureau, annual. Payson, Plaza, OCC Ref **HF5415.3 S78**

SOURCEBOOK OF DEMOGRAPHICS AND BUYING POWER FOR EVERY ZIP CODE IN THE
   USA. Arlington, VA: CACI, annual. Plaza and OCC Ref **HA203 S66**

STATISTICAL ABSTRACT OF THE UNITED STATES. U.S. Bureau of the Census, annual.

Payson, Plaza and Orange Ref **HA202 A2** 1991

SURVEY OF BUYING POWER: DATA SERVICE. S&MM (Sales & Marketing Management), annual. Data also appears in July and Oct issues of S&MM. Payson and Plaza Ref **HF5415.2 S94**

Periodicals

ADVERTISING AGE, weekly. Chicago: Crain.

AMERICAN DEMOGRAPHICS, monthly. Sections on U.S. Regions, Books, and People Puzzle in each issue.

CPI DETAILED REPORT, monthly. Washington, D.C.: U.S. Bureau of Labor Statistics.

JOURNAL OF MARKETING, quarterly. New York: American Marketing Association.

JMR, JOURNAL OF MARKETING RESEARCH, quarterly. Chicago: American Marketing Association.

MONTHLY LABOR REVIEW. Washington, D. C.: U. S. Bureau of Labor Statistics.

S&MM: SALES & MARKETING MANAGEMENT, monthly. New York: S&MM.

INTERNATIONAL TRADE, FINANCE & MULTINATIONAL CORPORATIONS
General Information

ENCYCLOPEDIA OF INTERNATIONAL COMMERCE, by William J. Miller, Centerville, MD: Cornell Maritime Press, 1985. Plaza Ref **HF1001 M55**

INFORMATION FOR INTERNATIONAL MARKETING: AN ANNOTATED GUIDE TO SOURCES, compiled by James K. Weekly and Mary K. Cary. New York: Greenwood Press, 1986. Plaza Ref **Z7164 C8 W4**

INTERNATIONAL BUSINESS KNOWLEDGE: MANAGING INTERNATIONAL FUNCTIONS IN THE 1990S, edited by William A. Dymszo and Robert G. Varnbery. New York: Praeger, 1987. Plaza **HD62.4 I56** 1987

INTERNATIONAL DIRECT INVESTMENT. Washington, D.C.: U.S. Dept. of Commerce, International Trade Administration, annual. Payson & Plaza Ref **HG4538 I57**

WORLD ECONOMIC OUTLOOK: A SURVEY BY THE STAFF OF THE INTERNATIONAL MONETARY FUND. Washington, D.C.: The Fund, biannual. Plaza Ref **HC10 W79**

WORLD ECONOMIC SURVEY: CURRENT TRENDS AND POLICIES IN THE WORLD ECONOMY. New York: United Nations. Dept. of International Economic and Social Affairs, annual. Plaza Ref **HC59 A169**

Country Economic and Financial Data

BALANCE OF PAYMENTS STATISTICS. YEARBOOK. Washington, D. C.: International
Monetary Fund, annual in 2 parts. Plaza Ref **HD3882 B34**

CORPORATE TAXES, A WORLDWIDE SUMMARY. New York: Price Waterhouse Center for
Transnational Taxation, annual. Plaza Ref **HD2753 A3 I54**

COUNTRY REPORT (Argentina, Brazil, Guatemala-El Salvador- Honduras, Mexico,
Peru-Bolivia). London: Economist Intelligence Unit, quarterly & annual.
Plaza Periodicals.

DEMOGRAPHIC YEARBOOK. Annuaire demographique. New York: United Nations. Dept. of
Economic and Social Affairs, annual. Payson & Plaza Ref **HA17 D45**

DOING BUSINESS IN ..... New York: Price Waterhouse. Plaza **HC14 P946**

EIU WORLD OUTLOOK. London: Economist Intelligence Unit, annual. Plaza Ref **HC59
E387a** 1989

FOREIGN ECONOMIC TRENDS AND THEIR IMPLICATIONS FOR THE UNITED STATES.
United States. Bureau of International Commerce. Washington, D.C.: U.S.
Government Printing Office. Series of semiannual or annual reports on over
100 countries. Plaza & Payson Ref **HC10 F6**

GOVERNMENT ECONOMIC AGENCIES OF THE WORLD, edited by Alan J. Day. Detroit: Gale
Research Company, 1985. Plaza Ref **HD87.25 G68** 1985B

INTERNATIONAL FINANCIAL STATISTICS. Washington, D. C.: International Monetary
Fund, monthly with yearbook. Payson & Plaza Periodicals

OVERSEAS BUSINESS REPORTS. United States. International Trade Administration.
Washington, D.C.: U.S. Government Printing Office. Reports on over 100
countries. Payson Ref **HP91 U482**

STATISTICAL YEARBOOK. Annuaire statistique. New York: United Nations.
statistical Office, annual. Updated by monthly Bulletin of Statistics
(Payson). Payson, Plaza, Orange Ref **HA12.5 U63**

WARDLEY GUIDE TO WORLD MONEY AND SECURITIES MARKETS, by Lynette J. Kemp.
London: Euromoney, 1984. Plaza Ref **HG4523 K35** 1984

WORLD DEBT TABLES: EXTERNAL DEBT OF DEVELOPING COUNTRIES. Washington: D. C.:
World Bank, annual. Plaza Ref **HJ8899 W672**

WORLD TABLES, 1989-1990 edition. Baltimore, MD: Published by Johns Hopkins
University Press for the World Bank, 1990. Payson, Plaza, Orange
Ref **HC59 W669**

Trade Data by Product

INTERNATIONAL MARKETING DATA & STATISTICS. London: Euromonitor, annual. Plaza & Payson Ref **HA42 I56** 1987

INTERNATIONAL TRADE STATISTICS YEARBOOK, v.1 Trade by Country, v. 2 Trade by Commodity. New York: United Nations. Plaza Ref **HF91 U473**

U.S. INDUSTRIAL OUTLOOK. Washington, D. C.: U.S. Dept. of Commerce, annual. Payson, Plaza Orange Ref **HC101 U54** (NTDB)

International Company Directories

INTERNATIONAL DIRECTORY OF CORPORATE AFFILIATIONS. Skokie, IL: National Register, annual. Payson & Plaza Ref **HD2741 I59**

MOODY'S INTERNATIONAL MANUAL. New York: Moody's Investors Service, annual. Payson & Plaza REf **HC4009 M66**

PRINCIPAL INTERNATIONAL BUSINESSES. New York: Dun & Bradstreet, annual. Payson & Plaza Ref **HF54 U5 P74**

Library of Congress Subject Headings

Commerce -- use for foreign trade
(country name) -- economic conditions
Foreign Trade Regulation
International Business Enterprises -- use for multinationals
International Finance -- Statistics
Investments, Foreign -- Statistics

Periodical Indexes

BUSINESS PERIODICAL INDEX. New York: H. G. Wilson, monthly with quarterly and annual cumulations.

JOURNAL OF ECONOMIC LITERATURE, quarterly. Classified listings of journal articles and book reviews (F = International Economics; F01 = global outlook)

PAIS INTERNATIONAL IN PRINT. Washington, D. C.: Public Affairs Information service, monthly with quarterly and annual cumulations

Selected Journals

COLUMBIA JOURNAL OF WORLD BUSINESS. New York: Columbia University, quarterly.

EUROMONEY. London: Euromoney, monthly. Supplements on special topics

FOREIGN AFFAIRS. New York: Foreign Relations Council, 5/yr.

INSTITUTIONAL INVESTOR, International Edition. New York: Institutional Investor, monthly.

JOURNAL OF INTERNATIONAL BUSINESS STUDIES. Columbia, SC: University of South Carolina, 3/yr.

MANAGEMENT INTERNATIONAL REVIEW. Weisbaden, Germany: Verlag, quarterly.

SURVEY OF CURRENT BUSINESS. Washington, D.C.: U.S. Dept. of Commerce, monthly.

Other Databases

ABI/Inform, produced by Data Courier, abstracts and indexing for over 800 journals, updated monthly. Long Beach Academic Computing Lab and San Fernando Valley Reference Center.

Business Periodicals On Disk, full image for over 400 journals on laser disk from journals indexed in ABI/Inform. Long Beach Academic Computing Lab and San Fernando Valley Reference Center.

National Trade Data Bank. Produced by the U.S. Dept. of Commerce with data from over 15 agencies including the CIA, International trade Administration and the Dept. of Agriculture. Full-text ASCII and spreadsheet documents may be downloaded to disk or printed. Updated monthly. Payson, Plaza and Orange County.

Wilson Business Abstracts. Indexing and abstracts from over 350 English language periodicals. Abstracts since 1990 and indexing since 1986. Payson, Plaza & Orange County.

Use this page to make a Large Name Card
to place on your desk
for the instructor to see.
Place the Name Card on your desk at each class.
Print your name in LARGE, BOLD, DARK BLACK marker pen.

BIOGRAPHY CARDS: SIDE A

NAME: . . . .
   (please print: first name first

Nickname: . . . .

(photo)

AGE:. . . . . ACADEMIC STATUS: . . . .

EXPECTED GRADUATION DATE: . . . .

CONCENTRATION: . . . .
(strength)

CONTACT PHONE NUMBERS

RESIDENCE: . . . .
BUSINESS: . . . .
FAX: . . . .

MAILING ADDRESSES . . . .
RESIDENCE

. . . .
BUSINESS

ACADEMIC EXPERIENCE: OTHER COLLEGES ATTENDED & DEGREES RECEIVED: (Majors)

. . . .

BUSINESS EXPERIENCE: PUT PRESENT COMPANY & POSITION FIRST

. . . .

. . . .

CAREER PLANS: RIGHT AFTER GRADUATION . . . .
. . . .

LONGER TERM PLANS . . . .

. . . .

. . . .

. . . .

. . . .

BIOGRAPHY CARDS: SIDE B

NAME: . . . .

CLASS: . . . .

(please print: first name first)

LEAVE THE REST OF THIS FORM BLANK... TO BE USED BY INSTRUCTOR

#1 . . . .

#2 . . . .

#3 . . . .

#4 . . . .

#5 . . . .

#6 . . . .

#7 . . . .

#8 . . . .

#9 . . . .

#10 . . . .

#11 . . . .

#12 . . . .

#13 . . . .

#14 . . . .

#15 . . . .

#16 . . . .

#17 . . . .

#18 . . . .

#19 . . . .

#20 . . . .

#21 . . . .

COMMENTS:

ADDITIONAL INFORMATION

NAME: . . . .
(please print: first name first)

CLASS: . . . .

DATE: . . . .

BUSINESS EXPERIENCE:
(Write "yes" or NA for "not applicable" for every item)

NON-OPERATING EXPERIENCE:

_____   I have invested personally in ____ businesses.

_____   I have served as a director or advisor to ____ businesses.

_____   I have served in some other non-operating role in ____ businesses. (please describe)

OPERATING EXPERIENCE:

_____   I have **full time** operating experience as the CEO of ____ businesses.

_____   I have **full time** operating experience as a senior member of a business team of ____ businesses.   (note role: CFO, Mkting VP, etc)

Please circle: My strongest area is:

Sales
Marketing
Finance
Accounting
MIS/Computers
Production

_____   I know an interesting CEO who could probably contribute to our study of business.

Who? . . . .

. . . .

TEAM FORMATION SHEET
(TO BE SUBMITTED TO YOUR PROFESSOR)

<u>PRINT NAME</u>   <u>PHONE</u>

1. . . . .

2. . . . .

3. . . . .

4. . . . .

5. . . . .

6. . . . .

TEAM # . . . .

ASSIGNED CASE: . . . .

PRESENTATION DATE(S): . . . .

COMMENTS: . . . .

. . . .

. . . .

. . . .

. . . .

TEAM FORMATION SHEET FOR STUDENTS

	PRINT NAME	PHONE

1. . . . .

2. . . . .

3. . . . .

4. . . . .

5. . . . .

6. . . . .

TEAM NAME OR # . . . .

SCHEDULED MEETING TIME: . . . .

SCHEDULED MEETING PLACE: . . . .

Other Information: . . . .

. . . .

. . . .

. . . .

. . . .

. . . .

. . . .

. . . .

. . . .

CASE PRESENTATION ASSIGNMENT SHEET

PRINT NAME   PHONE

1. . . . .

2. . . . .

3. . . . .

4. . . . .

5. . . . .

TEAM # . . . .

CASE TO BE PRESENTED: . . . .

CASE PRESENTATION DATE: . . . .

Field Reports Summary Sheet
Complete the attached summary.
Submit to your instructor.
Print clearly or type.

CLASS SECTION #_____   TEAM NUMBER #_____

NAMES OF TEAM MEMBERS:

. . . .

. . . .

. . . .

. . . .

. . . .

. . . .

. . . .

. . . .

NAME OF COMPANY: . . . .

TYPE OF COMPANY: . . . .

MAJOR PRODUCTS: . . . .

. . . .

. . . .

MAJOR MARKETS: . . . .

. . . .

INTERVIEWEES: . . . .

. . . .

MAJOR OBSERVATIONS: . . . .

. . . .

CASE PREPARATION SHEET
Complete for each case.

CASE NAME, CLASS, & DATE: ....

What is the situational context of the case? ....
....
....
....
....

Who are the principal players? ....
....
....
....
....

What are the pertinent facts provided in the text? ....
....
....
....
....
....

What are the pertinent facts provided in the exhibits? ....
....
....
....
....

What concepts apply? ....
....
....
....

What is difficult to understand? Why? Explain it! ....
....
....
....
....

CASE DISCUSSION SUMMARY SHEET
Complete for each case. Bring to class for discussion.

NAME OF CASE: . . . .

DATE: . . . .

CLASS: . . . .

KEY ISSUES OR CONCEPTS DISCUSSED: . . . .
. . . .
. . . .
. . . .

MAJOR POINTS OR LESSONS: . . . .
. . . .
. . . .
. . . .

OTHER FACTS, IDEAS OF INTEREST: . . . .
. . . .
. . . .
. . . .
. . . .
. . . .
. . . .
. . . .
. . . .
. . . .
. . . .
. . . .
. . . .
. . . .
. . . .
. . . .
. . . .

Case Presentation Assessment

Case: . . . . Group Member: Yes No

Group: . . . .

	Assessment		
Criteria	**Lousy**	**OK**	**Wow!**
1. Overall organization	1 2	3 4	5
2. Introduction	1 2	3 4	5
3. Organization of main body	1 2	3 4	5
4. Level of detail employed	1 2	3 4	5
5. Summary	1 2	3 4	5
6. Clarity of presentation	1 2	3 4	5
7. Relevance of presentation	1 2	3 4	5
8. Use of presentation aids	1 2	3 4	5
9. Quality of presentation aids	1 2	3 4	5
10. Presenter's handling of questions	1 2	3 4	5
11. Quality of quantitative assessment	1 2	3 4	5
12. Quality of qualitative assessment	1 2	3 4	5
13. Ability to relate trends to company	1 2	3 4	5
14. Identification of strategic problems	1 2	3 4	5
15. Identification of strategic options	1 2	3 4	5
16. Identification of existing (generic) strategy	1 2	3 4	5
17. Identification of (key idea) strategy. . . .	1 2	3 4	5
18. Identification of existing objectives and goals	1 2	3 4	5

(continued on next page)

Criteria	Assessment				
	Lousy		OK		Wow!
19. Identification of existing policies	1	2	3	4	5
20. Identification of existing plans	1	2	3	4	5
21. Development of detailed objectives & goals .	1	2	3	4	5
22. Development of detailed policies	1	2	3	4	5
23. Development of specific plans	1	2	3	4	5
24. Overall impression of <u>presentation</u>	1	2	3	4	5
25. Overall impression of <u>presenters</u>	1	2	3	4	5

Points which should have been covered but were not: . . . .

. . . .

. . . .

Questions which should have been answered but were not: . . . .

. . . .

. . . .

. . . .

Topics which <u>could</u> have been omitted/shorten: . . . .

. . . .

. . . .

. . . .

Other comments: . . . .

. . . .

. . . .

. . . .

CLASS PRESENTATIONS: CHECKLIST

_____1. Have you determined how each team member will participate in the presentation?

_____2. Have you scheduled a time to practice your presentation prior to class?

_____3. Have you determine how long the presentation should be and how much time should be devoted to Q&A?

_____4. Have you prepared a list of likely questions?

_____5. Have you discussed who will handle the introduction of each team member?

_____6. Have you determined explicitly how the transition from one team member (presenter) to another will be made?

_____7. Have you determined how to open and close the presentation in an interesting and professional way?

<u>FOR NON-PRESENTERS</u> (Class members who are <u>not</u> part of the presentation team)

_____1. I realize I'm expected to ask questions at the end of each presentation.

_____2. I realize I may be asked by the instructor to give my views on the strong and weak points of the presentation.

PRESENTATION WORKSHEET

CLASS, PROJECT NAME, & DATE: . . . .

. . . .

THESIS: . . . .
. . . .
. . . .
. . . .
. . . .

OPENING: A Real Attention Grabber . . . .
. . . .
. . . .
. . . .
. . . .

APPEARANCE (APPROPRIATE ATTIRE)
. . . .
. . . .
. . . .
. . . .

CONTENT: KEY POINTS OR MESSAGES IN SUPPORT OF YOUR THESIS OR MAJOR ARGUMENT.
. . . .
. . . .
. . . .

HOW TO MOTIVATE AUDIENCE TO BELIEVE IN MY THESIS:
. . . .
. . . .
. . . .
. . . .

PRESENTATION AIDS: WHEN, WHERE, HOW MOST EFFECTIVE:
. . . .
. . . .
. . . .
. . . .

HOW CLOSE WITH IMPACT: . . . .
. . . .
. . . .
. . . .
. . . .
. . . .

STUDENT FEEDBACK ON COURSE

DATE: . . . .

COURSE: . . . .

INSTRUCTOR: . . . .

1. What I <u>most liked</u> about the course:

     1. . . . .

     2. . . . .

     3. . . . .

2. What I <u>least liked</u> about the course:

     1. . . . .

     2. . . . .

     3. . . . .

3. I suggest the following improvements:

     1. . . . .

     2. . . . .

     3. . . . .

Comments:

. . . .

. . . .

. . . .

. . . .

. . . .

SOFTWARE

RONSTADT'S FINANCIALS

Software: Ronstadt's Financials will generate Forecasted Revenue Statement, Projected Income Statement, Balance Sheet, Projected Cash Flow, & instantly calculate over 175 Key Ratios and Measures, Breakeven Analyses & more. Faster and easier than any spreadsheet, Ronstadt's Financials includes pre-built financial models for all types of businesses. All you have to do is enter your basic assumptions, and the projected financials are created for you, FAST & EASY. Create a "best case scenario" and compare it to a "worst case scenario". Do the "WHAT IF" decisionmaking in half the time. Ronstadt's Financials is menu driven, includes a graphing capability, import and export data. IBM or compatibles with 640K Ram. *$139*

RONSTADT'S FINANCIALS PRO

Software: If you want to go beyond 640K with your financial model, you need Ronstadt's Financials PROfessional. If you want Windows in Ram, or you're on a network, or you want to compare as many as six scenarios simultaneously, you'll need more than 640K Ram. The PRO version gives you the memory management you require for those bigger jobs. $299

TEMPLATES

These add-on templates (software) enhance the value of your investment in Ronstadt's Financials.

EASYPLAN

As the name implies, this template is created for EASY customization and modeling of any business. In addition to the usual projected Income Statement, Balance Sheet, Cash Flow, Forecasted Revenues, you get a Schedule of Cost of Goods, amortized Schedule of Start-Up Costs, Payroll Schedule, Schedule of Advertising, Schedule of Fixed Assets, Schedule of Taxes, Accounts Receivable & Accounts Payable, and much more. Used by both product or service

companies. Sometimes includes with Version 2. When used with Ronstadt's Financials, this model is your best bet for doing CASE ANALYSIS! $69.

MARKETING & SALES MODEL

This template can be added into any of the library files which already come with Ronstadt's Financials, or it can be used as a stand-alone Marketing & Sales Plan. Used by marketing and sales professional, and also by marketing/sales departmental professionals, this template includes detailed budgets for Public Relations, Advertising, Marketing Research, Radio, Television, Catalog & Mailings, Collateral & Printed Materials, Direct Mail, Telemarketing, Trade Show, Packaging, Premiums & Promos, Travel & Entertainment, Marketing & Sales Payroll, Training & Professional Development Budget. If you're creating a Marketing and Sales Plan, this detailed plan is great. If you're writing a Business Plan, the Marketing & Sales Plan can be incorporated. IBM $39.95

FRANCHISE MODEL

This template has two models: one is a 12-month scenario and a 5-year annual model. The 12-month model includes Projected Revenue Statement, Income Statement, Balance Sheet, Cash Flow, Key Ratios & Measures, Breakeven Analysis, Schedule of Purchases & Inventory, and an Advertising & Promotional Budget. The assumptions are those you'd expect to see in making decisions pertaining to franchises: # of Existing Franchises, # of New Franchises, # of Conversions per year, each month, etc. The 5-year model contains the same, but looks at a longer plan. If you're a franchisor, or would like to consider becoming one, these templates are invaluable. If you're a franchisee, you'll do the usual financial projections with greater ease, clarity, and using an accurate model of a franchise business. $99.

SOFTWARE PUBLISHING

Although this template is set up for a Software

Publishing company, with a few easy modifications, it can also be used for any business where, for example, you have a product, you pay royalties, you go through multiple channels of distribution, have an R&D budget. Includes Assumptions Statement, Revenue Forecast, Income Statement, Balance Sheet, Cash Flow Projections, Key Ratios & Measures, detailed R&D budget, detailed standard product cost statement (for multiple products), and even a very detailed Marketing and Sales Plan, a Manpower Plan, Salary & Wage Schedule, and Schedule of Production and Purchasing Analysis. IBM $49.95

1-900 PHONE SERVICE MODEL

Have you ever considered using a 900 phone service telephone number as a potential revenue service. 900 telephone numbers are becoming more widely used by companies providing a service via the telephone. In fact, many software companies are now using 900 phone numbers for their customer technical support. Here's how it works: you call 1-900-phone number. The telephone number keeps track of the time used on that number, and bills that amount to the caller on their telephone bill at a rate determined by you. You then share those revenues with the telephone company. This model will help you determine how many calls you'll need to receive to breakeven. It will also show you the effect on your startup costs, your cash flow, and whether you'd lose or make money. IBM $49.95

PRIORITY CASH FLOW MODEL

Each of the library files that come with Ronstadt's Financials includes a Projected Cash Flow generated by the assumptions in your scenario. This standalone differs in that it looks at anticipated cash inflows and outflows with a view toward maximizing (stretching) cash flow to the limit! Whether you're cash short because you're growing the business, you're in a workout situation, or if you simply want to maximize your cash, this model will show you what the maximum amount of cash you could have available is. $49.95

VALUATION/DILUTION MODEL

This model will help you value a business using several different methods: the First Chicago Venture Group method; a simple compounding method, and others. In addition, it will compute for you the value of stock after each of up to as many as six rounds of equity financing. $49.95

LEASE vs. BUY ANALYSIS

Should you lease or buy? This model looks at all the alternatives under different assumptions. $39.95

PROJECTED PAYROLL MODEL

If you're anticipating a large payroll (over 6 employees), this model will help you be more precise about your projected payroll. Broken into three departments (which may be changed), the Sales & Marketing Department, Research and Development Department, and General and Administrative, you can have as many employees as the memory of your computer system can handle. This model may be tied into your projected Income Statement, or it may be used as a standalone.

BUSINESS PLAN on a Disk

Book with Optional Word Processing Diskette: This *fill-in-the-blank* word processing format Workbook and accompanying diskette helps you outline each section of your Business Plan. IBM *$39.95*

MARKETING PLAN on a Disk

Book with Optional Word Processing Diskette: With this Workbook and accompanying diskette, develop your Marketing Strategy, putting all the components of marketing together to identify and outline your Marketing Plan. Easy-to-use, *fill-in-the-blank* format. Helpful forms to help you organize your approach, determine customer needs and how you'll meet them. IBM *$39.95*

VENTURE FEASIBILITY PLAN

Book with Optional Word Processing Diskette:

Great Software & Books
Available from Lord Publishing

This Workbook is your first step *before* writing your Business Plan. It will help you determine if your business idea will meet your objectives, document you ideas, identify your customer opportunities, assess your financial resources. Better to go through this *"reality check"* before embarking upon writing your Business Plan. This Workbook may uncover weak areas in your concept, saving you time and money. *IBM $39.95*

SOURCES of CAPITAL FINDER

Software: Whether looking for seed capital, start-up funding, expansion or acquisition, this Database of Funding Sources will help you quickly identify the sources of capital critical to your business. Includes commercial finance firms, IPO underwriters, investment bankers, venture capitalists -- all potential sources of capital. With the stroke of a few keys, and in the privacy of your own home, this easy-to-use, menu-driven program asks you questions about your financing requirements and then sorts through the database to locate the company, contact name and address, phone number, investment criteria. Save time and uncertainty and find funding for your business now. *IBM $159*

ENTREPRENEURIAL FINANCE

Book: Also written by Dr. Robert Ronstadt, this book covers the financial aspects of "entrepreneuring". How much money does your business need? When is it needed? What form should it take ... debt or equity? If it's debt, how do you value the stock? How much is too much? How long can you survive with existing cash? What are the steps you can take to avoid disaster? What are the critical issues involved when raising money? Is your venture feasible? Keeping "control" and other equity issue. Who fails, and why? hc $39.95; pb $17.95

To Place Your Order
Call (800) 525-5673

198

14 Los Monteros Drive
Laguna Niguel, California
92629
(800) 525-5673

LORD PUBLISHING

BILL TO:

Name/Title

Organization

Street Address

City   State   Zip

YES! Please place my order for the following:

$129.00
Ronstadt's Financials Software, Version 2 (NEW)

$69.00
Update to Ronstadt's Financials, Version 2 (NEW)

$299.00
Ronstadt's Financials PROfessional *(Supports Extended Memory)*

$175.00
Update to Ronstadt's Financials Professional, Version 2 (NEW)

Disk Size: ☐ 5.25" ☐ 3.5"

SHIP TO:

Name/Title

Organization

Street Address

City   State   Zip

CHARGE TO MY CREDIT CARD ☐ VISA ☐ MasterCard ☐ AMEX

Credit Card Number _____ Expiration Date _____ mo. ___ yr. *

Name on Card (Print or Type) _____ Amount

Authorized Signature _____ Date

Telephone Number

* Add 5% Sales Tax for MA Residents.
Add $20.00 RUSH/Overnight shipping.
Add $5.00 C.O.D. orders.